IMPACTS OF INCARCERATION ON THE AFRICAN AMERICAN FAMILY

IMPACTS OF
INCARCERATION ON THE
AFRICAN AMERICAN
FAMILY

edited by
Othello Harris
R. Robin Miller

Transaction Publishers
New Brunswick (U.S.A.) and London (U.K.)

Third printing 2006

Copyright © 2003 by Transaction Publishers, New Brunswick, New Jersey.
Chapters 2-7 were originally published in *Journal of African American Men*,
Summer 2001, Vol. 6, No. 1.

This book is printed on acid-free paper that meets the American National
Standard for Permanence of Paper for Printed Library Materials.

Library of Congress Catalog Number: 2002032158
ISBN: 0-7658-0973-7
Printed in the United States of America

Library of Congress Cataloging-in-Publication Data

Impacts of incarceration on the African American family / Othello Harris,
    R. Robin Miller.
        p. cm.
    Includes bibliographical references and index.
    ISBN 0-7658-0973-7 (pbk. : alk. paper)
        1. African American prisoners—Family relationships. 2. African Ameri-
    can families—Effect of imprisonment on. 3. Prisoners' families—Effect
    of imprisonment on—United States. 4. Children of prisoners—Effect of
    imprisonment on—United States. 5. Social work with African Americans.
    6. Family social work—United States. 7. Criminal justice, Administra-
    tion of—United States. I. Harris, Othello. II. Miller, R. Robin.

HV9469 .I47 2002
306.88—dc21   2002032158

Contents

**Part 2: The Importance of Fatherhood and the Social Significance of
This Issue for African American Families**

Part 3: Policy Initiatives

Acknowledgments

The following chapters are reprinted by permission:

Part 1

Brad Tripp. 2001. "Incarcerated African American Fathers: Exploring Changes in Family Relationships and the Father Identity." *Journal of African American Men*, 6, 1: 13-29. Reprinted by permission of Transaction Publishers.

Mary L. Balthazar and Lula King. 2001. "The Loss of Protective Effects of Marital and Non-Marital Relationships of Incarcerated African American Men: Implications for Social Work." *Journal of African American Men*, 6, 1: 31-41. Reprinted by permission of Transaction Publishers.

Theresa Clark. 2001. "The Relationship Between Inmate Visitation and Behavior: Implications for African American Families." *Journal of African American Men*, 6, 1: 43-58. Reprinted by permission of Transaction Publishers.

Olga Grinstead, Bonnie Faigeles, Carrie Bancroft, and Barry Zack. 2001. "The Financial Cost of Maintaining Relationships with Incarcerated African American Men: Results From a Survey of Women Prison Visitors." *Journal of African American Men*, 6, 1: 59-69. Reprinted by permission of Transaction Publishers.

Patricia E. O'Connor. 2001. "Prison Cage as Home for African American Men." *Journal of African American Men*, 6, 1: 71-86. Reprinted by permission of Transaction Publishers.

Sandra Lee Browning, R. Robin Miller, and Lisa M. Spruance. 2001. "Criminal Incarceration Dividing the Ties that Bind: Black Men and Their Families." *Journal of African American Men*, 6, 1: 87-102. Reprinted by permission of Transaction Publishers.

Part 2

Stewart Gabel. 1992. "Behavioral Problems in Sons of Incarcerated or Otherwise Absent Fathers: The Issue of Separation." *Family Process* 31: 303-

Part 3

Part 1

Incarceration and African American Families

1

Various Implications of the "Race to Incarcerate" on Incarcerated African American Men and Their Families*

R. Robin Miller

> *"Freedom, too, the long-sought, we still seek—*
> *the freedom of life and limb, the freedom to work*
> *and think, the freedom to love and aspire."*
> *—W. E. B. DuBois, 1903*

Introduction

Marc Mauer, one of the contributors to this volume, once used the phrase "Race to Incarcerate" (1999) to capture the rapid increase in and the horrifying dimensions of the number of African Americans who came to be incarcerated in the 1980s and 1990s. More than implied in this brief and alarming phrase is the notion that the epidemic increase in the number of incarcerated African Americans was anything but happenstance. In fact, so effective was the "race to incarcerate" African Americans during this period that it is difficult to imagine a more successful endeavor were the actual intent of policy to incarcerate members of this group. Of course, this trend has been described by some as merely an unfortunate byproduct of misguided drug policies. Less investigated have been the many ways this disturbing trend has affected the families and family lives of those incarcerated.

This volume represents an attempt to answer an overwhelming need—to provide at least some empirical data and preliminary findings into an increas-

---

*An earlier version of this paper was published in the *Journal of African American Men*, Volume 6, Issue 1, Summer 2001.

ingly significant but little-known topic—the impacts of incarceration on the African American family. The reader will find included here studies of how, more specifically, incarcerated African American men are impacted emotionally, socially, and relationally by their incarceration; how the spouses of these men are affected financially and socio-emotionally; how extended family members are impacted; and how the dependent and grown children of these men are affected in myriad ways. This volume also includes classic works in the literature of incarcerated families by researchers such as Hairston, Lockett, Gabel, and King—works that are commonly referenced and considered by those of us working in the field.

The book also seeks to pull together theoretical pieces on some of the mammoth ramifications our race to incarcerate has held for the African American community. In this vein, papers in this volume investigate African American male and female relationships, relationships between African American fathers and sons, and the behavioral problems evidenced by some sons of incarcerated fathers. The significance of fatherhood for the black community, and the primacy marriage carries for the well-being of African American women and men is also explored.

Implications these findings carry for public policy are reviewed as well. For instance, measures and programs that should be developed within correctional institutions are described. Changes in social work protocol toward a more responsive approach are proposed. And of course, racial disparities in punishments, criminal justice handling, and justice system administration are addressed with an eye toward shaping a more equitable system. As a final note, it seems that part of the power of this volume as already mentioned rests with the timeliness of the research topic, and the original and classic works included. However, another point of strength stems from the cross-disciplinary nature of these works. Contributions come from the fields of sociology, criminology, social work, corrections, policy studies, medicine, and counseling. Similar volumes in this tradition are anticipated.

The incredibly high rate of incarceration has harmed the African American community in general and African American men, more specifically. While this point is obvious and surely needs no further arguments to be persuasive to most readers, an articulation of the specific ways African American men and their families are harmed is useful to our understanding. This introduction and brief review will detail some of the most critical impacts incarceration has had on the families of African American men—impacts which will then be further articulated by the research pieces included in this volume.

A Brief Review of the Literature

The rate at which African Americans have been jailed has increased drastically from the 1980s through the 1990s. In 1985, the incarceration rate of

African Americans was 368 per 100,000 in the population, and by 1995, that rate was almost double at 725 (Bureau of Justice Statistics, 1999). Concern for the families of those incarcerated increased during this period as well.

It must be noted, however, that the literature has been distinctly lacking in many respects. The role of men in the functioning of families has historically been ignored, and the familial roles performed by African American men have received very little attention, "In contrast to the volume of work focused on the position of black women, the role of black men in families is one of the most conspicuously neglected areas of family research." (Taylor, Chatters, Tucker, and Lewis, 1990). This brief review will include the impacts on African American men, on their relationships with their spouses, and on their relationships with their children.

Impacts Due to the Loss of Family on African American Men

Almost half of the men presently incarcerated are fathers (Harrison, 1997). While the common portrayal of the incarcerated male includes the depiction of a loner, a social misfit, or an individual who has been totally separated from the workings of society, many of these men are young, and many of them have formed families separate from their families of origin (Harrison, 1997).

Many of these men worry about how their spouses and children are faring in their absence. Financial difficulties faced by their families figure largely in the concern of many of these men since a majority of them contributed in some fashion to the finances of their families prior to incarceration (Gabel, 1992).

Part of this perceived loss of efficacy stems from the loss of what has been termed "the good provider role" for these men. This role involves the rights, responsibilities and expectations formed by a man who operates as the sole breadwinner for his family. Over time, it is argued, the man's identity is shaped and bolstered by this important familial role. Jesse Bernard (1982) documents how the good provider role previously enjoyed by men for roughly the last one hundred and fifty years has, unfortunately, been declining. Due to changes in the occupational structure as we have moved away from a manufacturing-based economy and toward a tertiary economy, as well as a decline in real wages since the 1970s, a growing number of families have faced the necessity of the dual-wage earner household. These changes have brought grief to the identities of many American men.

More specifically, William Julius Wilson (1987) has documented how a decline in our manufacturing sector for the last fifty years has differentially impacted African American families. While many explanations of the poor economic circumstances of some black families have focused on income transfers and in-kind benefits, we have virtually ignored the impact of male joblessness in explaining marital instability in the black family (Wilson,

1987). Factors that operate to remove African-American men from gainful employment, including incarceration, negatively impact both these men and the family unit economically, socially, and emotionally.

This perspective differs wildly from the culture-of-poverty-based explanation for family disruption common in earlier decades. Maxine Baca Zinn and Stanley Eitzen suggest that marital instability "...appears to represent the response of the poorest, most disadvantaged segment of the black population to the social and economic situation they have faced in our cities over the past few decades" (Baca Zinn and Eitzen, 1987: 356). Blacks and whites differ significantly in occupations and income, with about one-third of blacks living below the poverty line compared to approximately 9 percent of whites, and they are consistently twice as likely as whites to be unemployed. More specifically, the disparities between these two groups show that blacks are more likely to experience economic hardships and insecurities that lead to marital disruption (Baca Zinn and Eitzen, 1987). Given the record number of African American men removed from the black community by incarceration, any study of the stressors on the African-American family should include some discussion of the impacts of incarceration on the good provider role performed by African American men.

Besides the loss of their role as provider, many of these incarcerated men worry about negative impacts on their relationships with their spouses (Lanier, 1993). Through their loss of contact, they experience a loss of closeness. Many state that they worry about the real possibility of divorce before or after their release, and studies suggest that many families never reunite after his release (Hairston and Lockett, 1987; Lanier, 1993).

He may have been replaced in both her life, and in the lives of his children. Stressors on the relationship include sexual frustration on both his part and hers, intense loneliness, and the worry he feels knowing that she is experiencing crisis-provoking events alone (Dallao, 1997). In addition, he often has trouble coping with the positive changes she has experienced while he has been away. With increasing independence, she may have changed jobs, attained further schooling, and/or made new friends (Dallao, 1997). His role in the family dynamic has changed and this can be quite threatening. The questions of how he will fit back in the marital unit can be a continual stressor (Dallao, 1997).

The inmate can be frantically worried about what he sees as the deteriorating relationship between him and his child(ren). The relationship between incarceration and family breakup has been mentioned previously, and the deterioration of the marital relationship can have a horribly negative impact on his relationship with his children. When children are brought to visit, these visits can taper off, and sometimes stop altogether for a variety of reasons. The possibility that his relationship with his spouse is worsening has been described, but these visits can also desist simply because of the inconvenience or expense of the sometimes increasingly long distance between home and the prison (Lanier, 1993).

To complicate the negative effects of the decline in contact between the inmate and his child(ren) is whether he and the mother of his children were married before his incarceration. If he and she were never married, it is even more unlikely that he will be able to see his kids. Unfortunately, many of the African American males presently incarcerated have had children out of wedlock. And just as he misses being able to provide for his family, he misses being able to give gifts to his children. Closeness, involvement, and, of course, contact, all declined sharply for fathers and their children (Lanier, 1993), representing a considerable threat to the viability of these families. Unfortunately, "the absence of a reliable knowledge base on the role of black men in families has resulted in a portrayal of black men as peripheral to family and as performing poorly in the family roles of spouse and father" (Taylor et. al., 1990). Greater research on the role of African American fatherhood, in general, and of incarcerated fathers, more specifically, is called for.

Impacts on the Families of African American Men

The existing literature suggests that the impacts of his incarceration visited upon his family are many and varied. Most immediately, the family feels an echo of stigmatization along with the incarcerated family member. Early literature strongly supports this feeling of punishment. Morris (1965) states, "...many wives believe their husbands' punishment to have been imposed directly on the family," and Fishman (1981) reports that wives "...felt as if they, themselves, were doing time." As late as 1997, some family members reported that they felt punished, too (Dallao, 1997). This section will detail some of the effects on both spouses and children of incarcerated men.

Effects on Spouses

The spouse of an incarcerated man can miss his physical presence and she can also miss him as "companion, father, billpayer, income provider, and handyman" (Fishman, 1981). In actuality, many of the problems described by the spouses (married or unmarried) of incarcerated men can be divided into one of three categories: (1) problems which are financial or material in nature; (2) difficulties arising from more personal feelings of isolation; and (3) difficulties in managing children. Other important issues are mentioned in this section as well.

His separation from her can be immediate and devastating. Some women describe feelings of shock as their spouses are led from the courtroom after sentencing—even after having been told to expect that he would not be coming home with the family after the courtroom proceedings. Since some of these families lead a hand-to-mouth existence, she can face difficulties even in getting herself and her children home from the courtroom. Likewise, she feels the loss of the financial support of her spouse immediately, as paying the rent and other bills quickly becomes a problem.

One aggravating factor that comes into play in terms of financial difficulties is the increasing physical distance between many inmates and their families (Fishman, 1981). While this difficulty is financial in nature in a most immediate sense, it of course leads to less interaction between the inmate and his family members, which tends to exacerbate all the other problems of intimacy, closeness, and reintegration back into the family and the community as well.

In addition to the many financial problems she faces, she can experience extreme feelings of isolation (Gabel, 1992). These feelings can lead to a sense of abandonment which may keep her from visiting him in prison, or from sharing with him the problems she faces while he is not there (Gabel, 1992). She may be reluctant to tell him concerns with which she knows he cannot help and which may only distress him further. To complicate her feelings of psychological distress is the worry of coping with confusing and sometimes frightening court and prison systems.

She experiences sexual frustration and loneliness. To add to these feelings of frustration, isolation and abandonment is the loss of the personal privacy she once shared with her spouse. Personal business has now become part of the public domain. The reputation she and her spouse maintain in the eyes of the community can be damaged, and she can feel that sense of loss deeply (Fishman, 1981).

Finally, named among the most serious of the problems faced by many of these women is the problem she can feel in managing the children; in fact, she can experience extreme task overload in handling the additional problems with the children. First, she has lost whatever supervising he did with the children. She has also lost his disciplining of the children.

Effects on Children

Greater than 1.5 million children in America have a parent behind bars, and furthermore these children tend to be quite young (more than 43 percent of these children are seven years old or younger) (Dallao, 1997). It has been suggested that the impacts of incarceration on children have been largely ignored in the literature (Gabel, 1992).

In what is possibly the first problem to be addressed in detailing the impacts of incarceration on children, stands the fact that most parents do not acknowledge or recognize the distress of the children of incarcerated fathers (Morris, 1965; Dallao, 1997). Yet this failure can be one of the most troubling for the children of incarcerated fathers and, at times, this failure to address the issue of the missing parent can stem from a reluctance to trouble the child(ren). One large part of the small literature that exists on the affects on children is the impact of deception on children. While the harmful effects of deceiving children as to where their parents are can be mediated by other factors (namely, age of the child), most studies have found that this kind of deception is harmful, since children tend to become more confused and upset than when they are faced with the truth (Dallao, 1997). In addition, deception has been seen to lead to greater disobedience, temper outbursts, and even destructive or delinquent behaviors (Wilmer, Marks, and Pogue, 1966).

Children of incarcerated parents can suffer from feelings of rejection and guilt. Many exhibit discipline problems (Sack, 1977) and a decline in school performance (Friedman and Esselstyn, 1965). Most studies do not distinguish between affects on boys and girls and the ones that do emphasize studying boys with the explanation that boys are more likely to externalize (Gabel, 1992). Externalizing can include delinquent behaviors, and there is some evidence to suggest that some boys engage in delinquent behaviors to identify more fully with their incarcerated fathers (Sack, 1977). However, these studies are dated and also tend to be limited. Some of the newest studies on the impacts of incarceration on the socio-emotional development of children have revealed disturbing news, such as the possibility that the incarceration of a parent "…can alter and upset emotional development for years to come" (Dallao, 1997). Needless to say, this literature needs further elaboration.

Contributions of the Research in this Anthology

The readings in this volume tell us much more about how the loss of income affects African American families. In Part 1, Incarceration and African American Families, Brad Tripp's paper, "Incarcerated African American Fathers: Exploring Changes in Family Relationships and the Father Identity," investigates the identity of incarcerated African American fathers. Tripp finds that one of the most critical components of their perceived identity as fathers hinges on whether and to what extent these fathers saw themselves as good providers. Respondents reviewed the successes and mistakes they had made as fathers and what they perceived as the nature of fatherhood. This research found that incarceration has negatively impacted African American families in a number of critical ways. Many of these effects stemmed from the absence of these fathers from the home, and the many familial conflicts that arose due to the incarceration. What was most troubling for many of these fathers were the behavioral problems among their children that had erupted in part because of the incarceration—problems many of these men indicated might not have occurred had they remained in the home as active fathers. Fatherhood, as an identity, is further explored.

In "The Loss of Protective Effects of Marital and Non-Marital Relationships of Incarcerated African American Men: Implications for Social Work" Mary Balthazar and Lula King delve into the loss of the protective effects that marriage and familial relationships have for incarcerated African American men. It is well known that marriage tends to "protect" us from many harmful effects in society (Durkheim, 1897/1951) such as suicide, depression, and many common illnesses. This research finds that incarceration harms these familial ties in ways that negatively impact the mental well-being of these African American men, and further threatens the larger black community. These researchers suggest a number of family-oriented correctional programs to alleviate some of the worst stressors on these men.

Theresa Clark explored the relationship between visits by family and friends and the nature of inmate behavior in "The Relationship Between Inmate Visitation and Behavior: Implications for African American Families." Since the number of prison disturbances has increased in the last two decades, it is reasonable to look at the impact of visitations on the number of prison disturbances when controlling for the relative influences of other factors. This research revealed no relationship between inmate visitation and disturbances and possible policy implications are presented.

This volume pulls together research on the impacts of incarceration on the African American family, and Olga Grinstead, Bonnie Faigeles, Carrie Bancroft and Barry Zack investigate the actual costs families incur to maintain contact with and visit incarcerated African American family members. The costs explored with these data include the emotional, social and financial costs of visitations, telephone calls, and sending packages. This research suggests that these costs represent a considerable burden to these families and must be addressed institutionally.

Patricia O'Connor uses data from sociolinguistic interviews of male inmates from a maximum security prison operated by the District of Columbia's Department of Corrections in "The Prison Cage as Home for African-American Men." Using the extended narratives she collects, O'Connor studies how these men manage to continue to fulfill the fatherhood role long distance. Also explored are the ways these men continue to maintain family ties despite the growing spatial distance many of these men face as they are transferred further from their families. Ramifications of these difficulties are drawn, and suggestions for alleviating these stressors are made.

In the concluding paper for Part 1 entitled, "Criminal Incarceration Dividing the Ties that Bind: Black Men and Their Families," Sandra Lee Browning, R. Robin Miller, and Lisa Spruance extend some of the issues which have been addressed in Part 1 by focusing on actions of the criminal justice system that serve to destroy the black family, reasons black male inmate fathers are studied so rarely, and outlining the many other familial relationships (e.g., parents, siblings, and grandparents) which are rarely investigated. They also discuss the role restorative justice may play and explore the policy implications inherent in the findings of the papers in this volume.

Part 2, The Importance of Fatherhood and the Social Significance of This Issue for African American Families, contains papers which, taken together, describe a number of difficulties between separated fathers and sons, stressors on male and female relationships, and the critical importance marriage and family plays for the well-being of black adults. In "Behavioral Problems in Sons of Incarcerated or Otherwise Absent Fathers: The Issue of Separation," Stewart Gabel asks the question, "Is the separation between fathers and sons due to incarceration qualitatively different than that of other types of separation?" This paper explores the reactions of children to parental incarceration, paying particular attention to the interpretations and reactions of boys to the incarceration of their fathers. The literature on separation due to incarceration is then compared to that of separations due to other factors—most notably divorce. Gabel finds that adjustment and/or behavioral problems stem primarily from factors like household stressors before and after separation, meanings these children attach to the incarceration, characteristics of the caretaking parent, and the resources of the family more than simply the incarceration itself.

The theme of the importance of the relationship between father and son, which began in this volume with Stewart Gabel's work, is extended with "African American Fathers and Sons: Social, Historical, and Psychological Considerations," by Jay C. Wade. As has been mentioned previously, African American fatherhood has commonly been devalued and deemphasized. Perceptions about these fathers often include the consensus that they are either absent, or at the very least uninvolved. Wade challenges these misperceptions, reviewing the cultural forces that have historically influenced these families, and concludes that this familial dynamic is far from representative of the African American family. While in the research literature father-absence has traditionally been viewed to cause problems in sex-role identity or increased delinquency almost exclusively, this writer finds father-absence to contribute to more wide-ranging consequences for the development of these sons and therefore to present a problem easily worthy of future research.

The impacts of incarceration on the African American family obviously include influences on male and female relationships. McCreary and Wright explore the effects of stigma and wide misperceptions on these relationships in "The Effects of Negative Stereotypes on African American Male and Female Relationships." Due to a range of factors, including the propensity for many Americans to view African American families as dysfunctional and/or more likely to engage in deviant behaviors, misconceptions about the relationships between African American men and women abound. These contributors explore the influences of negative stereotypes on these dyadic relationships and suggest improvements in our collective understandings of these relationships.

Concluding Part 2 is Zollar and Williams' "The Contribution of Marriage to the Life Satisfaction of Black Adults." The protective effect of marriage is, arguably, one of the oldest research topics in sociology. Marital status and marital satisfaction have been found to increase global happiness in dozens of studies in the last century, and yet few studies have explored this topic using adequate African American samples. This lack of empirical research has exacerbated misunderstandings of the importance marriage holds in the black community at the same time that fewer black adults are marrying. In this paper, structural factors influencing the lower marriage rate (including imbalanced sex ratios, higher unemployment, and higher incarceration rates) are explored. Zollar and Williams find that marriage contributes to the global happiness and life satisfaction of black adults and should be viewed as vitally important to the black community.

The third and final part of the volume, Policy Initiatives, includes papers on how social service workers, social scientists, and public policy analysts can aid in alleviating some of the most significant problems suffered by the families of incarcerated African Americans. Anthony King, in "The Impact of Incarceration on African American Families: Implications for Practice," explores the scope of this disproportionate incarceration and effects on families. He further describes five program initiatives: culturally appropriate family-support groups; clinical services; community-based life education programs; family life education programs in correctional institutions; and family case-management services, designed to respond to the special needs of these inmates and their families.

Creasie Hairston and Patricia Lockett's paper, "Parents in Prison: New Directions for Social Services" is similar to Anthony King's paper in intent. These two authors also suggest program initiatives to support inmates and families. However, this paper details the landmark Parents in Prison program, which was developed and guided in part by these two authors, who have served on the Central Coordinating Committee since its inception in the early 1980s. These authors state that the purpose of this program is to "...increase participants' knowledge of child development, effective parenting styles and techniques, and family communication patterns; to strengthen inmate-family relationships during and following incarceration; and to increase inmates' understanding of the impact of incarceration and absence from the family on children and other family members." Inmates participate in: (1) home study courses; (2) structured classroom courses; (3) a monthly special event/rap session; and (4) special projects. This inmate organization is sanctioned by the Tennessee Department of Correction and stands as an example of the kind of coordination that inmates, families, social service workers, and prison administrators can achieve.

In "The Endangerment of African Americans: An Appeal for Social Work Actions," Paula Allen-Meares and Sondra Burman review factors in the disproportionate incarceration of African American men, various policy issues, and sound a call to arms for those in the social work profession to stand against what is, in effect, the crippling of the black community. These writers suggest program strategies to improve social support networks, greater financial and legal aid to these families, greater attention to the self-esteem and sense of self-worth of these men, and the eradication of discriminatory and racist laws and institutional policies. According to Allen-Meares and Burman, the profession of social work must become much more responsive to the needs of these men and their families.

Finally, Marc Mauer also surveys the disproportionalities in the incarceration of African American males and specifies influences in this unequal rate at various points in criminal justice handling. He describes various approaches to reducing the disparities seen in the criminal justice system, including legislative actions, the expansion of the use of alternative sentencing and community-based diversion programs, and community and justice system partnerships. In Mauer's words, the crisis of the treatment of African American males by the criminal justice system "...threatens the viability of an entire generation" and must be addressed for the continued well-being of the African American community.

Conclusion and Implications

There are many positives to improving the relationships inmates may maintain with their families. These positives include the critical role family can play in reintegrating the released offender back into the community (Holt and Miller, 1972; Fishman, 1981; Fishman, 1986) and the decline in recidivism evidenced by those inmates who are able to regain family ties after release (Hairston, 1991).

In addition, there are the many benefits to both the mental health of the inmate and his family (Hairston, 1991). Besides the purely practical matters of the benefits to the larger society and to the families of these inmates, is the simple question of social justice, "...unjust social arrangements are themselves a kind of extortion, even violence." (Rawls, 1971).

Policy implications suggested by the research contained in this volume include increasing the number of visiting hours per inmate, per month. We need to increase the length of each visit, and to increase the frequency of each visit. While not within the scope of this text, our collective understanding of the impacts of incarceration on the African American family is seriously limited by the continuing lack of research on female inmates and their families. While this body of research has been growing in the last decade (see Belknap, 1996 and Chesney-Lind and Shelden, 1998 for good reviews of the most current literature), given that the rate of African American women incarcerated rose from 183 per 100,000 in 1985 to 456 in 1996 (versus 73 for white females) (Kurki, 1999), the implications for family research are obvious. More and better research is called for.

Another question which has received little attention is the long-term impact of the incarceration of African American males on the perceptions of fatherhood for children. For instance, what about the effect on both boys and girls in regard to their perceptions of marriageability? Will boys receive different messages about their future familial roles than boys with fathers who have not been incarcerated? Will boys perceive themselves as marriageable? Will girls have different perceptions?

In a speech in 1963, Martin Luther King stated, "Injustice anywhere is a threat to justice everywhere" (King, 1963: 22). Evidence that we have created an *in*justice system that serves to negatively impact African American men and their families is mounting. Research that focuses national attention on these disparities is clearly warranted.

References

Baca Zinn, M., and Eitzen, S. (1987). *Diversity in American families.* New York: Harper and Row.

Belknap, J. (1996). *The invisible woman: Gender, crime, and justice.* New York: Wadsworth Publishing.

Bernard, J. (1982). *The future of marriage.* New Haven, CT: Yale University Press.

Bureau of Justice Statistics. (1999). The rate of jail incarceration for blacks is five times higher than the rate for whites. Washington, D.C.: U. S. Department of Justice.

Chesney-Lind, M., and Shelden, R. (1998). *Girls, delinquency, and juvenile justice.* New York: Wadsworth Publishing.

Dallao, M. (1997). Coping with incarceration: From the other side of the bars. *Corrections Today* 59(6): 96-98.

DuBois, W.E.B. (1903; 1989). *The souls of black folk.* New York: Bantam.

Durkheim, E. (1897; 1951). *Suicide: A study in sociology.* New York: Free Press.

Fishman, S. (1981). Losing a loved one to incarceration: The effect of imprisonment on family members. *Personnel and Guidance Journal* 32: 372-376.

Fishman, L. (1986). Repeating the cycle of hard living and crime: Wives' accommodations to husbands' parole performance. *Federal Probation* 2(1), 44-54.

Friedman, S., and Esselstyn, T. (1965). The adjustment of children of jail inmates. *federal probation* 29: 55-59.

Gabel, S. (1992). Behavioral problems in sons of incarcerated or otherwise absent fathers: The issue of separation. *Family Process* 31: 303-314.

Hairston, C. (1991). Family ties during imprisonment: Important to whom and for what? *Journal of Sociology and Social Welfare* 18(1): 85-104.

Hairston, C., and Lockett, P. (1987). Parents in prison: New directions for social services. *Social Work* 32: 162-164.

Harrison, K. (1997). Parental training for incarcerated fathers: Effects on attitudes, self-esteem, and children's self-perceptions. *Journal of Social Psychology* 137(5): 588-593.

Holt, N., and Miller, D. (1972). *Explorations in inmate—family relationships.* Sacramento, CA: California Department of Corrections.

King, M. L. (1983). *The words of Martin Luther King, Jr.* Selected by Coretta Scott King, New York: New Market Press.

Kurki, L. (1999). Racial incarceration disparities high, but decreasing. *Overcrowded Times* 10(6): 3-6.

Lanier, C. (1993). Affective states of fathers in prison. *Justice Quarterly* 19(1): 49-66.

Morris, P. (1965). *Prisoners and their families.* New York: Hart Press.

Rawls, J. (1971). *A theory of justice.* Cambridge, MA: Harvard University Press.

Sack, W. (1977). Children of imprisoned fathers. *Psychiatry* 40: 163-174.

Taylor, R. J., Chatters, L. M., Tucker, M. B., and Lewis, E. (1990). Developments in research on black families: A decade review. *Journal of Marriage and the Family* 52(Nov.): 993-1014.

Wilmer, H. A., Marks, I., and Pogue, E. (1966). Group treatment of prisoners and their families. *Mental Hygiene* 50: 380-389.

Wilson, W. J. (1987). *The truly disadvantaged: The inner city, the underclass, and public policy.* Chicago: University of Chicago Press.

2

Incarcerated African American Fathers: Exploring Changes in Family Relationships and the Father Identity

Brad Tripp

Introduction

Fathers comprise over one-half of the male prison population in the United States (Harrison, 1997). This number takes on a greater significance for African American communities as African American men comprise 48 percent of the prison population of state institutions (King, 1993). This figure particularly is staggering when viewed in light of the fact that African Americans account for only 12 percent of the United States' population, with African American men sitting slightly below 6 percent of the nation's populace (King, 1993).

According to Hairston (1998), the typical father in prison has a low educational background, was poor at the time of his arrest, and provided financially for his children before incarceration. Hairston (1998) also notes differences among the family forms that these men leave behind; less than one-fourth of imprisoned fathers are married, and nearly 50 percent of these fathers report multiple mothers for their children. The family relations that these men return to upon release are diverse in shape, size, and form. The multitude of family structures and issues that men encounter when released from prison is therefore another critical issue in the study of incarcerated fathers.

The imprisonment of fathers is often associated with a variety of social and psychological problems in children, especially among young boys (Gabel, 1992). Children who have little contact with their fathers during incarceration have higher levels of emotional problems than children who maintain frequent contact (McPeek and Tse, 1988). Due to a variety of circumstances, such as the distance between the family and the prison, incarcerated fathers rarely have the opportunity to see their children (Hairston, 1998). Perhaps the best predictor of child visits is the relationship between the father and the child's mother. Hairston (1998) reported that mothers often act as a gatekeeper between the child and the father, regulating the quantity and the type of interaction that the father can maintain with his child.

One of the most pressing issues that incarcerated fathers face is the decline in the quality of their relationship with their children, as the quality of the father-child relationship during paternal incarceration also acts as a strong predictor of children's emotional and social problems (Landreth and Lobaugh, 1998). With many incarcerated fathers reporting a deterioration in closeness with their children while in jail (Lanier, 1993), the separation of fathers from children, as a result of imprisonment, is a major issue for some African American families.

Fathers who perceive a decline in the quality in these relationships have a high tendency to report depression, or many of the symptoms of depression (Lanier, 1993). During their absence from home, many incarcerated fathers, especially men who are not married to the mothers of their children, fear that other men will replace them as father figures in their children's lives (Hairston, 1998). However, men who maintain healthy and substantial family relations during incarceration are less likely to recidivate compared to all other inmates (Carlos and Cevera, 1991).

Much of the research focusing on incarcerated fathers in the closing decade of the twentieth century examined specific programs centered on the importance of the father-child relationship. Perhaps the most ardent goal of these policies and programs attend to the maintenance of family relations, an important factor in minimizing recidivism (Carlos and Cevera, 1991; Hairston, 1998). Frequently, secondary socialization within the penal system leads inmates away from outside ties, such as family relations, and into the prison culture (Schmid and Jones, 1996). This process of "prisonization" (Brodsky, 1975) is often tied to a weakening of family ties and an increase in isolationist behavior, further decreasing the quality of relationships outside of prison walls (King, 1993). To combat isolation from family and inculcation into the prison culture, a variety of programs focusing on the father role have been brought into prisons (Lanier, 1987; Rudel and Hayes, 1990; Landreth and Lobaugh, 1998; Wilczak and Markstrom, 1999). These programs have yielded positive results in a variety of forms. Parent education courses for male prisoners have shown some promise in reducing recidivism (Rudel and Hayes, 1990). Other benefits from these programs have come in the form of improved father-child relationships, increases in self-worth as a father, improvements in child behavior, and increases in visitation quality (Landreth and Lobaugh, 1998; Wilczak and Markstrom, 1999).

Methods

This research began as an extension of a community service project, which started during the summer of 1998. The original program consisted of a two-hour course in which the research team familiarized inmates with some of the social and psychological studies that focused on the issues of incarcerated fathers. Participants were provided with supplies and assistance in the creation of letters for their children. Overall, the inmates provided positive responses to the program. The success of the initial program led the research team towards an extension of the project, which would provide an outreach service for the inmates, as well as various forms of qualitative data for research analysis.

The project acted as a pilot study on incarcerated fathers, allowing the research team to develop familiarity with the issues and lived experiences of men separated from their children as a result of imprisonment. The initial sample sought 20 participants willing to discuss their family relationships. As a result of the transient nature of the jail, only 16 of the initial 20 participants recruited were able to participate. Following in the form of the initial project, as well as modeling the project after most current research on incarcerated fathers that focuses on the father-child relationship, a six-week program was designed that focused on parent-child communication and interaction. Each weekly meeting would consist of focus groups of approximately eight men. Each group was led by a member of the research team. The research team consisted of one Caucasian male and three Caucasian females, with all team members in their early to mid-twenties. With a sample size of 16, the participants were divided into two groups, in order to provide smaller, more intimate groups in which each inmate could feel comfortable and could have the opportunity to express his opinion on the topic at hand.

Entrance Interviews

In addition to the weekly focus group meetings, all of the subjects participated in entrance and exit interviews. The main purpose of the entrance interviews, termed "Trust Building" interviews for this project, was to familiarize the inmates and the researchers with each other, as well as to provide the research team with family structures and issues that the participants face. These interviews comprise the bulk of the data used for this analysis because they provide deeper insight into the participants' lived realities than any of the focus group sessions. In addition, inmates seemed more comfortable discussing family issues with members of the research team than when in the company of other inmates. The inmates did discuss family issues during each of the focus group sessions, but with less intimacy and vulnerability as many inmates had displayed in the Trust Building interviews.

The Trust Building (i.e., entrance) interviews asked the fathers to talk about their children. Specifically, the interviews attempted to discern if the inmate acted as a father figure towards his own biological children, stepchildren, a girlfriend's child, or any combination of different children. The participants were asked to describe their relationship with each of their children, focusing on their own assessment of their performance as fathers. Men were asked to share memories of experiences in which they conceived of themselves as "good" fathers. They were also asked to share experiences in which they thought they were not good fathers.

The purpose of the entrance interviews was three-fold. First, these interviews were conducted to provide a basis for the relationship between the researchers and the participants, aiming to help the inmates feel at ease when sharing personal and familial information with the research team. Second, these interviews were used as a starting point from which the team could develop a program that would prove useful among different family forms. Using the entrance interviews as reference, the research team was able to approach each session with a base knowledge of the family situation of each inmate. Finally, these interviews, along with the exit interviews, formed the base of the content from which the analysis of the family issues and problems of incarcerated fathers was developed.

Weekly Focus Groups

Once the entrance interviews were complete, the inmates participated in three weekly focus group sessions. Although the 16 initial participants had been randomly divided into two groups, the size and compliment of each group varied slightly each week as a result of court dates or behavioral reprimands that restricted the inmates' participation. The first focus group session was modeled after the letter-writing portion of the exploratory study. The second focus group was a roundtable discussion of family visits. The final focus group session involved the creation of holiday cards for the inmates' children, providing the inmates with the ability to produce Thanksgiving cards.

The final week of the project involved exit interviews with each inmate. Similar to the entrance interviews, this segment of the project asked participants once again to focus on their self-perception of themselves as fathers. Changes and developments in each inmate's relations with their children were also questioned, along with inquiries regarding each subject's perceptions of the program.

The Sample

All participants were recruited from the Alachua County Jail in Gainesville, Florida. Additionally, all subjects were enrolled in the jail's Life Skills pro-

Table 1
Demographic and Familial Description of the Inmates Sampled

Inmate Pseudonym	# of Biological Children	# of "Step" Children	Age	Marital Status	Offense
Derrick	1	0	24	Single	Violation of probation
Lamar	2	4	42	Married	Burglary
James	5	2	33	Married	Violation of probation
Andre	1	4	40	Married	Grand theft
Tim	3	1	24	Single	Possession, sale of cocaine
Sean	2	2	30	Single	Violation of probation
Ed	3	2	47	Married	Violation of probation
William	2	0	29	Single	Burglary
Hank	2	0	26	Single	Possession of cocaine
Bryan	3	2	32	Single	Violation of probation
Sam	2	6	38	Single	Violation of probation
Joe	10	4	31	Single	Possession, sale of cannabis

gram. This program is available only to non-violent offenders, and offers inmates educational opportunities such as GED completion, conflict-management, and job search skills, among other classes. Male inmates with children were allowed to enroll in this project as one of their Life Skills courses.

Sixteen men signed up for the course, with 12 African Americans and four Caucasians enrolling. Given the small sample size, only the data from the African American participants will be examined here. The ages of the African American fathers ranged from 24 to 47, with the average age around 31 (Table 1). Nine of the 12 subjects reported having biological as well as other children towards whom they acted as "father figures," with the remaining three fathers reporting only their own biological children. All participants were incarcerated for either probation violation (N=6, 50 percent), burglary or theft (N=3, 25 percent), or drug possession or distribution (N=3, 25 percent).

Results

Entrance and Exit Interviews

A great deal of information regarding the impact of paternal incarceration on African American families was given during the entrance and exit interviews. As noted earlier, it was within the private settings of these interviews that inmates revealed personal, emotional, and familial issues in great depth. While the subjects noted how the focus groups allowed them greater comfort in discussing personal issues than in the broader setting of prison life, most participants seemed at greater ease, and revealed deep and introspective family issues when isolated with the researchers.

Within the individual interviews the fathers focused on three issues, specifically. The initial subject of which the inmates spoke was their identity as fathers. Since questions on their identities as fathers comprised the core of the entrance and exit interviews, the extensive data supplied by these subjects was expected. A second core subject of which the men spoke concerned their interpretations and emotions regarding their absence from their children's lives. This also was expected. However, it is important to acknowledge the strong association that most of the participants recognized between their absence from the home and their paternal identity. The third and final core subject to be discussed here is critical to our understanding of the effects that incarceration can have upon African American families. Ten of the 12 subjects (N=10, 83 percent) spoke at great length about conflict within the family. Neither the entrance nor the exit interview questions sought out measures of familial conflict; however, almost all of the participants spoke of conflict when describing their current family relationships. The inmates spoke of conflict with their wives, partners and former partners, as well as with their children. These conflictual relations, along with the inmates' father identities and their interpretations of their absence from the home, will be addressed in greater depth in the discussion.

Focus Groups

Letter Writing. During each focus group session the research team recorded observations and made note of relevant comments and themes. The first lesson, devoted to letter writing, gave the participants a chance to talk about whether they write letters to their children, and what issues they believe are important to include in the letters. The participants suggested topics such as: school, the child's attitude, encouraging words, and the fact that they love them. One inmate disclosed that he likes to draw pictures for his daughter. Another inmate, Lamar, uses his letters to give his children advice. He often tells his kids that they have to learn from their experiences. Discipline problems were of great importance to the men and they often wrote letters to their children about this. The inmates' comments about discipline during this focus group session are similar to some of the participants' comments about fatherhood during the entrance interviews. Many of the inmates focused on the structure and disciplinary strength provided by the presence of a father figure within the home.

Visitation. The second session on visitation was a shorter session in which only a discussion took place, without any scheduled craft activities. The men were asked probing questions about visits from their children and visitation policies of the jail. Inmates stated that visitation in the jail is limited to Friday, Saturday, and Sunday only. Visitation is for one hour each day and the inmate can only see two visitors each day. The Alachua County jail enforces non-contact visits where the inmates are separated from visitors by a plate of glass. The inmate is able to communicate with visitors using phones on each side.

There are many inmates who do not want their children to visit them in jail for various reasons. Most of the inmates viewed visits as a sad occasion, especially since they cannot touch their children. One inmate described how his daughter always puts her hand on the glass and that he responds by placing his hand on the divider as well. Another inmate expressed that he did not like his kids to visit because they always cry. Visits are not always sad though; one man talks of when his wife and children visit, he uses that time to take care of some business. He speaks to his wife about how to spend paychecks and takes the time to discipline his children.

Thanksgiving Cards. The last session was called "celebrating while you're away." At first, the men were reluctant to make cards. However, it only took a few minutes before they were all actively participating in creating Thanksgiving cards. Participants with young children showed a great deal of excitement while creating the cards, with the anticipation that their children would be delighted to receive handmade cards from their fathers.

Discussion

Father Identity

Acting as a Father Figure in Multiple Families. As mentioned, these interviews revealed a variety of different family forms and structures. One of the main facets that the participants shared was the presence of "step" children toward whom they acted as father figures. Nine of the 12 African American fathers (N=9, 75 percent) discussed acting as a father figure towards children that they did not sire. Within this subset of the sample, four of the nine "stepfathers" (N=4, 44 percent) took on this role legally through marriage to the child of orientation's mother. The remaining five "stepfathers" (N=5, 56 percent) took on the role of a father figure while cohabiting with a child's mother.

Some of the participants discussed acting as father figure when speaking about interactions with a relatives' child, such as nieces, nephews, or cousins. Therefore, many of the inmates held a variety of expectations for themselves within the role of a father. These expectations seemed to vary by different children and by different mothers. Some of the men seemed to suffer from multiple role strain while attempting to act as a father to multiple families. Inmates commented about the need to act as a provider to multiple families, both before incarceration and after release. Beyond the problems of acting as provider to more than one family, some of the inmates discussed how their relations with one of their child's mothers was hampering their continued relationship with their children.

Definitions of Fathering. Participants were prompted to talk about instances in which they perceived themselves as either a good father or a bad father. Building from current social depictions of fathers in either extremely positive or negative lights, the participants were asked to recall specific events in their lives as fathers in which they occupied one or both of these images of fathers. What resulted from these two questions was a vast field of responses that collectively begins to paint a portrait of how these men view fathering and fatherhood. Two approaches to how the inmates defined fatherhood will be noted as action orientation and child orientation.

Action Orientation. Participants who defined fatherhood within an action orientation tended to depict themselves as fathers in terms of the activities in which they engaged their children. Inmates adhering to this orientation also use minimal emotional descriptions when depicting themselves as "close" with their children. Activities such as taking children to church, McDonald's, and parks were cited by inmates. Participants also noted certain behaviors within the household as sources of pride in their father identity (i.e., helping child with homework). William, a 29-year-old father of two, followed the action orientation by defining his fathering successes as, "doing what a father supposed to do for them (children)…give them attention and sit down and study with them, and you know, let them go have fun…do things together…what a child like a father to do with them."

Another aspect of the action orientation to fatherhood identities dealt with more abstract ideas. Notions of providing guidance and discipline for their children arose in many interviews. Additionally, the majority of participants viewed the physical presence of a father within a household as extremely positive. James described this perceived difference between a house with and without the presence of a father figure.

JAMES: I know with a father being in the house is a whole lot different from a father not being in the house, because you know as a child how far I could push my mother, and I could push her right to the edge, and I could stop. But see, with dad you can't push dad that far because dad don't go that far...dad already know what you're trying.

James' statement reflects the beliefs that many of the inmates held regarding the relation between a father's presence and household order, structure, and discipline. The third component of the action orientation is that of a financial provider. Nearly every participant spoke of supporting his children when assessing his father identity. This theme was so prevalent in the trust building interviews that it will be covered in depth in a later section of the discussion.

Child Orientation. The other orientation to one's father identity was in relation to the children themselves. These men tended to judge themselves as fathers not on their own behaviors so much as on their relationship with their children. Respect was one of the qualities frequently mentioned by participants as a marker of their fatherhood viability. These participants believed that they were good fathers when their children treated them with respect and acted with responsibility. The absence of positive affective qualities in the relationship between father and child was also a facet of this orientation to fatherhood. One inmate cited how his son did not trust him, and that this was why he felt he was a bad father. These men seemed to move back and forth between positive and negative assessments of themselves as fathers depending on the status of their relationship with their children.

Another component of the child orientation to fatherhood revolved around the behavior of the children. When asked to talk about a time when he viewed himself as a good father, Andre responded, "there been a lot of times that I feel like I have been a good father, since, when he comes home from school saying that the teachers tell him how good he dress and keep his hair cut, his homework done." Andre judges himself to be a good father when his son is well behaved and doing well in school. He judges his successful performance of the father role not on his own behavior but on his son's behavior, which he feels is under his influence.

Financial Aspects of Fatherhood. Many of the inmates based elements of their father identity on their ability to provide financially for their children or on their ability to purchase gifts for their children. Based out of an action orientation, these participants spoke of fatherhood in relation to their ability to purchase or provide financially for their children. Derrick said, "I see myself as a good father as far as supporting my child...but at the same time...me being in here, that taking away from that I want to buy her school clothes and stuff, you know what I'm saying, that be bad." Other inmates related the provider aspect of their father role to specific instances such as holidays. Sam explicitly linked his performance of the provider role during holidays to his evaluation of himself as a father:

RESEARCHER: Can you tell us when you did something and thought of yourself as a good father, you thought you did a real good job?

SAM: Um, like when Christmas time comes, buy 'em gifts and stuff like that.

RESEARCHER: When have you thought of yourself negatively?

SAM: Like right now, Christmas time is coming up.

Similar to many other participants, Sam defined himself as a father using an action orientation, while focusing specifically on the fatherhood role of a provider. Like many fathers in America, Sam explicitly focuses on the role of provider during holidays, judging his performance of the father role on the gift-giving aspect of Christmas.

Absence. Absence from the home as a result of incarceration acts as a major factor in changes in inmates' perceptions of themselves as fathers. As stated earlier, many of the participants expressed distress regarding their inability to provide financially for their children while incarcerated. However, many of the fathers spoke of other ways in which their incarceration and separation from the family had affected their concept of their performance of the father role. For some of the participants, being removed from their family caused them to feel as if they were no longer a part of the family. Hank, a 26-year-old father of two, said, "I am not one hundred percent a father because I'm locked up, and I can't do the things that I supposed to do as a father and I can't take care of them like I want to." His inability to engage in paternal duties causes Hank to feel that he is not being a father. Sam echoed Hank's comments about losing his father role while in jail, stating that, "I'm not really that (a father) right now…I ain't there for them like I should be."

In addition to Sam's perception of himself as a poor father, Sam also considers the notion of paternal replacement. He notes that, "they got so many relationships, I ain't gonna deal with that part." Sam feels that while he is incarcerated and, in his view, unable to be a father, other men who are in his former partner's life will replace him as a father figure. The combination of Sam's views of a father's responsibilities and his visions of replacement seem to push Sam away from his identity as a father. Many of the participants expressed similar sentiment, reflecting upon the loss of power they have experienced in prison. When the inmates spoke of themselves as fathers, their notions of fatherhood invariably focused on the loss of power in their personal role fulfillment, as well as a loss of control in family issues and problems.

Inmates spoke not only about the ways that separation from the family had affected their views of themselves as fathers, as many of the men noted how their absence through incarceration had affected their children. James cited how his incarceration has changed his relationship with some of his children, and talked of the readjustment that his children will have to make once he is released from jail.

JAMES: Sitting in here is driving me crazy, because it takes so much away…there's so much…that I've missed to where I can't make up for what I've missed, but then we've got to go through this getting familiar with each other again…when I look at them I see it in their look, it's like all of this is strange to them again.

However, the key issue that the inmates spoke of when addressing their children and their absence was behavioral problems. Many of the inmates felt that the presence of a father in the house was a source of structure and guidance for the children. Joe noted how his children have been acting out since he was placed in jail. Since he has been incarcerated, four of his 10 children have been brought home by the police. Joe feels that this type of behavior would not occur if he were at home stating that, "When I'm out there they know that any trouble caused and I'm gonna come over and deal with it."

Conflict

Conflict with Wives or Partners. As stated earlier, inmates addressed conflict within the family more than any other subject. Some of the participants spoke of marital or dating problems that have resulted in limited contact or arguments with their partners. Lamar told the researchers that he still maintains weekly contact with his children, but that he does not speak with his wife when he calls. The couple has had difficulties that they were not able to work out, and they have not spoken since his incarceration. The couple's problems are based on Lamar's drug problem, the causal factor in his arrest for burglarizing a home.

Ed, a 29-year-old father of two, also spoke deeply about conflict with his wife since his incarceration. Unlike Lamar's situation, Ed's wife confronted him about her perception of their situation. Ed told the research team, "me and my wife just had a serious confrontation because I forgot about my wife and focused all of my attention on the kids." Ed explained that he apologized to his wife and told her that he felt secure in their relationship, and was deeply concerned about the children's well being while he was away. Despite this couple's success in overcoming family problems during incarceration, the conflict between spouses was a common theme discussed by all four of the married inmates. However, conflict between partners was not limited solely among married couples. William told the interviewers that his girlfriend was "cheating" on him while he was in jail, and that he asked for a paternity test when the child was born (it was his child). Infidelity concerns are common among incarcerated men (King, 1993), and add to the strife experienced by couples when one of the members is imprisoned.

Conflict with Former Partner. Conflict with the mother of one's child was a common subject among inmates who were no longer involved with the child's mother in a relationship. Derrick spoke about how his poor relationship with his ex-girlfriend is preventing him from maintaining his father-child relationship while in prison. When the researchers asked Derrick about his relationship with his youngest daughter, he replied, "her mom is like, in another relationship, so I kind of stray away from that (his relationship with his daughter)." Derrick still maintains phone contact with his daughter, but he seemed to feel powerless as a father in jail, and sought to avoid a confrontation with his ex-girlfriend. Derrick's comments also serve as a reflection of the notions of paternal replacement addressed in the analysis of the inmates' fatherhood identity.

Conclusion

During imprisonment familial relationships and identities are constrained and must readjust to the enforcement of paternal separation. While this project is limited in scope to the family life perceptions of fathers only, this research has isolated a series of issues that confront African American families during the incarceration of the family's father figure. Imprisonment has the potential to damage an inmate's perception of himself as a father. When asked to discuss their lives as fathers, many of the participants cited their incarceration as a reason for perceiving themselves as "bad" fathers.

While many of the participants noted their imprisonment as a factor in their perception of themselves as poor fathers, the underlying theme behind this notion varied from inmate to inmate. Some of the men discussed their physical separation from their children and partners, and spoke of the emotional pains that they have experienced during their prison term. Other men discussed how incarceration has prevented them from fathering. These men focused on the importance of a father figure in the home, and believed that their children were missing out on a source of guidance, structure, and discipline. Another concern that affected these men's perceptions of themselves as fathers was the development of financial concerns and the loss of the role as a financial provider. Nine of the 12 African American fathers (N=9, 75 percent) mentioned the loss of their ability to provide financially for their family. Many of the inmates also talked at length about the financial troubles that have fallen upon their families during their imprisonment. These three concerns, emotional pains, the loss of a father figure in the home, and the loss of the provider role, all act as sources of negative influences on these men's perceptions of themselves as fathers.

Some of the inmates responded to their new identity as poor fathers by distancing themselves from their families. This behavior is the most troubling facet of incarceration reported by the participants for a variety of reasons. First, these inmates are isolating themselves from an important source of support during the incarceration process. The family is an even greater source of support for prisoners when they are released, as the presence of healthy family relations acts as an outstanding predictor of non-recidivation (Carlos and Cevera, 1991). Second, distancing oneself from father-child relationships can result in a minimization of the father role in these inmates' sense of themselves. Based on Lamb, Pleck, Charnov, and Levine's (1987) determinants of father involvement, the act of distancing oneself from the family during imprisonment can result in decreases in three of the four determinant factors.

Inmates who distance themselves from the family are prone to lose motivation, skills, and support. These inmates may lose motivation as a result of limited contact, and emotional sentiment in which they degrade themselves as fathers during incarceration. These behaviors may decrease these men's level of motivation to act as fathers after imprisonment. Second, decreased contact between the inmate and his family can result in decreases in familiarity and interaction skills among family members. Men who distance themselves from their family life while in prison often engage in prisonization (Brodsky, 1975) wherein they develop a new identity based on the prison culture, while minimizing their previous identity. The inculcation into the prison culture can result in a loss of family and child-rearing skills, thereby reducing yet another factor in the prediction of father involvement. The final determinant of paternal involvement that incarcerated fathers who distance themselves from family relations while in jail are at risk of losing is the notion of support. Men who actively engage their role as an involved father often receive great support from their wives, partners, or other members of the family. Inmates who enact the distancing behavioral patterns alienate themselves from their families and decrease the sources of support they might receive upon release.

Finally, the families of incarcerated African American fathers seem to be at great risk of conflict within the family. Conflict between husband and wives, with former partners, and among parents and children was a central subject in most of the inmate's descriptions of their current family relations. Unfortunately, this research is limited in the measurement of familial conflict in a variety of ways. A pre-test measure of family conflict before incarceration is not available. Inmates were not asked to describe changes in the level of conflict within their family since their imprisonment. While some of the inmates described family troubles that have arisen since their incarceration, a valid measurement of their pre-incarceration family life is nonexistent.

While damage to the father identity during incarceration is the most significant issue for African American families discussed in this research, it is not the only problem confronting the families of African American inmates. Perhaps the most pressing issue for African American families dwells within the disproportionate incarceration rates of African American males. While prisons across the United States are overpopulated by a distinctly disproportionate amount of African American fathers, neither the justice system nor legislative bodies have offered assistance to the families left without a father figure outside of prison walls. Contrary to the nominal status of prisons as correctional institutions, punishment, security, and the overall safety of the facility are the focus of prison policies, not family relations (Cripe, 1997). This policy directive has resulted in a pattern of restrictions, further curtailing the minimal contact that fathers are able to maintain with their children (Hairston and Hess, 1989). African American families are losing access to fathers and father figures at both ends of the justice system, via the courts with a disproportionate imprisonment rate for African American males, as well as within prison as a result of policies that ignore the families of inmates.

A great deal of research remains unexplored regarding the perceptions and experiences of the families that African American men are separated from by prison walls. More research is needed concerning the coping strategies utilized by the wives and partners of incarcerated African American fathers. Examining how these women address the physical loss of a partner, as well as exploring how these families adjust to the financial difficulties during paternal incarceration are important issues that are essential in the development of a deeper understanding of the lived experiences of these families. Further research on the effects of paternal incarceration on children is also needed. Finally, research exploring the effects of diverse educational and familial interaction programs is needed. Future prison programs focusing on incarcerated fathers should be developed in response to the social, emotional, familial, and financial needs of inmates families.

References

Brodsky, S. L. (1975). *Family and friends of men in prison*. Lexington, MA: Lexington Books.

Carlos, B. S. and Cevera, N. (1991). Inmates and their families. *Criminal Justice and Behavior* 13, 318-339.

Cripe, C. (1997). *Legal aspects of corrections management*. Githersberg, MD: Aspen Publishers, Inc.

Gabel, S. (1992). Behavior problems in sons of incarcerated or otherwise absent fathers: The issue of separation. *Family Process* 31, 303-314.

Hairston, C. F. (1998). The forgotten parent: Understanding the forces that influence incarcerated fathers' relationships with their children. *Child Welfare* 77, 5: 617-639.

Hairston, C. F., and Hess, P. (1989). Family ties: Maintaining child-parent bond is important. *Corrections Today* 51, 102-106.

Harrison, K. (1997). Parental training for incarcerated fathers: Effects on attitudes, self-esteem, and children's self perceptions. *The Journal of Social Psychology* 137, 5: 588-593.

King, A. E. O. (1993). The impact of incarceration on African American families: Implications for practice. *The Journal of Contemporary Human Services* (Spring).

Lamb, M. E., Pleck, J. H., Charnov, E. L., and Levine, J. A. (1987). A biosocial perspective on paternal behavior and involvement. In J. B. Lancaster, J. Altman, A. Rossi, and L. R. Sherrod (Eds.), *Parenting across the lifespan: Biosocial perspectives* (pp. 11-42). New York: Academic Press.

Landreth, G.L. and Lobaugh, A.F. (1998). Filial therapy with incarcerated fathers: Effects on parental acceptance of child, parental stress, and child adjustment. *Journal of Counseling and Development* 76, 157-165.

Lanier, Jr., C. S. (1987). Fathers in prison: A psychosocial exploration. Unpublished master's thesis, New Paltz College of the State University of New York.

Lanier, Jr., C. S. (1993). Affective states of fathers in prison. *Justice Quarterly* 10, 49-65.

McPeek, S. and Tse, S. (1988). *Bureau of prisons parenting programs: Use, costs, and benefits*. Washington, D.C.: Federal Office of Research and Evaluation.

Rudel, C. H. and Hayes, M. C. (1990). Behind no bars. *Children Today* 19, 20-23.

Schmid, T. J. and Jones, R. S. (1996). Suspended identity: Identity transformation in a maximum security prison. In D. H. Kelly, *Deviant Behavior* (5th ed., 427-443). New York: St. Martin's Press.

Wilczak, G. L. and Markstrom, C. A. (1999). The effects of parent education on parental locus of control and satisfaction of incarcerated fathers. *International Journal of Offender Therapy and Comparative Criminology* 43, 1: 90-102.

3

The Loss of the Protective Effects of Marital and Non-Marital Relationships of Incarcerated African American Men: Implications for Social Work

Mary L. Balthazar and Lula King

Introduction

The incarceration rate for African American males is staggering, and the projected rates for the prison population in the United States for 2005 is mind-boggling. From 1973 to 1993, the nation's prison population grew from 350,000 to 1.4 million (Bureau of Justice Statistics, 1993; Department of Justice, 1993). Current data show that the combined federal, state and local adult correctional population grew by 163,800 men and women during 1998 to reach a new high of 5.9 million people. This includes incarcerated inmates, probationers, and parolees in the community. Almost 3 percent of the nation's adult population, or about 1 in every 34 adults, was incarcerated or on probation or parole at the end of the 1990s (Bureau of Justice Statistics, 1999).

The racial, ethnic, and gender breakdowns in the incarcerated population reveal some disturbing trends. The incarceration rate, in 1997, for African American males in their late twenties was 8,630 per 100,000 residents, compared to 2,703 among Hispanic males, and 868 among white males. The rate among African American males age 45 to 54, in 1997, was larger than the highest rate among Hispanic males, age 20 to 29, and 3 times larger than the highest rate among white males, age 30 to 34. African American men and women were at least 6 times more likely than whites to have been in prison by the end of 1997 (Bureau of Justice Statistics, 1999). The potential consequences of these high rates of incarceration for African American men, women, their families, and communities are enormous.

Reasons for Disparities

Several explanations have been identified in the literature for the disparities in the rates of incarceration:

1. change in sentencing policies, which began during the 1970s;
2. the sentencing guideline systems;
3. mandatory minimum sentences for various crimes beginning in the early 1980s; and
4. racial bias (Mauer, 1995).

As a result of liberal and conservative support for a more fixed and determinate sentencing structure with decreased emphasis in rehabilitation, the stage was set for a shift in the sentencing policy (Mauer, 1995). By 1990, almost every state and federal government had adopted some form of mandatory sentencing policy (Bureau of Justice Statistics, 1992). The premise behind mandatory minimums was that for a given crime, an offender would be required to receive a set minimum prison term regardless of any mitigating circumstances. The mandatory sentencings for drunk driving were modest, but for drug offenses, penalties were harsher (Mauer, 1995).

Racial disparity in the criminal justice system is a product of both high crime rates among some groups and differential treatment by the criminal justice system. Policies that have contributed to racial disparity include law enforcement policies that unduly punish African Americans and policing policies that focus on inner-city communities (Mauer, 1995).

The Ecological Perspective

The Ecological Perspective, postulated by Germain (1979) as a conceptual framework, later elaborated and refined (Germain and Gitterman, 1987), provides the analytical tools for understanding the plight of incarcerated African American males. This perspective provides a multidimensional parameter for viewing the complex interrelationships of the world of African American males. The following concepts from the Ecological Perspective provide understanding of the impact of incarceration on African American males; their families and communities will be used in the paper:

Life stressors—generated by critical life issues that people perceive as exceeding their personal and environmental resources for managing them.

They include difficult social or developmental transitions, traumatic life events, and any other life issues that disturb the existing fit between the individual and his/her environment.

Stress—an internal response to a life stressor and is characterized by troubled emotional or psychological states, or both. Associated negative feelings may include anxiety, guilt, anger, fear, depression, helplessness, or despair and are usually accompanied by lowered levels of relatedness, sense of competence, self-esteem, and self direction.

Relatedness—refers to attachments, friendships, positive kin relationships, and a sense of belonging to a supportive social network.

Habitat and Niche—the former includes dwelling places, physical layouts of urban and rural communities. The latter refers to the status occupied by an individual or family in the social structure of a community (Germain and Gitterman, 1987).

Impact of Incarceration on African American Men

African American men represent a vulnerable, "endangered" segment of the American population (Gibbs, 1988; Taylor, 1987; Gary, 1981; Rasheed and Rasheed, 1999). Gary and Leashore (1982) state that African American men have higher morbidity and mortality rates, experience greater unemployment, earn less, and have higher rates of incarceration than do white men. They argue that these circumstances have crippling consequences for mental health of African American men, their families, and communities. Intimate relationships are very important to the maintenance of mental health and to the prisoner's post-release success. Problems related to the maintenance of these relationships have been identified as a principal deprivation for prisoners. They describe their inability to be involved in the daily lives of their children and loved ones as a source of great psychological stress and pain (Baunach, 1985; Hairston, 1991).

Research on married men and women further underscores the importance of intimate relationships. Studies show that married men and women, compared to their unmarried counterparts, especially those who are divorced and separated, experience lower mortality and morbidity; better mental health; lower rates of alcoholism, suicide; and higher levels of reported happiness and satisfaction with life (Campbell, Converse and Rodgers, 1976; Coombs, 1991; Goves, Style and Hughes, 1990; Lee, Seccombe and Shehan, 1991; Williams, 1988; Zollar and Williams, 1987). Research also shows significant benefits from involvement in intimate relationships for unmarried adults

(Orthner, Bower, Zimmermann and Short, 1992). The preponderance of evidence supports the view that intimate relationships provide a "protective barrier" for individuals as they negotiate life-stressful situations.

The ecological concept of relatedness broadens the range of significant relationships. It refers to attachments, friendship, positive kin relationships, and a sense of belonging to a supportive social network (Germain and Gitterman, 1987). This concept captures the multilevel relationship network in the African American community. It represents important nurturing and sustaining resources for African American men. This network functions as a therapeutic buffer to both the internal and external stressors in the lives of African American men. The disconnection from these therapeutic networks, as a result of incarceration, can be very traumatic for the men, because incarceration severely limits African American men's access to these sources of psychological and social supports.

Impact of Incarceration on African American Families

The number of incarcerated African American men does not represent lone individuals without intimate ties, social roles, commitments, and expectations. It represents partners, friends, families, and communities that operate as intimate network systems. The high rate of incarceration of African American men has a devastating ripple effect on their families. Of course, the extent of the impact will largely depend on whether the incarcerated male is viewed as an asset or a liability to his family. If he were perceived as an asset, the loss of his role within the family will be experienced with a greater sense of loss and disruption. This disconnection of ties and roles can result in both psychological and financial distress for the family (Hairston, 1991).

Research shows that offenders can be both assets and liabilities to their families. Carlson and Cervera (1992) found that women had to rely on family and friends to fill the role of their incarcerated husbands in terms of money, companionship, and baby-sitting. In her study of partners of incarcerated men, Fishman (1990) found that women exhibited a strong commitment to their male partners and put forth much effort to maintain intimate ties across prison walls. Some of the women's lives seem to improve with the man's removal, others deteriorated. While the women display admirable fortitude when confronted with the loss of their partners, for almost all of them this represents a challenge to their resources and a profound interruption in their lives (Fishman, 1990).

Children suffer when parents are removed from the home. Some studies found that some children of incarcerated men experience significant psychological stress and acting-out behavior following their father's incarceration, while others exhibit fewer systems of stress (Brodsky, 1975; Fishman, 1990; Carlson and Cervera, 1992; King, 1993). These studies show that the negative psychological and circumstantial impact on children from the removal of a parent for incarceration is similar, in form though not in degree, to that produced by removal due to divorce or death. Children suffer both psychological and financial distress resulting from loss of parent and income from their support. Hagan (1996) shows that theories of strain, socialization, and stigmatization each confirm the potential for negative developmental outcomes when a father is imprisoned. This is especially true if there was positive parenting prior to incarceration.

All of the factors potentially disrupt family cohesiveness, which studies show would predict serious delinquency (Sampson, 1987). Children's internalization of social norms may also be disrupted by high levels of incarceration. Changes in parental working conditions and family circumstances are known to affect children's social adjustment and norm transmission across generations (Parcel and Menaghan, 1993). Due to high rates of incarceration of African American men in their late twenties, and those aged 45 to 54, it would seem that a large number of African American children and families are being negatively impacted.

Impact of Incarceration of African American Communities

The ecological concepts of habitat and niche provide understanding of how the high rate of incarceration of African American men impacts their communities. Habitat refers to the physical characteristics of the community, whereas, niche refers to the person's status position in that community. A large percentage of incarcerated African American men come from low-income, inner-city communities. Research shows that offenders can be both assets and liabilities to their communities (Fleisher, 1995; Decker and Van Winkle, 1996; Venkatesh, 1997). The extent to which the community will experience loss of the assets of the offenders will depend on its level of organization and nurturing and sustaining resources. If the community is organized and has sufficient nurturing and sustaining resources, it can readily overcome the loss of the offender's assets when the offenders are removed from the community. On the other hand, in disorganized communities in which there are insufficient nurturing and sustaining resources, and where assets are already depleted, the loss of the offenders' assets will be more intensely experienced.

Research shows that most criminals also have legal employment. Their removal from the community through incarceration also removes employees from the local economy (Fagan, 1997). Prior to incarceration, most males are an economic resource to their communities and immediate families. Sullivan's (1989) research suggests that in impoverished communities, a work-age male generates economic activity that translates into purchases at the local deli, child support, and other material support. Once these males are incarcerated, this economic value is transformed and transferred. It is transformed into penal capital via salaried correctional employees to provide security. It is also transferred to the locality of the prison, where the penal system's employees reside (Sullivan, 1989).

Economic hardship is one of the strongest geographical predictors of crime rate (Hagan, 1993). There is a circular relationship between a high rate of incarceration and a high rate of unemployment within a community. Individuals who are incarcerated numerous times tend to become more hostile to legal legitimacy, less willing to work, and less able to get a job (Sampson, 1989). This is supported by Wilson (1987) who argues that a community experiencing economic loss as a result of incarceration will experience an increase in crime. Economic hardship is one of the strongest geographic predictors of crime rates. The social interrelationship of crime and unemployment suggests that communities that are deprived of other resources experience greater criminal involvement among residents (Hagan, 1993). It is reasonable to assume that a community experiencing economic loss as a result of a high rate of incarceration of African American males will experience an increase in crime (Wilson, 1987).

Incarceration not only has an economic effect on the community in which the offenders reside; it also has a permanent impact on their earning potential. The criminal justice system leaves economic scars on the incarcerated males long after their formal involvement with the system has ended (Freeman, 1992; Crutchfield and Pitchford, 1997). Grogger (1995) demonstrated that merely being arrested has a short-term, negative impact on earnings, while Freeman (1992) has shown that suffering a conviction and imprisonment has a permanent impact on earning potential. Crutchfield and Pitchford (1997) argue that individuals who are deficit in educational and training skills are destined to have low-level jobs, which not only do not pay well but also offer no promotional opportunities for future advancement.

The absence of males restricts the number of adults to supervise young people in a community. The presence of large numbers of unsupervised youth is predictive of serious crime at the community level (Sampson and Groves, 1989).

The incarceration of large numbers of parent-age African American males also restricts the number of available male partners within the community. This means that African American women experience more competition for partners and male parents for their children. As a result, some women with children might be reluctant to end relationships that are unsuitable for their children and themselves, partially because prospects for a more suitable replacement are perceived as poor. On the other hand, African American males may also be reluctant to commit to or remain committed in parenting partnerships due to the availability of female partners (Gary, 1981; Wilson, 1987).

Family-Oriented Correctional Programs

Most family-oriented correctional programs have been established since the 1980s, although the need for them was recognized as a formal corrections principle since 1953 (Hopper, 1994). The primary focus of public policies regarding family-oriented programs has traditionally been to provide minimal support for the maintenance of family relationship and the well-being of individuals who have a family member involved in the criminal justice system. This lack of focus on family-oriented programs can be found throughout the criminal justice system beginning with the arrest, sentencing, imprisonment, and after release from prison. There has been a lack of focus on family-oriented programs until recently because the emphasis of the criminal justice system has been on punishment (Hairston, 1995).

Currently, prison communication policies acknowledge the importance of families; however, there remain some barriers to effectively implementing those policies. Hairston (1995) identified the following barriers: (1) the remote location of prisons from the residences of families; (2) highly regulated visiting polices that restrict visiting days, hours, and who can visit and accompany children; (3) the type of acceptable visitors' identification and clothing; (4) the regulation of behavior during visits; and (5) limitations on physical contact.

Family-oriented programs are helpful in reducing the stress associated with incarceration. They also help to maintain emotional attachments and physical contacts, which are conducive to family reunification. There is a relationship among maintenance of emotional attachments and physical contacts and recidivism rates. Studies of prisoners show consistently that those who maintain strong family and friendship ties during incarceration and assume responsible marital and parental roles on release have lower recidivism rates than those who function without family ties, expectations, and obligations (Curtis and Shulman, 1984; Hairston, 1988).

Several obstacles to family-oriented correctional programs have been identified by Hairston (1995). First, there is minimal support for families at all levels of the criminal justice system. Secondly, there is the enormity of the financial and social burdens on families who try to maintain contact with the incarcerated member. Thirdly, there is the lack of social services support for prisoners and their families from social workers.

Although family-oriented correctional programs are limited, some can be found in various areas of the correctional system. Hairston (1995) identified the more common types. These are: (1) visiting programs with inmates at the prison; (2) parent education (only at a few prisons for men); (3) support groups; and (4) residential centers (primarily for women prisoners). Family-oriented correctional programs for male prisoners are severely limited. For example, almost all prisons for women, some jails, and a few prisons for men provide parent education courses that teach child development and parenting skills and techniques (Boudouris, 1985; Lillis 1994). Additionally, residential programs that permit children to live with their incarcerated parents are rare in U.S. correction facilities. These programs enable women serving time for nonviolent offenses to live in a group residence with their children, rather than in prison. There are no such programs that provide group residences for incarcerated men and their children (Hairston, 1995).

The Role of Social Work

The social work profession has not been very supportive of prisoners and their families. Neither has it been very supportive of those social workers who provide limited services to these families (Hairston, 1995; Allen-Meares and Burman, 1995; Swan, 1981). Only a few schools of social work prepare students to work in corrections, and social work degrees are not required in all prisons for the provision of social services (Hairston, 1995). Crucial service needs for this population remain unmet, especially for African American prisoners and their families.

Hairston (1995) argues that the social work profession and the schools of social work have not been very supportive of prisoners and their families. Allen-Meares and Burman (1995) also acknowledge the "discomforting silence" from the social work profession. The appallingly high rate of incarceration of African American males and the resulting impact on marriages, families, children, and communities demand more than silence and lack of support from the social work profession. In keeping with its stated mission and purpose, and its commitment to social justice, the profession must advocate for changes in societal structures and social processes that contribute to the high rate of incarceration of African American males. There is a need for social workers to advocate for more services to families of incarcerated males, and for increased diversion from the criminal justice system to community-based programs.

The Role of Schools of Social Work

In order for social workers to be prepared to work effectively with African American males, schools of social work must include content on them. Content must also be included on the rate of incarceration of African American males and its impact on their families and community. Graduate and undergraduate students should be taught this content and be provided experiences to work with this population in their field placements. Emphasis should be on both community and clinical practice.

Community-Based Programs

A variety of community-based programs have been identified and recommended in the literature. They include a variety of formats to address the needs of prisoners and their families. They include: (1) visiting programs; (2) educational programs; (3) residential programs; (4) life education programs; and (5) support groups (Hairston, 1995; King 1993). These are programs developed and administered by professionals. The authors also recommend these programs and propose additional formats to be administered by groups indigenous to the African American community. They include: (1) churches; (2) fraternities; (3) sororities; (4) social and pleasure clubs; (5) grassroots organizations; (6) Masonic and Lions organizations; (7) American Association of Retired Persons; and other non-traditional organizations that are indigenous to the community. These organizations have a long history of helping the African American community. Schools of social work could collaborate with these organizations to develop preventive and service programs to address the special needs of African American men and their families. Since most of the organizations exist in the African community, it can be an empowering experience to find solutions for problems within the offenders' own community. Such programs can include mentoring, tutoring, and other services for the offenders and their families while simultaneously addressing factors in the community that might contribute to the high rate of incarceration of African American males.

Implication for Future Research

Research on African American men needs to be conducted so as to inform us of their gender roles from a scientific perspective (Rasheed and Rasheed, 1999). Information needs to be generated on African American men at different developmental, class, and age levels in order to gain a fuller understanding of their strengths rather than their pathology. This type of research will enhance our understanding of the life cycle development and behaviors of African American men. Research on the interrelationship of micro and macro systems factors will help to understand how African American men's lives are shaped by them. This will require a broader range of instruments to collect data, which should be culturally relative.

Additional research needs to be conducted on the effects of incarceration on African American males, their children and families. It is important to understand not only the negative impacts of incarcerations but also the positive coping strategies that are used to maintain family functioning in spite of incarceration.

Although there has been a mixed history of success, alternative programs to incarceration offer possibilities of diverting a large segment of African American men from the criminal justice system, especially those who are involved in drugs and other less severe criminal activities. Research on the effectiveness of these programs can aid in restructuring them to more effectively meet the needs of the participants and their families. There is a need for research that aids in identifying programs and policies that can have a long-term impact on crime. Research has indicated the potential crime control impacts of programs such as Head Start and Job Corp. Data from other types of interventions is needed (Mauer, 1995).

References

Allen-Meares, P. and Burman, S. (1995). The endangerment of African American: An appeal for social work actions. *Social Work* 40(2), 268-274.

Baunach, P. J. (1985). *Mothers in prison.* New Brunswick, NJ: Transaction Publishers

Boudouris, J. (1985). *Prisons and kids.* Laurel, MD: American Corrections Association.

Brodsky, S. (1975). *Families and friends of men in prison.* Lexington, MA: Lexington Book.

Bureau of Justice Statistics. (1992). *State justice sourcebook of statistics and research.*Washington, D.C.: Marc Mauer.

_____. (1993). *Jail inmates 1992.* Washington, D.C.: Marc Mauer

_____. (1999, August 22). *U.S. correctional population reaches 5.9 million offenders.* (Press release). Washington, D.C.: Stu Smith.

Campbell, A. Converse, P. E., and Rodgers, W. L. (1976). *The quality of American life: Perceptions, evaluations, and satisfactions.* New York: Russell Sage Foundation.

Carlson, B., and Cervera N. (1992). *Inmates and their wives.* Westport, CT: Greenwood Press.

Coombs, R.H. (1991). Marital status and personal well-being: A literature review. *Family Relations* 40, 97-102.

Crutchfield, R. D., and Pitchford, S. R. (1997). Work and crime: The effects of labor stratification. *Social Forces* 76, 93-118.

Curtis, R., and Shulman, S. (1984). Ex-offenders' family relations and economic supports: The significant women study of the TRAP project *crime and delinquency* 30, 507-528.

Decker, S. H., and Van Winkle, B (1996). *Life in the gang; Family, friends and violence.* New York: Cambridge University Press.

Department of Justice.(1993, October, 3). Half year increase pushes prison population to record high. (Press release). Washington, D.C.: Marc Mauer.

Fagan, J. (1997). Legal and illegal work: Crime, work and unemployment. In Burton Weisbrod and James Worthy (Eds.), *Dealing with urban crises.* Evanston, IL: Northwestern University Press.

Fishman, L. (1990). *Women at the wall.* Albany, NY: Suny Press.

Fleisher, M. S. (1995). *Beggars and thieves: Lives of urban street criminals.* Madison: University of Wisconsin Press.

Freeman, R. B. (1992). Crime and unemployment of disadvantaged youth. In Adele Harrell and George Peterson (Eds.). *Drugs, crime and social isolation barriers to urban opportunity:* Washington, D.C.: Urban Institute.

Gary, L. (Ed.). (1981). *Black men.* Beverly Hills, CA: Sage.

Gary, L., and Leashore, B. (1982). The high risk status of black men. *Social work* 27, 54-58.

Germain, C. B. (1979). Introduction: Ecology and social work. In C. B. Germain (Ed.), *Social work practice: People and environments.* New York: Columbia University Press.

Germain, C. B., and Gitterman, A. (1987). Ecological perspective. In A. Minahan (Editor in-Chief), *Encyclopedia of social work* (18th ed., Vol. 1, 488-499). Silver Spring, MD: National Association of Social Workers.

Gibbs, J. (Ed.) (1988). *Young ,black and male in America: An endangered species.* Dover, MA: Auburn House.

Goves, W. R., Style, C. B., and Hughes, M. (1990). The effect of marriage on the well-being of adults. *Journal of Family Issues* 11, 4-35.

Grogger, J. (1995). The effects of arrest on the employment and earning of young men. *Quarterly Journal of Economics* 110(1), 51-71.

Hagan, J. (1993). The social embeddedness of crime and unemployment. *Criminology* 31: 465-492.

_____. (1996). The next generation: Children of prisoners. *The unintended consequences of incarceration.* New York: Vera Institution of Justice.

Hairston, C. F. (1988). Family ties during imprisonment: Do they influence future criminal activity? *Federal Probation* 52, 481-52.

_____. *(1991).* Family ties during imprisonment: Important to whom and for what? *Journal of Sociology and Social Welfare* 18, 87-104.

_____. (1995). Family views in correctional programs. In Richard L. Edwards (Editor in-Chief), *Encyclopedia of social work* (19th ed. Vol. 1, 991-996). Silver Spring MD: National Association of Social Workers.

Hopper, C. B. (1994). The status of prison visitation. Paper presented at the Annual Meeting of the Academy of Criminal.

King, A. E. O. (1993). The impact of incarceration on African American families: Implications for practice. *Families in Society: The Journal of Contemporary Human services* 3, 145-153.

Lee, G. R., Seccombe, K., and Shehan, C. L. (1991). Marital status and personal happiness: An analysis of trend data. *Journal of Marriage and the Family* 53, 839-844.

Lillis, J. (1994). Family service groups and programs. *Corrections Compendium* 19 (1), 1-3, 18.

Mauer, M. (1995). Sentencing of criminal offenders. In R. L. Edwards (Editor-in-Chief), *Encyclopedia of social work* (19th ed., 2123-2129). Silver Spring, MD: National Association of Social Workers.

Orthner, D. K., Bowen, G. L., Zimmermann, L. D. and Short, K. A. (1992). *Young, single soldiers and relationships* (technical report). Alexandria, VA: U.S. Army Research Institute for the Behavioral and Social Sciences.

Parcel, T. L. and Menaghan, G. G. (1993). Family social capital and children's behavior problems. *Social Psychology Quarterly* 56, 120-135.

Rasheed, J. M., and Rasheed, M. (1999). *Social work practice with African American men: The invisible presence.* Thousand Oaks, CA: Sage.

Sampson, R. J. (1987). Communities and crime. In Michael R. Gottfredson and Travis Hirschi (Eds.), *Positive criminology.* Beverly Hills, CA: Sage.

Sampson, R. J., and Groves, W. B. (1989). Community structure and crime: Testing social disorganization theory. *American Journal of Sociology* 94: 744-802.

Sullivan, M. L. (1989). *Getting paid: Youth, crime and work in the inner city.* Ithaca, NY: Cornell University Press.

Swan, A. (1981). *Families of black prisoners: Survival and progress.* Boston: G. K. Hall.

Taylor, R. L. (1987). Black youth in crisis. *Humboldt Journal of Social Relations* 14, 106-133.

Venkatesk, S. A. (1997). The social organization of street gang activities in urban ghetto. *American Journal of Sociology* 103: 82-111.

Williams, G. G. (1988). Gender, marriage and psychological well-being. *Journal of Family Issues* 9, 452-468.

Wilson, W. J. (1987). *The truly dis-advantaged: The inner city, the underclass and public policy*. Chicago: University of Chicago Press.

Zollar, A. C., and Williams, J. S. (1987). The contribution of marriage to the life satisfaction of black adults. *Journal of Marriage and the Family* 49, 87-92.

4

The Relationship Between Inmate Visitation and Behavior: Implications for African American Families

Theresa A. Clark

Introduction

Behavior of persons incarcerated has become an increasing issue for prisons and a primary focus of government officials in the Commonwealth of Virginia during the past decade. During this time period, the number of prison disturbances has increased (Bureau of Justice Statistics, 1990). The increase in behavior problems not only raises concern about the safety of inmates, correctional personnel, and the community, but also becomes a critical fiscal issue for the commonwealth because of costs associated with daily operations. Behavior problems are of special concern to social workers who work in numerous correctional capacities or to those who have external responsibilities with the families of prisoners. These problems can interfere with the social worker's interventive strategies and empowerment process. As professionals, social workers focus on person-in-environment processes. Whether employed by the prisons or other human service agencies, social workers cannot afford to ignore behavioral implications for the functioning of individual prisoners and their family systems.

The Scope of the Problem

In a national survey of state prison inmates, the Bureau of Justice Statistics (1990) reported that the majority of male inmates were charged with rule violations at some point during their stay in prison. Rule violators were

45

defined as, "inmates who were formally charged with or written up for breaking prison rules or regulations" (p. 138). The type of behavior exhibited by an inmate, while in prison, is as important to the prison system as it is to the inmate. The inmate is faced with the possibility of increasing time actually spent in prison or additional punishment, which in the most severe form is solitary confinement. The prison system in America is increasingly being forced to operate under conditions of overcrowding and severe fiscal constraints. Therefore, needing to address any situation outside of the regular daily activity of prison operations appears to be costly in both money and person hours.

It is not surprising that prison problems have increased at the same time as severe overcrowding in our state prisons. "Since 1983, Virginia's incarceration population has grown on the average at more than 8.9% annually" (Virginia Commission on Prison and Jail Overcrowding, 1989: 1). Data indicate that the numbers of prisoners in our state prisons exceed capacity. "On December 31, 1998, State prisons were operating at between 13% and 22% above capacity, while Federal prisons were operating at 27% above capacity" (Virginia Statistical Abstract, 2000). A major alternative being used to reduce this overcrowding has been relocating prisoners from Virginia prisons to those in other states.

Overcrowding is undoubtedly a significant contributor to the increase in prison disturbances; however, a solution that moves prisoners to other states has the consequence of reducing the likelihood that prisoners will receive visits from their families and friends. A study conducted by Jackson, Templer, Reimer, and LeBaron (1997) indicates that "incarcerating inmates in a prison closer to their home would increase the probability of visitation" (p. 83). While the general public may have little sympathy for this situation, there is some indication that visitation has positive effects for prisoners, and ultimately, the community. For example, research has shown a link between the frequency of visitation and postrelease success for prisoners (Bayse, Allgood, and Wyk, 1991; Brodsky, 1975; Carlson and Cervera, 1991; Holt and Miller, 1972). Visitations can strengthen family systems that have been negatively impacted by the absence of husbands, sons, and fathers. There is also some suggestion that regular visitation may reduce the number of behavior problems among incarcerated individuals (Bennett, 1987). In predicting an inmate's psychological well being, frequency of visitation was one of the variables found to be significant in a study conducted by Wooldredge (1999). However, more study is needed to determine if there is a significant relationship between visitation and inmates' behavior while incarcerated.

Prison Population

State prison systems are experiencing increased problems in serving inmates, in part, due to overcrowding, inadequate funds, employee attrition rates, inadequate facilities, and increased crime within prison walls. Administrations attuned to social work values are particularly frustrated by the limitations of the systems that employ them. Statistics indicate that the number of individuals in contact with the criminal justice system in the United States is overwhelming, and that the number of those incarcerated has increased each year (Bureau of Justice Statistics, 1991). The national corrections population, which includes individuals on probation, in jail, in prison and on parole, grew from over 1.8 million, in 1980 to more than four million in 1989, a 120.4 percent change (Bureau of Justice Statistics, 1990). More recent data indicate that "5.5 million adults in the United States were under correctional supervision in 1996" (Bureau of Justice Statistics, 1999:1). The number of adult prisoners in the United States has grown from 882,500 in 1992 to 1,302,019 in 1998 (Bureau of Justice Statistics, 1998). During this time period, 94 percent of the total inmate population were males, which remained constant at 94 percent (Bureau of Justice Statistics, 1998).

The Bureau of Justice Statistics reported that despite the increase in the nation's prison inmate population, certain characteristics remained the same (1991). For example, "the population remained mostly male, minority, young, low-income, high-school dropouts, drug users or offenders, teen parents and recidivists" (1991: 3; 1996). Approximately 65 percent were racial or ethnic minorities (Bureau of Justice Statistics, 1991) and unchanged at year end 1997 (Bureau of Justice Statistics, 1998), suggesting that this group is going to be disproportionately affected by what happens inside the prison.

African American Men in Prison

Although the adult male prison population was comprised of approximately 42 percent African American males in 1997 (Bureau of Justice Statistics, 1998), which has remained relatively stable over a seven-year period, African American males represent just 6 percent of the national population (U.S. Statistical Abstracts, 1999). The over-representation of African American males in the U.S. prison system appears to have a deleterious effect on the development and maintenance of African American families. Some of the strengths historically germane to the African American family may be weakened. For example, "strong kinship bonds, strong work orientation and high achievement orientation" (Hill, 1972: 37) may be interrupted due to the incarceration of the African American male. Hill defines strengths as, "those traits which facilitate the ability of the family to meet the needs of its members and the demands made upon it by systems outside the family unit, necessary for the survival and maintenance of effective family networks" (1972: 3). More current work by Hill (1993) indicates that contact with the criminal justice system, especially the disproportional incarceration of African American men, contributes to the disintegration of the African American family unit.

According to Hill, some of the factors contributing to the disintegration of the African American family unit are "the formation of black single-parent families, males less available as marriage partners, barriers to legitimate employment or steady employment, and that incarceration keeps them [inmates] from their wives and girlfriends for long periods of time" (Hill, 1993: 81). When families disintegrate, additional stress is placed on human service systems.

Barriers to Maintaining Family Ties

Incarceration of prisoners is painful for the prisoner and causes disruption of relationships and communication with the outside world, especially with the family. The only means of maintaining contact is through letters, telephone calls, and visitation. But, there are limitations to using these methods to maintain family ties (Carlson and Cervera, 1992). Some of the limitations are imposed by prison policy. For example, policy pertaining to face-to-face visitation is stringent and limited. In part, this is due to the costs and person-hours for staff needed to supervise the visitation (White, personal communication, 1994). Within the prison system, visitation programs are sometimes inadequate when coupled with limited physical resources and understaffed correctional institutions. Inmate visitation requires the implementation of policy procedures that are in addition to the daily responsibilities of the prison staff.

Visitation is allowed only on Saturdays, Sundays, and legal holidays in the Commonwealth of Virginia. Moreover, in some states, visitation may be interrupted by prison policy, which mandates a minimum of four prison lock-downs a year (Virginia Department of Corrections, personal communication, 1994). Prison lock-downs mandate that inmates remain in their individual cells for a specified period of time. The length of time depends on the time required by prison staff to search for contraband or to resolve an emergency situation.

There have been a number of attempts to encourage visitation of family members to inmates in prison by concerned groups in Virginia. For example, several of the policy recommendations were made by the First National Leadership Conference on Families of Adult Offenders held in Virginia in 1986 relative to strengthening the offender family unit.

Despite policy recommendations pertaining to family contact to strengthen the family ties of adult offenders, family members and inmates still face barriers. For example, prisons are usually built in remote and rural areas, while most inmate families live in metropolitan areas (Bennett, 1987). The combination of low family income and the distance to the prison facility reduces the chance of regular visitation, especially if the family does not own a vehicle, or is without funds to utilize public transportation, if available. In addition, if there are means of public transportation available such as buses, they generally stop in towns close to the prison, and this leaves the visitor with problems reaching the facility from the bus stop. Family members who have to rely on others, such as relatives and friends, to obtain transportation, child care, or financial assistance, find that these are not always reliable resources (Jorgensen, Hernandez, and Warren, 1986; White, personal communication, 1994).

Visitation and Prisoner Behavior

The importance of family systems does not appear to represent a significant rehabilitating factor to prison administration. This, in part, is a result of a societal movement over the past three decades to punish criminals as opposed to rehabilitating them. The increase in crime rates and recidivism in the United States, during this period of time, provided the impetus for society to question the effectiveness of prison rehabilitation programs and the punishment given for criminal activity. As a result, a decrease in the emphasis on rehabilitation and an increase in stiffer penalties, especially the use of prisons, have emerged (Flanagan, 1995; Blumstein, 1989; Selke, 1993). Moreover, Jorgensen, Hernadez, and Warren (1986) indicate that families are not the focal point in the rehabilitation planning process for inmates. Also, social service agencies, which may be equipped to strengthen family ties, may not be providing sufficient services to families of those incarcerated. Hairston and Lockett (1987) noted that many social service agencies have ignored the need to strengthen the family relationships between parents who are in prison and their children, and other family members.

The maintenance of family relations through regular visitation to individuals incarcerated in prisons and the effect on recidivism has been the focus of a number of studies over the past several decades. For example, the frequency of visits between family members and prisoners has been linked to positive outcomes, both in prison and post-institutional release, according to a study conducted by Bennett (1987). A significant number of studies have indicated a positive correlation between family visits and the reduction in recidivism (Brodsky, 1975; Fishman and Alissi, 1979; Holt and Miller, 1972). Moreover, several studies have found that the maintenance of healthy family relations while a family member was incarcerated was a key indicator in reducing recidivism (Bayce, Allgood and Wyk, 1991; Bennett, 1987; Carlson and Cervera, 1992; Holt and Miller, 1972; Jorgensen, Hernandez and Warren, 1986).

Although recent studies of visits to inmates focused on the relationship between the visits to inmates and the family system, there appears to be a paucity of empirical research on the relationship of prison visitation to the inmate's behavior while in prison. Yet, this is also an important issue to the individual, family, and the institution. Bennett, in his study of prison visitation noted, "there are very few studies available about inmate visits and the relationships of such visits to institutional adjustment, program participation, continuation of the marriage or general post-institutional adjustment" (1987: 2). An individual who is in a new environment will encounter physical, social, emotional, and psychological changes. Maintaining contacts through telephone, letters, or visits from those closely associated with the inmate could facilitate adjustments that would reduce the possibility of the inmate exhibiting negative behavior.

Inmate behavior has been studied from different perspectives to include race as a salient variable. There are indications that a relationship between societal experiences and inmate behavior of black males exists and that blacks view the prison system similarly regardless of the geographic area from which they come (Leger and Barnes, 1986). "Many blacks believe they are victims of a racist criminal justice system, and these beliefs are intensified as the number of encounters with the system increases" (Leger and Barnes, 1986, p. 120). It is therefore logical to assume from this study and others that there is a need to provide support networks for inmates, especially black inmates, to reduce behavior problems.

It is possible that prisoners will continue to have hope for their future if they maintain contact with their families, and there may be a reduction in the prisoner's negative adaptation to the prison environment (Jorgensen, Hernandez and Warren, 1986). This type of negative adaptation has been termed prisonization and has been defined as

> a process that includes accepting the subordinate role into which one is thrust as an inmate, developing new habits of sleeping, dressing, eating, and working; undergoing status degradation; adopting a new language; and learning that one is dependent on others (including one's fellow inmates) for the scarce pleasures found in incarceration, including food, work assignment, freedom from assault, and privileges. (Allen and Simonsen, 1992: 379-380)

The process of becoming prisonized will have an impact on the behavior of the prisoner. While not all inmates become prisonized, according to a study conducted by Wheeler (1978), those who do become prisonized are less likely to conform to staff expectations.

There appears to be a correlation between prisonization and visitation. Schwartz and Weintraub (1974) found that infrequent visits led to an increase in prisonization. Conversely, "the maintenance of contact between the inmate and his spouse, children, extended family members, and friends assists him in [positively] adjusting to the prison environment" (Carlson and Cervera, 1992 : 36). Adjustment to the prison environment may reduce the level of inmate prisonization and could lead to a reduction in behavioral problems. Secondly, the prison culture requires new roles for the inmate.

This new prison culture rarely leads to the development of new positive roles for the prisoner. Prisonization appears to thrust the inmate into a subordinate role (Allen and Simonsen, 1992). This process could lead to a decrease in positive feelings about self and thus the development of a lower self-esteem. For example, if the inmate desires to, but is unable to maintain the role of head of household simply because of his current situation, he becomes frustrated (Jorgensen, Hernandez and Warren, 1986). Consequently, it is probable that prisonization could foster negative behavior by the inmate.

Importance of Study

National statistics and studies indicate the need to further investigate the relationship between visitation and inmate behavior. Also, the importance of using visitation as a rehabilitative tool, if supported by research, could positively impact both inmate adjustments to prison and prison costs. The national survey of state prison inmates in 1986 reported that punishments for rule violators were diverse. For example, punishments involved "solitary confinement or segregation, forfeiting of good time, confined to cell or quarters, loss of entertainment or recreation liberties and loss of commissary privileges, formal reprimands, extra work or transfers to other institutions or higher custody levels and a small percentage received no punishment or received suspended punishment" (Bureau of Justice Statistics, 1990: 138). "The state and, ultimately, the taxpayer build prisons and hire personnel to monitor and control inmates. Institutional misconduct requires not only the use of special facilities designed for prisoners who pose behavior problems, but also the special attention of prison staff, and can be viewed as financially costly. Other monetary costs can be measured in terms of health care and lost work time resulting from incidents where misconduct assumes the form of serious interpersonal violence" (Goetting and Howsen, 1986: 50).

The need to investigate the relationship between visitation and inmate behavior is significant to the development of future prison rehabilitation policies and programs. Also, the understanding of how the relationship, positive or negative, impacts the individual system (inmate), family system, or the prison system will offer theoretical and methodological concepts to aid in social work practice. Additionally, the following are significant reasons to justify this study: (a) the potential use of visitation as a rehabilitative tool in future prison planning and policy issues; (b) the concern for the level of prisonization and its relationship to the behavior of male inmates; (c) the recognition of the positive relationship between visits, inmate recidivism and inmate behavior; and (d) the issue of concern of disproportionately represented black males in the prison system impact on the black family.

The importance of the relationship of regular visitation by family and friends to male prison inmates and their behavior while in prison should be examined using the most rigorous research methods possible. An investigation to determine if a relationship exists between visitation and inmate behavior will increase the awareness and the knowledge base in social work and in criminal justice fields.

Methodology

Data used in this study were collected from inmate files maintained in two prison facilities housing male felons in the Commonwealth of Virginia. A random sample was drawn from the total prison populations of inmates who were incarcerated in fiscal year 1995. It was determined that a 12-month time period would provide a general pattern of visitation and inmate behavior. Inmate records were examined to determine the frequency of visits from relatives and friends, the positive and negative behavior of the inmates, and demographic information on each inmate.

Research Design

A non-experimental, longitudinal research design is employed in this study to determine if there is a relationship between visitation and inmate behavior. This design was selected to allow the researcher to gather data over an extended time to allow for identification of variances and patterns in visitation and behavior of inmates.

Using this research design, several variables were included to control for demographic differences among inmates that may potentially influence visitation or behavior. These variables include age, race, marital status, and number of children. In addition, variables related to their incarceration status were also included. These were the types of previous crimes committed, the number of previous incarcerations, incarceration date, length of prison sentence, and with whom the inmate resided at the time of incarceration.

Data Sources

The data sources in this study were comprised of written and computerized prison administrative files. They included: (a) inmate files, (b) disciplinary infraction records, (c) prison program participation records and (d) visitation records.

The primary independent variable, visitation, was defined as the number of face-to-face contacts each month, between the visitor and inmate, during prison visitation, from July 1, 1994 to June 30, 1995. Visitor names are recorded individually in the prison visitation records.

To address reliability and validity of the count, approximately 10 percent of the sample was reviewed for accuracy. Ten inmate files were reviewed in Prison Site Min and 25 were reviewed in Prison Site Max. Data were collected for each variable in the study. On a follow-up visit, the files were again reviewed and a comparison of the collected data to the information in the files revealed no discrepancies. In addition, the researcher was the only individual collecting the data, thus insuring a level of consistency.

The dependent variable, institutional infractions, was defined by the number of documented rule infractions an inmate accrued during the sample time frame. Rule infractions are violations of the Code of Inmate Offenses or posted institutional rules.

A computerized program (PRSN) was developed by Bell Services of Roanoke, Virginia, to enter the data collected in this study. The program allowed the data to be entered and retrieved alphabetically (inmate names), by sample number, or by inmate identification number. Safety features were built into the program to lessen data entry error rates.

Statistical Analyses

In this study, univariate procedures were employed to describe the sample population and multivariate procedures were employed to answer the research question. Multiple regression analyses allowed several independent variables to be entered into an equation to investigate their predictive power relative to the dependent variable.

Results

Three hundred thirty-nine male felons from two Virginia prison sites comprised the sample for this study. Demographic and background variable information, which is listed in Table 1, was obtained through univariate analysis. These data provide an overview of the sample characteristics. In summary, the profile of this inmate sample appears to be representative of male felon inmates housed in Virginia prisons and across the United States. Specifically, there is a disproportionate number of African American males incarcerated and the total sample has less than a high school education (Selke, 1993; Carlson and Cervera, 1991). The mean age reported by inmates was 34.3 years. Data also show that the majority of inmates had never been married. However, slightly more than one half (51 percent) of the inmates reported having children. Criminal history and incarceration variables, listed in Table 2, were also obtained through univariate analysis.

Through multivariate analysis, five different models were tested to answer the research question. The first model tested included an analysis of the total sample of the primary independent variable, total visitation, and all of the other independent variables. The results of this test contributed to the decision to explore this study's research question through the development of four additional models. One model included the total sample and four models selected out sub-samples from the data set.

All of the models were significant in predicting variation in the dependent variable of the number of inmate infractions, but visitation by family and friends to incarcerated males was not found to be a significant predictor variable in any of the models (Table 3). Age was consistently a significant predictor variable in four of the five models, with younger inmates receiving higher numbers of institutional infractions. Furthermore, in Model 1, which involved analysis of the total sample, number of years incarcerated, race, prison education program participation, and also prison self-help program participation emerged as significant predictor variables. Some of these vari-

Table 1
General Demographic and Background Variables

Variable		Test Statistics
Age		M + 34.3, SD + 7.86
Race		
	African-American	67%, n = 228
	Caucasian	31%, n = 105
	Hispanic	1%, n = 4
	Asian	.3%, n = 1
	Native American	.3%, n = 1
	Other	.3%, n = 1
Education		M = 9.7, SD = 2.52
Marital Status		
	Married	17%, n = 58
	Never Married	62%, n = 212
	Divorced	12%, n = 40
	Widowed	3%, n = 9
	Separated	7%, n = 22
Number of Children		M = .91, SD = 1
Living Status		
	Wife/Girlfriend	22%, n = 74
	Child(ren)	2%, n = 5
	Mother	36%, n = 122
	Father	9%, n = 32
	Stepmother	2%, n = 6
	Stepfather	2%, n = 8
	Other	38%, n = 129

ables emerged in the other models tested, as well; significant at either the p<. 05 or p<. 10 level (number of years incarcerated, participation in self-help programs, and participation in prison education programs).

Two additional variables also emerged in the analysis of late models. Specifically, offense levels were significant at the p<. 10, with more serious offenses being associated with higher numbers of institutional infractions. Participation in prison work programs may also be a significant predictor (p<. 10), with those inmates who did not participate in work having higher numbers of infractions. Taken as a whole, findings from the five models suggested the following. African American participants received a higher number of infractions, while the more years that one was incarcerated was associated with lower number of infractions. Also, participation in prison education or work programs was associated with more institutional infractions. Finally, inmates with more serious offenses were more likely to have more institutional infractions.

Table 2
Criminal History and Incarceration Variables

Variable		Test Statistic
Prison		
	Min	25%, n = 85
	Max	74%, n = 250
Current Offense		
	Most Serious	44%, n = 151
	Serious	35%, n = 118
	Less Serious	8%, n = 28
	Least Serious	3%, n = 44
Sentence		M = 59, SD = 84
Years of Incarceration		M = 8, SD = 5
Previous Incarceration		M = .69, SD = .89
Prison education program		77%, n = 264
Prison self-help program		82%, n = 280
Prison work program		84%, n = 286
Number of Visits		M = 7, SD = 16
Institutional Infractions		M = .82, SD = .15

Table 3
Summary of Five Models of Multiple Regression Analyses:
Significant Predictors of Institutional Infractions

Model	Sample Size	Significant Predictor Variables
Model 1 (total sample)	325	Age (negative relationship)*
		Number of Years Incarcerated (negative relationship)*
		Prison Self-help Program (positive relationship)*
		Prison Education Program (negative relationship)*
		Race (African-American participants)*
Model 2 (African-American)	221	Age (negative relationship)*
		Prison Education Program (negative relationship)^t
		Prison Self-help Program (positive relationship)^t
Model 3 (non African-American)	102	Age (negative relationship)*
Model 4 (Maximum Prison Site)	244	Age (negative relationship)*
		Race (African-American participant)
		Prison Self-help (positive relationship)^t
		Prison Education Program (negative relationship)^t
		Number of Years Incarcerated (negative relationship)^t
		Offense (negative relationship)^t
Model 5 (Minimum Prison Site)	79	Number of Years Incarcerated (negative relationship)*
		Prison Self-help Program (positive relationship)*
		Prison Work Program (negative relationship)^t

Note: * = significant, $p < .05$; ^{t} = statistical trend, $p < .10$

Discussion

The findings from this study must be interpreted within the limitations of the study's methodology. Methodological limitations are evident in the areas of design, sampling, measurement, and data analysis restrictions. Specifically, due to the longitudinal, correlational nature of the study design, no causal inferences can be made about the relationship between any of the significant independent variables identified and the dependent variable. Although some of the independent variables are associated with the dependent variable in this study, a cause and effect relationship cannot be established. Prison policies and protection of human rights prevented the use of an experimental design to answer the multivariate research question in this study.

Second, the method of sampling in this study was systematic sampling. Although this sampling method meets the requirements for probability sampling, the findings in this study can be generalized only to the two prison sites during the time frame of this study. Further, generalizations to other prison sites in Virginia or throughout the United States cannot be made.

Third, data collected in this study were collected from existing information, or secondary analysis of available data. Fourth, one of the assumptions of regression analyses is that variables are measured in a continuous data format. Three variables were recoded using dummy variables to comply with this rule. Fifth, there were data restrictions, which prevented the full exploration of the dependent (institutional infractions) and primary independent variable (number of visits). Data on the type of institutional infraction were not collected. For example, it is not known if the infraction was for being in the wrong place or for physically assaulting another inmate or correctional employee.

Further studies are needed to determine if a relationship exists between visitation and institutional infractions. Other approaches to studying inmate institutional behavior, other than utilization of institutional records, must be considered. For example, self-report measures or observations of inmates may be effective. Future research might focus on diverse methods to prepare data for statistical analyses. The dependent variable, institutional infractions, could be dichotomized into zero infractions and some infractions, which would allow the data to be analyzed employing different methods, such as logistic regression or discriminant function analysis.

Since, in other studies, visitation to inmates has been found to relate to positive family functioning and lower recidivism, further investigation of the concept and its relationship to inmate behavior should be explored. In this study, the exploration of the relationship between visitation and inmate behavior was limited because of the use of secondary data analyses. Full exploration of this relationship has not occurred in this study, but this study has used rigorous research methods in an area not previously studied. Although there was no relationship found in this study between visitation and inmate infractions, logically one would think that the potential of a relationship exists. Given the relatively low explained variance in all of the tested models, it is possible that other variables, upon examination, might have a relationship to inmate infractions. For example, the concept of prisonization or gang affiliation might be explored in relationship to institutional infractions.

This study appears to be the only existing study to examine the relationship between visitation and institutional infractions by defining visitation and infractions as actual counts of the number of visits or the number of institutional infractions. Therefore, no definitive conclusions may be drawn. That this study is preliminary continued research, using diverse definitions of each variable should occur as a follow-up to this study. Only with further knowledge of the relationship between visitation and inmate behavior can we begin to suggest possible interventive strategies for Social Workers and other helping professionals.

References

Allen, H. E., and Simonsen, C. F. (1992). *Corrections in America: An introduction.* New York: Macmillan.

Bayse, D. J., Allgood, S. M., and Wyk, P. H. (1991). Family life education: An effective tool for prisoner rehabilitation. *Family Relations* 40, 254-257.

Bennett, L. A. (1987). What has happened to prison visiting? Current use of a rehabilitative tool. Paper presented at the annual meeting, American Society of Criminology, Montreal, Canada.

Blumstein, A. (1989). American prisons in a time of crisis. The American prison: Issues in research and policy. *Law, Society, and Policy* 4, 13-22.

Brodsky, S. L. (1975). *Families and friends of men in prison: The uncertain relationship.* Boston, MA: D.C. Heath and Co.

Bureau of Justice Statistics. (1990). Washington, D.C.: Government Printing Office.

_____. (1991). Washington, D.C.: Government Printing Office.

_____. (1998). Washington, D.C.: Government Printing Office.

_____. (1999). Washington, D.C.: Government Printing Office.

Carlson, B. E., and Cervera, J. J. (1991). Incarceration, coping, and support. *Social Work* 36(4), 279-285.

_____. (1992). *Inmates and their wives: Incarceration and family life.* Westport, CT: Greenwood Press.

Fishman, S. H., and Alissi, A. S. (1979). Strengthening families as natural support systems for offenders. *Federal Probation* 16-21.

Flanagan, T. J. (Ed.). (1995). *Long-term imprisonment policy, science, and correctional practice.* Thousand Oaks, CA: Sage.

Goetting, A., and Howsen, R. M. (1986). Correlates of prisoners misconduct. *Journal of Quantitative Criminology* 2(1), 49-67.

Hairston, C. F. and Lockett, P. W. (1987). Parents in prison: New directions for social services. *Social Work* 32, 162-164.

Hill, R. (1972). *The strengths of black families.* New York: Emerson Hall.

_____. (1993). *Research on the African-American family: A holistic perspective.* Dover, MA: Auburn House.

Holt, N., and Miller, D. (1972). *Explorations in inmate-family relationships.* Sacramento: California Department of Corrections.

Jackson, P., Templer, D. I., Reimer, W., and LeBaron, D. (1997). *Correlates of Visitation in Criminology* 41 (1), 79-85.

Jorgensen, J. D., Hernandez, S. H., and Warren, R. C. (1986). Addressing the social needs of families of prisoners: A tool for inmate rehabilitation. *Federal Probation* 50(4), 47-52.

Leger, B. R., and Barnes, H. G. (1986). Black attitudes in prison: A sociological analysis. *Journal of Criminal Justice* 14, 105-122.

Selke, W. L. (Ed.). (1993). *Prisons in crisis.* Bloomington, IN: Indiana University.

Schwartz, M. C., and Weintraub, J. (1974). The prisoner's wife: A study in crisis. *Federal Probation* 38(20-26).

U.S. Census Bureau, Statistical Abstract of the United States: 1999 (119th ed.). Washington, D.C.

Virginia Commission on Prison and Jail Overcrowding. (1989). *Commission on prison and jail overcrowding* (NCJ Publication No. 121577).

Virginia Statistical Abstract. (2000). Weldon Cooper Center for Public Service. University of Virginia, Charlottesville.

Virginia Department of Corrections. (1994). (Personal Communication).

Wheeler, G. R. (1978). *Counterdeterrence: A report on juvenile sentencing and effects of prisonization.* Chicago: Nelson Hall.

White, S. (1994). (Personal communication).

Wooldredge, J. D. (1999). Inmate experiences and psychological well-being. *Criminal Justice and Behavior* 26(2), 235-250.

5

The Financial Cost of Maintaining Relationships with Incarcerated African American Men: Results from a Survey of Women Prison Visitors

*Olga Grinstead, Bonnie Faigeles,
Carrie Bancroft, and Barry Zack*

Introduction

There is an incarceration epidemic in the United States. There are currently 1.8 million people in custody in the United States and about half of these inmates are African American (U.S. Department of Justice, 1999). African American men, in particular, have been disproportionately impacted by incarceration. One in every 14 African American men in the United States is now incarcerated, and one in four will be incarcerated at some point in his life (Schlosser, 1998).

For every man who is incarcerated, there are women and children who suffer social, psychological and financial consequences. In addition to the loss of income that can result when a family member is incarcerated, families face the additional financial burden of prison visiting, telephone calls and other contacts with the incarcerated (Girshick, 1996).

One of the most consistent findings in criminal justice is that visiting during incarceration promotes family reunification and reduces recidivism (Schafer, 1994; Hairston, 1991), and programs have been developed to encourage family support and reunification (e.g., Jorgensen, Hernandez and Warren, 1986). Maintaining contact with an inmate, however, is also stressful, costly and potentially stigmatizing for the family and other visitors (Hairston,

1991). While the psychological costs and stigma of imprisonment of a family member and of prison visiting has been well-documented (Girshick, 1996; Daniel and Barrett, 1981; Moerings, 1992; Fishman, 1988a), and the financial burdens of visiting and maintaining contact with an incarcerated person have been described qualitatively (Girshick, 1996), the actual financial costs have not been assessed quantitatively.

Here we report on the demographics, income, relationship to the person being visited, patterns of contact and the costs of visits, telephone calls and packages sent to the inmate among a group of women visiting male inmates at a large state prison. We also discuss implications for the health of African American families and offer policy recommendations.

Methods

Data Collection Site

Data were collected in August 1998 at a large state prison in California. Approximately 6,000 inmates are currently housed at this prison. Inmates are 40 percent African American, 25 percent Latino, 30 percent European American and 5 percent other ethnicities. Visiting is permitted for several hours in the visiting room on four days of the week, Thursday through Sunday. Inmates in certain programs are also allowed "ranch" or "picnic" visits in which family members share a meal in a more relaxed setting. Some inmates who are legally married are also allowed family visits in which family members visit for three days and two nights in a family housing unit on the prison grounds. All visitors enter and leave the prison through a hallway known as "the tube." A house across the street from the main prison entrance serves as the visiting center and provides childcare as well as a place for visitors to rest, have a snack and, if necessary to meet prison rules, to change their clothes before visiting. The visiting center also has a peer health education program, assists with transportation for visiting, and offers referrals for other services.

Survey Methods

Data were collected during five days in August 1998. Interviewers stood at either end of "the tube" at tables displaying snacks and gifts. Each woman leaving from the visiting area when an interviewer was free was approached and asked if she would like to participate in a survey. Interviewers were available to offer the interview in English and Spanish, although no interviews were conducted in Spanish. Women were told that the survey would take about ten minutes and that after the survey they could choose a gift to thank them for their time. Gifts included video games, costume jewelry, computer games, watches and other items that had been donated to the visiting center. The survey was anonymous. Women who agreed to answer the survey were read a summary of information for research participants and given a copy of this information to keep. In addition to the individual surveys, we also counted all of the women who left the prison and categorized them by ethnicity based on our observation. This count allowed us to estimate what percentage of the entire population of women leaving the prison that day were surveyed and if we were able to recruit a representative sample. This project was approved by the Committee on Human Subjects at the University of California, San Francisco.

Survey Instrument

The survey instrument was designed to be administered verbally in approximately ten minutes and included the following topics: demographics (age, income, education, ethnicity, ethnicity of person she was visiting, whether she was raising children), frequency and patterns of visiting, relationship to the person being visited, use of visiting services and the amount of money spent on visiting, telephone calls and packages sent to the inmate. To protect privacy, each woman was asked to point to the income category that most closely matched her income in the previous year. Costs of contact with the inmate were assessed by asking how much each woman spent on an average visiting day, the frequency of visiting and her monthly costs for telephone calls to the prison. Participants were asked if they had ever sent a quarterly package, and if so the cost of that package. They were also asked if they had any other types of visits (such as overnight family visits), and if so the frequency and cost of these visits. Monthly costs of maintaining contact with the inmate were calculated by summing the following: amount spent per visit multiplied by the frequency of visits per month; amount spent monthly on other visits; amount spent monthly on phone calls; and amount spent on quarterly packages divided by three. This sum was then multiplied by 12 to create the annual cost of visiting. Descriptive statistics presented include means for continuous variables and frequencies for categorical variables. For this report on the impact of incarceration on the African American family we describe a sub-sample of respondents who were either themselves African American, who were visiting an African American man, or who were both African American themselves and visiting an African American man (African American sub-sample).

Results

During data collection periods on the five days of data collection, 981 women were counted leaving the prison visiting area. Based on appearance, the observers estimated that 34 percent of these women were African American, 20 percent Latina, 39 percent European-American and 4 percent Asian. Of the 981 women who were counted, 153 (16 percent) completed a survey. Those who completed a survey had the same ethnic representation as the overall Population of women leaving the prison (37% African American, 16% as Latina, 38% as European-American, 1% as Asian and the remainder of mixed ethnicity) suggesting that a representative sample was achieved.

Women who were African American, visiting African American men, or both, included 75 of the 153 women who were surveyed. Demographic characteristics of this sub-sample are shown in Table 1. Most women in the sub-

Table 1
Demographic Characteristics

	N = 75
Age	
17-25	24%
26-35	27%
46-45	32%
>45	16%
Ethnicity	
African-American	76%
European-American	17%
Latino	4%
Asian	1%
Have children	91%
Education	
<High school	12%
Completed high school	20%
Some college or vocational school	35%
Completed college	24%
Any graduate school	8%
Household income	
<$10,000	17%
$10,000-$19,999	23%
$20,000-$29,999	23%
$30,000-$40,000	11%
>$40,000	19%
Don't know or refused	1%

aCategories are not mutually exclusive.

sample were African American (76 percent) and the remaining European-American (17 percent), Latina (4 percent) and Asian (1 percent) women who were visiting African American men. The most common educational level was having completed high school as well as some college or vocational school. Nearly a quarter of the women had completed college. Overall, this was a relatively low-income sample. Only one in five women earned more than $40,000 per year. Ninety-one percent reported that they had children, and 75 percent reported living with their children.

Characteristics of the women's relationships and visiting patterns are shown in Table 2. Most of the women reported that they were visiting their husbands (39 percent) followed by their fiancée (19 percent), boyfriend (12 percent), friend (14 percent) or other relative (16 percent). A majority of women, then, were visiting their intimate partners. The most common visiting frequency reported was two to three times per week (36 percent), followed by once a

Table 2
Relationship to Man Visiting and Visiting Patterns

Relationship to man visiting	
Husband	39%
Fiancée	19%
Boyfriend	12%
Friend	14%
Relative (not husband)	16%
Frequency of visits/frequency planning to visit (if first visit)	
4 times per week	4%
2-3 times per week	36%
1 time per week	25%
2-3 times per month	18%
1 time per month	13%
Has he been incarcerated before this time?	
Yes	76%
Did you visit him during a previous incarceration?	
Yes	41%
How long have you been visiting him in prison?	
>1 year	56%
1-3 years	23%
4-6 years	4%
7-9 years	3%
>10 years	9%

week (25 percent). Most women had been visiting for less than one year (56 percent), although there were a number of women who had been visiting for 10 years or more (9 percent). Over three-quarters of the women surveyed reported that the men they were visiting had been incarcerated previously, and 41 percent had visited them during a previous incarceration.

All but one of the women surveyed had been to the visiting center at the prison. The most frequently mentioned reason for going to the visiting center was for childcare. Other services that were mentioned (in order of frequency) were to attend a health education program, to use the bathroom, to get food, to wait or "hang out," to change clothes or to remove the underwires from her bra (to pass through the metal detector). Only one or two women mentioned using the telephone, arranging transportation, or for a place to leave her belongings.

The overall average monthly cost of visiting, calling and sending packages was $292. Table 3 shows the relative amount spent on various types of contact per month. The most expensive type of contact was regular visiting (visits in the prison visiting room). Visits cost an average of $43 each, but because many women visited frequently, the overall average monthly cost of visiting was $168. Telephone calls were the next most expensive contact at an average of $85 per month. Most women (64 percent) had sent a quarterly package; quarterly packages cost an average of $82 which equals a monthly cost of just over $27. Twelve women reported having had other types of visits such as "ranch" or family visits. Because these types of visits were infrequent,

Table 3
Average Monthly Cost of Contact with Inmate

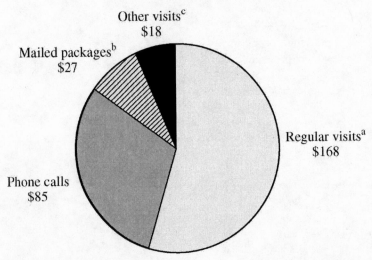

Other visits[c]
$18

Mailed packages[b]
$27

Phone calls
$85

Regular visits[a]
$168

the overall average monthly cost was low ($18). However, these types of visits could be expensive; women reported spending up to $200 on one family visit. These cost estimates did not include the cost of time off from work when needed.

The overall annual costs of maintaining contact with an inmate relative to annual income is shown in Table 4. The amount spent on contact was not proportional to income; women in the second lowest income group spent, on average, the largest amount of money on visits, phone calls and packages combined. When we consider the proportion of income spent on contact with the inmate, women in the lower income groups spent a larger proportion of their entire income than did women with higher incomes (shown in Table 5). While women in the lowest income category spent 26 percent of their income on visits, telephone calls and packages, women in the highest income group spent only 9 percent of their income on these activities.

The remainder of the original sample included 78 women who were not themselves African American and who were not visiting African-American men. This sub-sample included European American (58 percent), Latino (27 percent), Native American (8 percent) and Asian (1 percent) women. They reported a similar distribution of household income, educational level, age and relationship to the inmate being visited and nearly identical average spending ($289/month and $3,464/year) as the African American sub-sample. Women in the highest income category spent the smallest amount. Although the overall amount was the same, women in this sub-sample spent more per visit ($63 versus $43), less on telephone calls ($63 versus $85/month), less

Table 4
Annual Income and Annual Amount Spent on Inmate

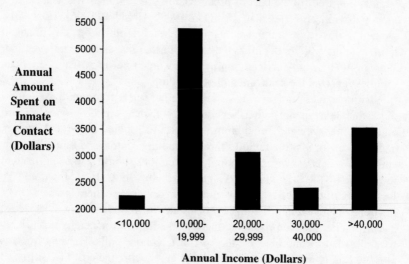

Annual Income (Dollars)

Table 5
Percentage of Annual Income Spent on Inmate Contact

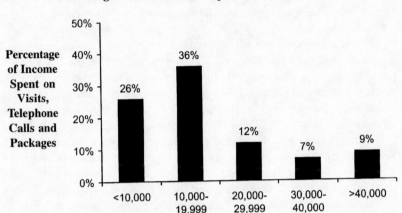

on other visits ($4 versus $17/month) and more on packages ($103 versus $81) than women in the African American sub-sample.

Discussion and Policy Recommendations

Women visitors in our sample, particularly low-income women, reported spending a large proportion of their income on prison visiting and other costs of maintaining contact with incarcerated men. While the specific impacts of this financial burden were not explored qualitatively in this study, others have described in detail the severe budgeting, self-denial and financial constraints imposed by the cost of prison visiting, telephone calls and sending money to an incarcerated man (Fishman, 1988b; Girshick, 1996). Most of the women in this study were also raising children; the impact of this financial burden on the welfare of children deserves further research and intervention. Women in African American families and women not in African American families reported the same amount of spending.

Visiting centers can provide social and other services to families attempting to maintain contact with incarcerated men such as support groups, referral and case management. In addition to efforts to provide individual support and services for visiting families through visiting centers and family reunification programs, however, structural interventions should also be initiated to reduce the high cost of visiting (Fishman, 1988b; Hinds, 1981; Light, 1993). Prisons are often placed far away from urban centers and there is also a growing trend to move inmates from crowded states to "rental cells" in other states. These practices make prison visiting logistically and financially prohibitive for most visitors and increase the cost of telephone calls. Housing inmates close to family members would be useful in reducing the cost of visiting.

Phone calls are another source of expense that could be addressed via structural intervention. Inmates are allowed only collect calls, which are already expensive, to which surcharges are added by the state, making collect telephone calls from prison one of the most expensive types of calls in the nation (Soloman, 1999; Schlosser, 1998). This should and is being addressed legislatively; in the meantime, visitors need to be fully informed of the costs of telephone calls and letter writing assistance should be provided to visitors with limited literacy.

Another major cost of visiting is food. No food may be taken into the visiting room, thus obligating purchases from the vending machines, and new, unopened food packages must be brought for family visits. This problem could be addressed by providing low-cost, nutritious food for visitors or by allowing packaged foods to be brought into the visiting room, particularly for children. While packages of goods may still be sent to inmates on a quarterly basis, the content of packages has been restricted. In some cases, all goods sent to inmates must be purchased through mail order houses specializing in sending approved items to inmates. In addition to the impersonal nature of this exchange, families are no longer allowed the option of economizing by comparing prices.

Finally, legislators and the public should be made aware of how these regulations increase the financial burden of maintaining contact with the incarcerated, and be informed that visiting during incarceration promotes family reunification and reduces recidivism (Schafer, 1994; Hairston, 1991). Visiting centers may also present opportunities to develop and support advocacy and empowerment of women visitors to challenge the structural barriers that support and maintain the high cost of maintaining contact with incarcerated men.

References

Daniel, S. W., and Barrett, C. J. (1981). The needs of prisoners' wives: A challenge for the mental health professions. *Community Mental Health Journal* 17(4), 310-322.

Fishman, L. T. (1988a). Stigmatization and prisoners' wives' feelings of shame. *Deviant Behavior* 9, 169-192.

_____. (1988b). Prisoners and their wives: Marital and domestic effects of telephone contacts and home visits. *International Journal of Offender Therapy and Comparative Criminology* 32(1), 55-66.

Girshick, L. B. (1996). *Soledad women: Wives of prisoners speak out.* Westport, CT: Praeger.

Hairston, C. F. (1991). Family ties during imprisonment: Important to whom and for what? *Journal of Sociology and Social Welfare* 18(1), 85-104.

Hinds, L. S. (1981). The impact of incarceration on low-income families. *Journal of Offender Counseling, Services and Rehabilitation* 5(3/4), 5-12.

Jorgensen, J. D., Hernandez, S. H., and Warren, R. C. (1986). Addressing the social needs of families of prisoners: A tool for inmate rehabilitation. *Federal Probation* 50(4), 47-52.

Light, R. (1993). Why support prisoners' family-tie groups? *The Howard Journal* 32(4), 322-329.

Moerings, M. (1992). Role transitions and the wives of prisoners. *Environment and Behavior* 24(2), 239-259.

Schafer, N. E. (1994). Exploring the link between visits and parole success: a survey of prison visitors. *International Journal of Offender Therapy and Comparative Criminology* 38(1), 17-32.

Schlosser, E. (1998). The prison-industrial complex. *The Atlantic Monthly* (December): 51-77.

Solomon, D. (1999). Senators urge end to fees on prison calls. *San Francisco Chronicle*, August 17.

U.S. Department of Justice, Bureau of Justice Statistics. (1999). *HIV in prison and jails 1996*. Washington, D.C.: U.S. Department of Justice.

6

The Prison Cage as Home for African American Men

Patricia E. O'Connor

How does one make a life in prison? An inmate whom I call Roman and who is serving a 40-year sentence puts it this way when speaking of his future life in prison:[1]

> You had a choice, to make your life here, this part of your life. Get up, go to work. You LIVE here…this is home for a while, whether we like it or not. This is home for a while. This is home for a while.

Sociolinguistic discourse analysis of narratives of prisoners can help interpret the import of these lines not only to a listener or reader, but to the speaker as well. We may be struck with his clarity. Prior to these lines in the interview he has told me that he is faced with a 40-year sentence. He has admitted in his narrative to shooting two people whom he says attempted to rob him during a drug deal. He "blew them away" and now two people are dead and Roman will spend most of the rest of his life in prison. This will be "home" and he shows understanding that he will need to normalize that experience, make of it the greater part of his life.

This paper is primarily based on data from 19 sociolinguistic interviews which include life stories of maximum security inmates from the District of Columbia's Department of Corrections. Using critical discourse analysis, I describe the impact of imprisonment on African Americans in American prisons and the impact of that placement on their roles in families and communities. Much of my prisoner research detailed in *Speaking of Crime* (2000) illustrates how narratives can show the moral agency required for rehabilitation. This paper shows the context into which that moral agency fits and discusses in particular the cyclical nature of imprisonment in African Ameri-

71

can families in D.C.; notes how inmates desire education and training and how that educational search helps them influence their children as well as other inmates to study; and details the methods inmates use to create and/or maintain family in spite of distance caused by incarceration itself and exacerbated by the recent forced diaspora in which the criminal justice system now sends most D.C. prisoners hundreds of miles from Washington for their sentences.

Methodology of the Study

Inside the cellblocks, using the social network (Milroy, 1987) of inmates whom I had taught, I elicited a corpus of 191 taped narratives. I used an open-ended questioning method similar to linguist William Labov's (1972) work detailing African American speech in the inner city. I designated as a narrative a report of a specific event (Labov, 1972; Labov and Waletsky, 1967), noticeably bound by opening and closing markers (Schegloff and Sacks, 1973). Questions "How did you end up at Lorton?" and "Have you ever been in danger of death?" garnered detailed narratives of crimes and of victimizations. Crimes for which the men were incarcerated included murder or voluntary manslaughter, burglary, armed robbery, armed burglary, theft, and/or armed assault, drug distribution, child molestation, indecent acts, rape and sodomy.

As a critical discourse analyst I examine units as small as the pronoun, as large as whole stories embedded within other stories, in an effort to gain more understanding of how prisoners view their acts, and ultimately their selves within the broader context of incarceration. Discourse units that show reflexive thinking include pronouns "I" and "you" which are used by speakers to locate themselves in discourse about actions and states. In reflexive language, verbs show actions and states indexed to the speaker by those pronouns. In epistemic structures (utterances about knowledge states), speakers reveal their information about a situation. These three reflexive elements—pronouns, verbs, and meta comments—assist us in determining agency in discourse. Whole narratives placed within the context of imprisonment and family disruption help us to see a lack of community agency toward the effects of incarceration.

If we return to the original quotation from Roman we note the way Roman uses four instances of second-person pronouns "you" and "your" rather than "*I* had a choice, to make *my* life here," etc. in the excerpt from the beginning of the paper. I have noted elsewhere (O'Connor, 1994, 1997) that switching to the pronoun "you" in autobiographical discourse indicates several operations can be going on in the speaking event: the speaker is considering his personal experience as if it were generic—things that you, i.e., other people as well as me, do; he is interpersonally involving others, the audience in particular, into his autobiographical experience inviting identification and perhaps empathy; he is also intra-personally involving the storytelling self with the storyworld self. The latter concept is one that helps the inmate to see himself as an agent in his past—in this case, one who chose to shoot others— and as an active self in the current situation, the speaking self of the interview and of the prison setting where he can choose (you LIVE here) to live his life in his new "home," informed by an understanding of those past and criminal acts.

Not only by doing, but also by telling about doing, people are agentive: people go about sense-making in the construction of narratives in a life story. The entire narrative, offered as part of a life story can, as well, be considered a large reflexive discourse unit. In seeking a reflexive understanding in prisoners' narratives I focus on their display of knowledge not only of their acts but of those acts within the context of forming, indeed re-forming, a life, a life rather more often now to be lived outside their family community. Thus, I analyze material relevant both within and beyond the world of criminal justice, for narrative is a powerful tool of self- and social-formation, a powerful tool in building family life. But what will that life be? What kind of "home" is prison?

Contexts of Imprisonment

Within the contexts and culture of prison we quickly note the cyclical nature of imprisonment, in particular in African American lives in Washington, D.C. The high incarceration rate for African Americans in the District of Columbia shows that 2,966 per 100,000 blacks are put in prison or jail, a rate more than 10 times the rate of whites (Mauer, 1997b:3) who make up over 30 percent of the District population, yet less than 1 percent of its prisoners. Within this concentration of D.C. prisoners, many inmates seek to make prison more homelike by gaining access to education and training and by seeking to maintain contacts with their families and influencing children to study and to avoid the fast life. They try to maintain and even create family in spite of distance caused by the isolation and diaspora. This paper contends that, in spite of an inmate's individual efforts, the current effect of incarceration, especially on African American families, is contributing to the cyclical nature of crime and incarceration affecting all of America by destroying the fabric of community life and productive employment. That said, incarceration does not remove the desire or the efficacy of one person's choice to change a life; it merely states how futile Roman's choice to "LIVE here" can seem when faced with the violent experiences many endure or perpetrate in prison.

Review of Literature, History, Statistics, and Demographics of Imprisonment

Michel Foucault wrote *Discipline and Punish* "as a historical background to various studies of the power of normalization and the formation of knowledge in modern society" (1979: 308). He discussed the many changes that came about when an enlightened world got rid of attacks upon the body of the prisoner (public dismemberment through drawing and quartering, for instance) and replaced these with systems of incarceration. He expressly noted that the concern about prison today is not "whether it is to be corrective or not," but that prisons have become "mechanisms of normalization"(1979: 306), ways to make or mark behavior. Ironically, going to prison has become far too normal, rather than normalizing in American society, particularly so in African American society. The Bureau of Justice Statistics website notes that the number of people under U.S. Criminal Justice supervision has grown to 5.5 million, which includes 3,318,500 whites; blacks[2] added another 2,099,500 and others added 105,000. Of these, 1.8 million are incarcerated in prisons and jails (Beck and Mumola, 1999: 1).

The rate of prisoners per capita in the United States rose from 292 per 100,000 in 1990 to 420 per 100,000 in 1996 (Gilliard and Beck, 1997: 1). The state of Texas recently had the highest incarceration rate of the 50 states with 717 per 100,000 (Gilliard and Beck, 1998: 5). As high as that rate appears, many cities have even higher concentrations. In Washington, D.C., the rate was an astounding 1,583 persons per 100,000 when I began my study in 1991: by 1998 that rate had grown to 1,913 per 100,000 (Beck and Mumola, 1999: 3).

The United States vies now only with Russia for highest rates of incarceration internationally (Mauer, 1999: 9; see also Mauer, 1997a). As not-for-profit Sentencing Project author Marc Mauer puts it, America is in a "race to incarcerate" that has mushroomed to the point that it "perpetuate[s] a societal commitment to imprisonment through the expansion of vested economic interests" (1999: 10). That economic interest includes many profit-making companies that build and run prisons in the United States. Inmates put it more simply, "We're being warehoused," and it is a warehouse with a definite color line. It is a warehousing that is deeply affecting the African American family structure.

Racial demographics have been steadily changing in United States prisons and jails, making the over-representation of African Americans, Latinos, Asians and Native Americans more and more stunning. On December 31, 1993, nearly two-thirds of all sentenced prison inmates in America were black, Asian, Native American, or Hispanic (Beck and Gilliard, 1995: 9). An adult black male was 8 times as likely to be incarcerated as a white male adult at the time of my study in 1991 (Maguire and Pastore, 1995: 548) and as I noted previously, that likelihood has risen to 10 times now, in spite of the fact that blacks in America comprise only 12 percent of the entire population. The interview data that I collected comes exclusively from African American male prisoners in the District of Columbia[3] where those incarcerated are 99 percent African American, while the city itself is only 65.9 percent African American according to the 1990 U.S. Census. (See Collins, 1997; Siegel, 1992 for more on racial disparity in sentencing.) Such disparity and the resultant concentration of African American men and women in prisons directly diminishes opportunities for family life. As William Julius Wilson's 1987 study of *The Truly Disadvantaged* points out, joblessness, concentration of migrating blacks to inner cities, prejudice, and the switch to a service economy all have contributed to diminishing opportunity for changing the face of poverty among the underclass in the inner cities. He notes that along with joblessness, high black-male mortality and incarceration rates terribly reduce the proportion of black men in stable economic situations conducive to strong family life (Wilson, 1987: 83). This leads us to examine how an imprisoned man can view himself as part of a family, or larger community, given the constraints of prison.

Images of Self and Other: Whom Do We See When We Look Behind Bars?

Prisoners differ from each other due to their past as well as to their current situations. Rarely do two inmates serve the same sentence for a similar crime.[4] Confusion and a sense of non-distributive justice pervade the American prison system as a result of conflicting sentencing practices between local and federal guidelines, practices that have differed over time as well as across jurisdictions. These elements contribute to a prisoner's sense of violation and make taking measures into one's own hands seem reasonable inside prisons—a point of view taken sometimes by guards as well as inmates as all struggle with the caged man syndrome where destructiveness to others or the self becomes the norm. The iconic caged man bears more examination.

During monarchial times in Europe, murderers and assassins were publicly displayed in cages loaded onto carts and trundled through the streets on public view. An interesting parallel can be drawn to the 1906 caging of a man from the Congo put on display at the New York Bronx Zoo (see Potts, 1997). A master craftsman of fine instruments in his African homeland, Ota Benga had been brought to the U.S. by a missionary/anthropologist named Samuel Phillips Verner and exhibited as an example of so-called pygmy life along with other indigenous peoples (the Ainu of Japan, the Eskimo, and the Apache [including the prisoner of war, Geronimo] and others) in an Anthropology exhibit in St. Louis at the 1904 World's Fair, where Ota Benga was a crowd favorite (Bradford and Blume, 1992: 113-126).

Two years later in New York, though Ota Benga at first had the run of the new Zoological Gardens as well as the Museum of Natural History, he was later reduced to mere spectacle at the Bronx Zoo where he was caged for a time with a chimpanzee, with bones scattered about the cage to present a semblance of the purported cannibalism of pygmies (Bradford and Blume,

1992: 181).[5] In 1916, after protests had closed the human exhibit, Ota Benga committed suicide, in despair at not being able to afford passage home to Africa—all contact with the missionary Verner having been lost (Bradford and Blume, 1992: 216-218). Thus, an African man is presented as a curiosity, wild, caged, dangerous and ultimately self-destructive—quite similar to the view about African Americans today in much of American society. (See Walker, Spohn, DeLone, 1996: 37 on self-destructive self-views; Carroll, 1998: 17 on media depictions.)

Cokley asserts that the misrepresentation of images of Africans and African Americans contributes to the sense of black youths' "callousness toward black people which upon closer inspection indicates a level of self-denigration" (1996: 6). Potts'(1997) familiar reference to the "dangerous black man" as depicted in the Ota Benga caging and Foucault's crowd pleasing dangerous criminal in the cage-cart of the monarchial times in France are now conflated as the word prisoner connotes to most a black man behind bars, too unable to be rehabilitated, too dangerous to be released. Indeed, bare statistics assist in making that image: According to the Bureau of Justice (1999) website, about 9 percent of the black population in the United States was under some form of correctional supervision compared to 2 percent of the white population and over 1 percent of other races. Missing, however, are ways to interpret what cannot be captured with statistics, such as the impact of racial profiling on arrest rates. Mauer (1999) in *Race to Incarcerate* puts it more bluntly for the future: three of ten black male babies born today will be incarcerated at some time in their lives (1999: 118). He notes that prison is made to seem inevitable in communities that lack resources (1999: 6).

Researchers McCreary and Wright (1997) discuss the effects of such negative images: "African Americans are consistently pictured by American Society and media as criminals. Drug users, drug sellers, absent fathers, and adolescent mothers" (1997: 24). Such images pervade the data I collected. Many of the men in D.C.'s prisons are addicts and as such have committed crimes in pursuit of drugs or through working inside the equal opportunity employment of the drug economy. Their early and profligate sexual experiences have produced numerous children. Their incarceration now contributes heavily to maintaining a status of absentee fathers. Often, they are as well the sons of absentee fathers. Inmate reports reflect the symbiosis of crime and poverty. McCreary and Wright (1997) say that inability to access economic and educational resources for generations has led some African American men to "compensate for their low social status by overinflating the importance of concepts like respect and honor" (1997: 30) This is a familiar concept to those who go inside prisons, where we see some of the results of what McCreary and Wright call the "bad man reputation" which has been sustained through killing and maiming and which continues on the inside of prisons. For Roman, "getting the respect" that came with drug dealing was one of its major appeals. Keeping that respect through not allowing his enterprise to be robbed cost two lives as well as his own freedom. Yet, he and many others still live by that credo for they believe that in the streets and in prison it keeps them alive. Another inmate in my data, Malcolm-Bey, put it this way as he spoke of prison dangers: "If you're afraid to die, this is the wrong place to be."

Data: Dangers of Street Life/Dangers of Prison Life: Hardly a Family Model

Inmates' recollections of their street life and of their current life in prison are replete with violence. Such a concentration of violence builds a picture of harsh and desperate lives. Roman's reminiscences of his early years include running away, being beaten by his father ("when I was ten I got my first punch up side of the head"), sleeping under the steps of his elementary school, recalling near death experiences: "I was with these older guys and one of 'em took his gun out, and stuck it in my face. I was about thirteen." He tells further that the cocaine gang he joined was dangerous: "It's worse than people think, worse than what the public sees. Inside stuff, like getting killed for any— most people say it's because he's messed up with drugs. That's one, just one reason. It is worse. One mistake will cost you your life." Later he remarks, "We called it 'being in the way.'" As he put it, "I got caught up on the life, the fast life, the women, the money…being able to walk through a neighborhood and have everybody, you know, who had the drug, give their respect." Getting the respect, developing self-respect, outside these contexts of crime would appear as justifiable goals. Perhaps what they are is normal goals, normal to us as humans, but normalized to the situation in which lack of legitimate economic advantage has skewed the meaning of respect.

"Normal" inside prison I found to be uncompromisingly dangerous. Below is but one example from the "stabbing stories" I collected (see O'Connor, 1994, and 2000) within the life story study. This man, whom I call Edward, was attacked at night inside his supposedly locked, single occupant cell:

> and uh. I was stabbed eight times. I was stabbed… once in the face. Once in the… right lung… hit in the shoulder and back. And uh… I was stabbed twice, before I even woke up. N'but, when I turned over and looked up… I saw this… three-hundred-pound man you know. With a, a, a, a, a, short mach-machete, in his hand, you know. (Extra periods indicate pausing.)

Stories such as this, a story of survival against blind attack in prison, reveal the extreme danger that inmates and families of the incarcerated must feel when their family member is put away.

Prison is dangerous for all who enter. Families of those who work inside prisons, as well as families of the incarcerated, face the fear of daily danger and intimidation. In 1993, American prisons and federal incarceration facilities officially reported numerous incidents of violence: 46 inmates killed by inmates; 4,829 assaults by inmates on staff; 8,220 assaults by inmates upon inmates; and 100 inmate suicides (Maguire and Pastore, 1995: 586). If an inmate does not die in such an assault, or if the inmate can manage without hospitalization, many such acts of violence of prisoners on other prisoners go unreported. An inmate code of silence prevails which contributes to the private settlements of scores, adding to yet another cycle of violence. These acts of violence or merely the images of danger that are commonly associated with prisoners follow them to the outside when they are released.

Trying to Reclaim Community and Family Standing

Inmates who have been incarcerated and released and who are trying to take on a legitimate life, leaving crime behind, report many difficulties in getting jobs—lack of recent job experience and references, to name two of the obvious ones.[6] Inmates I have interviewed talk as well about the self-respect that they expected, but which didn't result when they did earn honest money. For instance, an inmate I call Kingston discussed a job he held for three months:

> When I got my check the next week, I didn't have but a hundred and sixty-two dollars...and uh...you know...I'm living with a, with a young lady. And... She's working. She's bringing in a nice dollar... and I, you know, I looked at that check and I couldn't believe it.

Kingston says he then called one of his former crime friends who was also out of prison. He retells this conversation:

> So he say, "What's going on?" I say, "Man, you know what's happening, you know, for three months now...I've been trying to do it their way...and proving it to myself I can do it. I think I've done that. And...you know, it's not helping me any. I'm scared. Bills still due and everything, man. It makes me feel bad... to come home every week, and...my woman bringing home, home almost, almost three times as much as I'm bringing home."

Such is the unrealistic and idealized view of what family life should be for Kingston: he wants to be the chief breadwinner, he wants wages, status, and respect on his job commensurate with a career-long employment. This disappointment bears little logic when the girlfriend has been in her profession (as a prison guard) for many years and Kingston has had only three months. Yet, his expectations are that the male be the chief earner and it is this that ultimately galls him the most. He turns back to cocaine sales, then moves on to bank robberies, ultimately returning himself to prison, for a much longer time. Home now will be not where he earns his keep, but where he is kept, a place wherein he, like Roman, will conduct his life.

Life Inside Prison as a Way of Making Home, Making Community

Coming back to prison, the plight of most of those inside (Beck et al., 1993: 11, Haigler, Harlow, O'Connor, and Campbell, 1994: 60), does not, however, totally thwart inmate efforts to establish family, or family-like connections. Many inmates speak with great concern about young people, about helping prevent their future warehousing in prisons. While few report marriages that have survived incarceration, family is still important to most inmates in my interviews. They relate most deeply to their families of origin, in particular to their mothers or grandmothers as important influences in their lives. Similar to the desire to connect with family and community, inmates join groups, especially those that offer educational and vocational training in prison, which has also been correlated with increased educational proficiency (Haigler et al., 1994: 58). For another way of increasing family-like activity, some inmates counsel young offenders who are brought to prisons for a "look at their future"; others join groups such as Lorton Prison's Concerned Fathers program which teach parenting skills to maintain contact with their children. In the interview data, Kingston, mentioned above in relation to the disappointment of slow money earned legally, speaks lovingly of his children: "My son is twenty-four. I'm most proud of him. I've got a boy and a girl. My daughter's eight." He tells that his son graduated from high school, spent three years in the Army in Germany and luckily was out before the Gulf War. When his children visited Kingston's mother, he sometimes got to talk with them on the phone. Not so much unlike busy professionals in two-income families, inmates, too, parent by telephone. While inmates still write letters at rates higher than householders (Haigler et al., 1994: 73), they now also use the phone to check up on their own children or children of their girlfriends to see what they are doing, to offer encouragement in school, to discipline by voice for infractions reported by their mothers.

The use of phone time, though, is strictly regulated in prisons and is lucrative to the sole source contractors who bid for and gain monopolies on outgoing calls, which are all collect. The burden on families for these collect calls is great, yet a cost accepted by many who wish to maintain contact with the prisoner. Not all want that contact and children cannot control their own access to talk with or to visit an incarcerated parent. Hairston estimates that the number of fathers in prison who have dependent children is at least half a million and the number of children with a father in prison is a million (1995: 31). That estimate is climbing as numbers of incarcerated have risen to nearly 2 million as we enter the new millennium. Whether for lack of resources caused by long distances from prisons to home communities or from use as pawns to exact revenge, many children are denied visits. "Most incarcerated fathers do not share a marital bond or an ongoing relationship with the mothers of their children" note Johnston and Gabel (1995: 7). Unless fathers lived with the children prior to incarceration, there is little chance that they will see them while incarcerated (Fritsch and Burkhead, 1982, cited in Johnston and Gabel, 1995: 8).

The lack of marital bonds in a traditional sense is supported by the interviews I conducted. Language used to describe family and children reveals much about the condition of relationships prior to as well as during prison. Kingston's discussion of going back to work omits the words wife or girlfriend or the children's mother's name. Instead women are called "my young lady" and "my woman" or "my children's mother," "my son's mother." Many of the men refer to women with only a scientific term, female. Such phrases reveal a distancing that signals loss or doubt in family relationships.

The story of family, then, in many prisoners' lives often looks like one of missing pieces, yet they are found in a puzzle that forms a repeating pattern of loss. An inmate I call Kevin spoke at length about his own home-life in our interview, stating that he had run away from home often as a child, as did his older sister. "I've never seen my father," he states. "My father is dead. This is what I hear from my family." Kevin also says, "I have a brother I've never seen." The missing pieces could be looked at in another way, though. In Kevin's own reproductive life he has fathered a child, but is not with him not only due to incarceration, but because he and his son's mother no longer get along: "she had problems far as you know me being locked up, 'cause she, she had the baby. My sister give her a place to stay, plus, plus my sister kept my son." Thus, he reveals that his sister replaces or supplements the mother role. Replacement is a familiar refrain in the stories of those who are children of the incarcerated. Families and sometimes friends take in incarcerated relatives' offspring. This may not be the "village" imagined raising the child, but it is the network willing to do so. Inmates I've interviewed also help raise other inmates' children upon their release, helping the children make contact with inmates who desperately want to be visited. With 75 to 80 percent of incarcerated women and 65 percent of incarcerated men having children (Harris, 1995: vii), the absentee parenting, the loss of contact, the despair of both children and parents, and the harsh economic deprivation all contribute to the cycles of imprisonment wherein prison has become all too often the inevitable path of some member of many families.

In my data, men speak of consulting their uncles, cousins, brothers, and even their children who are also incarcerated inside the facility. The instinct to help one's young takes interesting twists inside the volatile prison setting. In an interview with the man I call Roland, he tells:

> while I was in jail, I got into an incident, right, where I had to stab a dude because he came to me for sex. So, uh, I happened to see my uncle who was there, right. And uh, I was talking to him and he tell me like uh, "you gotta be a man, or a girl." He say, "What you gonna do?" I say, "Man, I can't beat that big old dude." So he, he gave me a knife, say, "you gotta do what you gotta do."

And Roland did what he figured he had to do. He stabbed the man when he came to his cell. Thus, the uncle, a seasoned inmate, gives the neophyte Roland the key to survival—a weapon and advice to strike first. As Roland put it, his reputation "came behind that." Thus, even though Roland is incarcerated, he uses family ties to help solve a problem—a rather typical act in families everywhere—to ask for and get advice and assistance. The uncle's knowledge of the harsh life of prisoners who are taken advantage of is needed. He not only advises but also assists materially in making his nephew's life in prison tolerable. This happens, of course, within a skewed (to the outside world) sense that violence can prevent intimidation. In Roland's case his violence thwarts the other man sufficiently to build Roland a reputation which eliminates further sexual advances. Roland has learned a coping strategy from his uncle.

Maintaining Family Ties Long Distance

While nationwide America is building more prisons, the U. S. Congress has bowed to local Virginia pressure to close the Lorton prison complex where the District of Columbia has housed most of its prisoners, 25 miles from D.C.. The once prison farm of seven facilities, some of it originally built by prison labor, is slated to close by 2001. Overcrowding, as well as mismanagement and economic concerns were cited as major causes for the closure, which will return to public and commercial use valuable acres of land. Prisoners have, since well before this closure plan, been sent far afield due to overcrowding. This displacement from the community has a dramatic effect on prisoners' relationships with their families and a negative impact on arranging work contacts upon their eventual release. For example, inmate William "T" Lawson, whom I taught in Washington, D.C.'s maximum facility at Lorton, Virginia, wrote to me a few years ago from a private prison in Youngstown, Ohio, and listed all the places he had been shipped to during his 20 years in custody with the District of Columbia: Federal facilities in Leavenworth, Kansas; El Reno, Oklahoma; Terre Haute, Indiana; Oxford, Wisconsin; Atlanta, Georgia; and Lewisburg, Pennsylvania; county facilities in Spokane, Washington, and Jamestown, North Dakota; private for-profit prisons run by Corrections Corporation of America in West Tennessee and North East Ohio. He began incarceration in D.C.'s Maximum and Central facilities, and is returned to one of these whenever the contract expires in the rented spaces. He is currently incarcerated long distance in the Sussex facility near Richmond, Virginia. He is serving a 60-year sentence. For 15 of those years I have been his correspondent, following his attempts to maintain contact with his family, to join positive groups, to participate in programs, to take courses, which have included college classes such as the ones I taught in English, or industrial arts courses such as photography and printing, among others. He is going about the business of making a life inside in spite of the upheavals from removals and the wait in new facilities to get on the "list" to do activities and take courses, privileges not often allotted to newcomers.

A further illustration of maintaining family relationships comes from Lawson's application of learning received in our classes. Lawson told me once of his use of the literature we examined in our English class when his young nephew visited him while he remained at the Lorton complex. An accomplished artist, especially of cartoon art, Lawson drew for his nephew the picture of a "hat" from Antoine De Saint-Exupery's (1943) philosophical *The Little Prince*. Lawson reported with delight his nephew's confusion, then amazement and pleasure that the "hat" was indeed a boa constrictor consuming his large meal. Appearances (like uncles in prison) are not always what they seem. A small moment to treasure from a visit, a visit now impossible due to Lawson's relocation hundreds of miles from family.

According to inmates I interviewed, even men who are illiterate arrange to have others write letters on their behalf to people on the outside. Ironies of some for-profit prisons, though, include the rule forbidding anyone to mail stamps or writing materials to prisoners. Incidences of LSD on stamps seemed a reasonable cause for this caution, but that must be considered alongside the fact that some prisons sell stamps to inmates and allow only postal money orders to be given so that purchase of stamps, paper, pens, etc., is required and at a profit for the prison.

Conlusions and Implications: Critical Literacy

The picture thus portrayed of prison life sullies our concepts of criminal justice. Efforts made by prisons toward rehabilitation have been thwarted by rising rates of incarceration due to mandatory sentencing and influxes of prisoners with drug-related crimes due to addiction and its concomitant illegal acts. Combine these with shrinking interests and resources for programming and counseling. The results are often dangerously chaotic. In spite of a lowered crime rate, prison populations continue to rise; funds for rehabilitation do not. The Crime Bill of 1994 eliminated use of Pell Grants to fund higher education of prisoners, removing from most facilities all college-credit-bearing programs, courses that offer skills deemed to be a major reason why some inmates do not return to prison (Haigler et al., 1994: 59).[7] I have been fortunate in that Georgetown University has sponsored gratis the college level courses we teach to about 50 inmates annually, a rare situation.

What then is needed? Missing across the board in incarceration is in-depth attention to the life of the mind and its role in shaping actions. Perhaps, because people in prison are less educated we believe they are less educable, a fallacy in reasoning. Instead of working with the minds, we focus our attention on the bodies of the incarcerated and we dangerously and erroneously assume that prisoners will be changed to do good merely by the fact of caging these bodies. Return rates to prison as well as violence inside defy that assumption. My research collecting life stories revealed at a minimum that we need to get *more* people into prisons, not more criminals, more non-criminal citizens. We need average citizens to see what is going on, to allow inmates to articulate their pasts in light of a potentially changed future, to listen to inmates, to officers and to families of all these affected by crime and by criminal justice. To begin to understand the terrible dangers for officers, administrators, inmates, and communities alike, we as citizens, not just employees or researchers, need to witness the conditions that our large prison complex promotes. We should also, as Helen Prejean (1993) has revealed in her work with offenders in *Dead Man Walking*, concentrate on the damage to the victims and their families to give ourselves a full picture of the costs of crime. Rather than turning only an amused eye upon the caged man and the increasingly more common caged woman, we need to turn discerning eyes and ears toward the stories of incarceration and crime in order to begin to comprehend the rational and the rationalized explanations for criminal behaviors. Doing that is what I am calling a critical literacy for communities. Part of a critical literacy for communities means we need to know in person what our institutions of incarceration are doing to prevent the return of criminals to crime and to prison. Without the personal intervention, we leave to a bureaucracy what needs a hands-on touch—the everyday comprehension of knowing enough about another to promote belief in changing one's life. Incarceration is not only fracturing families, it is polarizing whole communities. Providing forums for visitation and education by communities who could invest time in promoting a positive future would be a dramatic departure from our seeming contentment with stereotypes of caged and self-destructive humans. We need to reconsider the cage before it becomes the iconic representation of America worldwide.

Notes

1. Extra periods indicate lengthening pauses between words. All CAPS shows increased emphasis on a word.
2. U.S. Department of Justice Bureau of Justice Statistics uses the term "black" rather than African American.
3. Speculations on the under-representation of whites in prisons in D.C. include assertions that whites can more often afford private legal counsel and thus mount better defenses, avoid prosecution, and seek alternatives to incarceration by paying fines where applicable. White prisoners are also sometimes sent to federal prisons (ostensibly for their safety) where they would not be as pronounced a minority.
4. See Mauer, 1999: Ch 4 on the shift from indeterminate to mandatory sentencing and various states' rulings.
5. Keepers often urged Ota Benga "to charge the bars of a cage, his mouth open wide, his teeth bared, to give spectators the impressions of the wildman and to give

children a fright," note Bradford and Blume (187). After the exhibit closed due to protests and to Ota Benga's increasingly "unmanageable" behavior, he was placed in the custody of the Howard Colored Orphan Asylum. He chose to remain in the U.S., occupant of the orphan asylum and later as a student at the Lynchburg Seminary in Lynchburg, Virginia, where he adapted his nomadic African lifestyle to the woods and countryside where he could hunt, study, and even work for a time in tobacco before he took his life.

6.   Former inmate, now *Washington Post* journalist and author, Nathan McCall described in his *Makes Me Wanna Holler* (1994) how honesty on application forms resulted in his not being hired as a writer and dishonesty about his having a criminal record resulted in subsequent firing at places that had hired him and that had been pleased with his skills.

7.   They draw from studies on Alabama prisoners: M. O'Neil (1990). "Correctional Higher Education: Reduced Recidivism?" *Journal of Correctional Education* 41, 28-31. State of Alabama Department of Post-secondary Education (1992). "A Study of Alabama Prison Recidivism Rates of Inmates Having Completed Vocational and Academic Programs While Incarcerated Between the Years of 1987 through 1991."

References

Beck, A. J., and Gilliard, D. K. (1995). *Prisoners in 1994*. Washington, D.C.: U.S. Dept. of Justice, Bureau of Justice Statistics.

Beck, A. J., and Mumola, C. (1999). *Prisoners in 1998*. Washington, D.C.: U.S. Dept. of Justice, Bureau of Justice Statistics.

Beck, A. J. et al. (1993). *Survey of state prison inmates, 1991*. Washington, D.C.: U.S. Dept. of Justice, Bureau of Justice Statistics.

Bureau of Justice Statistics. (1999, September). *For all races, the number of adults in the correctional population*. BJS online. Retrieved September 24, 1999 from the World Wide Web: http://www.ojp.usdoj.gov/bjs/gcorpop.htm.

Bradford, P. V. ,and Blume, H. (1992). *Ota: The pygmy in the zoo*. New York: St. Martin's Press.

Carroll, G. (1998). *Environmental stress and African Americans*. Westport, CT: Praeger.

Cokley, K. (1996). The psychological and sociohistorical antecedents of violence: Africentric Analyses. *Journal of African American Men* 2(1), 3-13.

Collins, C. F. (1997). *The imprisonment of African American women*. Jefferson, NC: McFarland and Co.

Foucault, M. (1979). *Discipline and punish*. Trans. Alan Sheridan. New York: Vintage Books.

Fritsch, T. A., and Burkhead, J. D. (1982). Behavioral reactions of children to parental absence due to imprisonment. *Family Relations* 30:83-88.

Gilliard, D. K., and Beck, A .J. (1997). *Prison and jail inmates at midyear 1996*. Washington, D.C.: U.S. Department of Justice, Bureau of Justice Statistics.

_____. (1998). *Prisoners in 1997*. Washington, D.C.: U.S. Department of Justice, Bureau of Justice Statistics.

Haigler, K., Harlow, C., O'Connor, P. E., and Campbell, A. (1994). *Literacy behind prison walls*. Washington, D.C.: U.S. Dept. of Education.

Hairston, C. F. (1995). Effects of parental incarceration. Katherine Gabel and Denise Johnston (Eds.), *Children of incarcerated parents*. New York: Lexington Books.

Harris, J. (1995). Introduction. Katherine Gabel and Denise Johnston (Eds.), *Children of incarcerated parents*. New York: Lexington Books.

Johnston, D., and Gabel, K.(1995). Incarcerated parents. Katherine Gabel and Denise Johnston (Eds.), *Children of incarcerated parents*. New York: Lexington Books.

Labov, W. (1972). *Language in the inner city*. Philadelphia: University of Pennsylvania Press.

Labov, W., and Waletsky, J. (1967). Narrative analysis: Oral versions of personal experience. In *Essays on the verbal and visual arts*. (Proceedings of 1966 spring meeting, American Ethnological Society) June Helm (Ed.). Seattle: University of Washington.

Mauer, M. (1999). *The race to incarcerate*. New York: The New Press.

_____. (1997a). *Americans behind bars: U.S. and international use of incarceration 1995*. Washington, D.C.: The Sentencing Project.

_____.(1997b). *Intended and unintended consequences: State racial disparities in imprisonment*. Washington, D.C.: The Sentencing Project.

Maguire, K., and Pastore, A. L. 1995. *Sourcebook of criminal justice statistics—1994*. Washington, D.C.: U.S. Department of Justice, Bureau of Justice Statistics.

McCall, N. (1994.) *Makes me wanna holler: A young black man in America*. New York: Random House.

McCreary, M. L., and Wright, R.C. (1997). The effects of negative stereotypes on African American male and female relationships. *Journal of African American Men* 2&4, 25-46.

Milroy, L. (1987). *Observing and analyzing natural language: A critical account of sociolinguistic method*. New York: Basil Blackwell.

O'Connor, P. E. (2000). *Speaking of crime: Narratives of prisoners*. Lincoln: University of Nebraska.

_____.(1997)."You gotta be a man or a girl": Constructed dialogue and reflexivity in the discourse of violence. *Pragmatics* 7(4), 575-599.

_____.(1994). "You could feel it through the skin": Agency and positioning in prisoners' narratives. *Text* 14(1), 45-75.

Potts, R. G. (1997) The social construction and social marketing of the "dangerous black man." *Journal of African American Men* 2(3),11-24.

Prejean, H. (1993). *Dead man walking: An eyewitness account of the death penalty in the United States*. New York: Random House.

Saint-Exupery, A. (1943). *The little prince*. Trans. Katherine Woods. New York: Harcourt, Brace.

Schegloff, E. A., and Sacks, H. (1973). Opening up closings. *Semiotica* 8:289-327.

Siegel, L. J. (1992). *Criminology*. St. Paul: West Publishers.

Walker, S., Spohn, C., and DeLone, M. (1996). *The color of justice: Race, ethnicity, and crime in America*. Belmont, CA: Wadsworth Publishing Co.

Wilson, W. J. (1987). *The truly disadvantaged: The inner city, the underclass, and public policy*. Chicago: University of Chicago Press.

7

Criminal Incarceration Dividing the Ties That Bind: Black Men and Their Families

Sandra Lee Browning, R. Robin Miller, and Lisa M. Spruance

In 1958 Gresham Sykes published his now seminal work, *The Society of Captives: A Study of A Maximum Security Prison* in which he wrote about the "pains of imprisonment." The pains or deprivations that one suffers in prison include the losses of liberty, goods and services, heterosexual relationships, autonomy, and security. While incarcerated, an inmate's basic needs are met (food, clothing, shelter, and medical care), but nonessentials are in limited supply. His forced same-sex confinement eliminates the opportunity to engage in heterosexual relationships. During his incarceration he is subjected to endless rules and commands that regulate his every waking moment. His very safety is in constant question. Often surrounded by very dangerous inmates, he is the potential target of violence, aggression, and exploitation. It is, however, the deprivation of liberty that is of issue in this paper. Once deprived of liberty an inmate's movements are restricted within the institution, but, more importantly, the inmate is involuntarily cut off from his or her family, friends and relatives.

Those family and kinship ties that have helped define the identity and the sense of self of these persons, and have served as a source of social support, have abruptly ended with the inmate's incarceration. While through visitation, correspondence, and phone calls, the inmate and his family can maintain contact, it is those relationships that bind us together in a cyclical pattern of both support and dependency that, in a very real sense, ends during the period of incarceration. The inmate is isolated, and separated from his parents, siblings, grandparents, and significant other. While theoretically reserved for the most serious offenders, imprisonment in our nation's jails and prisons drives a wedge between inmates and their kinship web. By denying the various liberties of the inmate, our correctional system also deprives a parent of a child, a sibling of sibling, a grandparent of a grandchild, a child of a parent and a partner of a mate. These problems, which are rarely acknowledged, are exacerbated by unprecedented prison growth—growth that has been directly linked to the War on Drugs. This is a war that has captured a growing number of young black men. In the year 2000, there were nearly 2 million Americans behind bars. Although blacks make up about 13 percent of the U.S. population, they constitute 50 percent of the state and federal prison population (Beck and Karberg, 2001). This is an alarming number, as some 353,851 blacks were arrested on drug charges (Uniform Crime Reports, 1999). The casualties are not only the accused offenders and victims but their families as well—families that are involuntarily separated from their love ones, who face the daily stressors, anxieties, and problems caused by the separation.

The hidden victims in the correctional system are the family members of the incarcerated. Nearly 1.5 million U.S. children—2 percent of the nation's minors—had a parent in prison at the end of the twentieth century. And black children are nearly nine times more likely to have a parent in prison (Mumola, 2000). To the extent that research has focused on incarcerated parents and their children, researchers have almost exclusively looked at the problems of incarcerated women and their children. While no doubt a subject worthy of intervention and scholarly attention, at 93 percent the "imprisoned gender" is, by far, male. More to the point, the "imprisoned race/gender" is that of a black male. Due to the disproportionate numbers of black men involved in the criminal justice system, issues of fathering behind bars have direct implications for the black parent-child relationship. The children left behind are often in the care of the mother, or over-burdened relatives—the imprisoned's parents, siblings, or grandparents. Those who cannot stay with family members are frequently placed with an assortment of under-funded or otherwise inadequate social services providers. While often shouldering the responsibilities of keeping the family together, the imprisoned man's wife or girlfriend is left to negotiate her life alone. She has to juggle the care and support of the children, while maintaining contact through visits, letters, and phone calls, and at the same time deal with the loss of her partner's support and companionship.

Traditionally, we think of criminal incarceration as only affecting the offender. This paper argues that imprisonment affects not only the incarcerated, but the hidden victims of incarceration—the inmate's family. This is never more the case than with the black male inmate. Comprising anywhere from half to a majority of the men who are imprisoned, his plight affects the black community as a whole, and specifically his family: parents, grandparents, siblings, children, wife or girlfriend. The research discussed in this paper will be placed in the context of a restorative justice model, with the emphasis being on restoring the relationship between the black male offender, his family, and the community.

Nearly 2 Million in 2000

The United States has experienced unprecedented growth in the number of people it incarcerates. The U.S. incarceration rate is the highest in the world surpassing the incarceration rate for the former Soviet Union (Mauer, 1991), making the United States the world leader in imprisonment. As of mid-year 2000, our prisons swelled to nearly 2,000,000 incarcerated adults. Ninety-five percent of those prison inmates were male, and almost 50 percent of these males were black. The incarceration rate for black men is seven times the rate for white men—3,250 per 100,000 compared with 461 per 100,000 (Beck and Karberg, 2001). A black male has a 29 percent chance within his lifetime of serving time in prison. This is compared to a mere 4 percent chance for white men (Bonczar and Beck, 1997). When jails are added to the equation, roughly eight in 10 black men will spend some time locked up during their lifetimes—typically before the age of 40 (Miller, 1996).

In 1990, The Sentencing Project, a sentencing alternative advocacy group, issued a report entitled "Young Black Men and the Criminal Justice System." The report found that almost one in four black men between the ages of 20 and 29 was under some form of criminal justice supervision (Mauer, 1990). In a follow-up study, "Young Black Americans and the Criminal Justice System: Five Years Later," the authors documented how the conditions for young black men had worsened. In just five years, the numbers rose from one in four black men to one in three black men ages 20 to 29 being under the supervision of the criminal justice system (Mauer and Huling, 1995). Sparking the growth in criminal incarceration was the explosion in drug arrests. Within the 10-year period between 1983 to 1993 our country experienced a 510 percent increase in the number of incarcerated drug offenders, rising from 57,975 to 353,563. As noted by the authors, while blacks made up 13 percent of monthly drug users, blacks comprised 35 percent of those arrested for drug possession, 55 percent of the convictions, and 74 percent of those sentenced to prison (Mauer and Huling, 1995).

In their 2001 World Report, Human Rights Watch using Department of Justice Statistics argued that the War on Drugs disproportionately affects blacks, with some 46 percent of state prisoners and another 40 percent of federal prisoners being sentenced for drug offenses. This occurs with blacks comprising approximately 13 percent of the U.S. population. Black men were more than 13 times more likely to be charged with drug offenses than were white men. The racial disparities are more striking on a state-by-state basis. The report found that in some states the racial disparities were worse, with blacks constituting between 80 percent and 90 percent of all drug offenders sent to prison on drug charges. Black males in 15 states were anywhere from 20 to 50 times more likely to be sentenced for drug offenses (see the Human Rights Watch World Report 2001 for a full discussion).

Human Rights Watch is just the latest in a series of research that links our nation's War on Drugs and young black men to the increasing incarceration rate (Tonry, 1995; Lusane, 1991; Shelden, 2001). While the injustices of our current War on Drugs, and the burgeoning criminal justice industrial complex, are outside the scope of this paper, within its bounds is the discussion of how increasing black male incarceration impacts on the man and on his kinship network. The disenfranchisement of black men is most often discussed in terms of their inability to vote once convicted of a felony (Fellner and Mauer, 1998; Shapiro, 1997). The disenfranchisement of black men occurs not only at the voting booth but also in our nation's prisons and jails. Their involuntary separation coupled with the correctional system's inability to recognize the importance of continued fathering strikes at the heart of the family. While almost all prisons make some sort of arrangements for prisoners to maintain some social ties with the outside world, without real efforts to maintain and strengthen the ties of the father-child bond, the correctional system plays a significant role in dividing the ties that bind, and supplying the next generation of incarcerated black men—namely the children of current prisoners.

The Forgotten Parent—Black Male Inmates

State and Federal prisons held an estimated 721,500 parents with minor children in 1999. Nearly 1.5 million U.S. children (2 percent of all minor children in our country) had a parent in prison, a growth of more than 500,000 children since the early 1990s. The majority of these children, some 58 percent, were younger than 10 years old, with an average age of 8 years old. An estimated 336,300 households with minor children had an imprisoned parent. In state prisons, blacks made up 49 percent of the parents with minor children. Federal prisons housed 44 percent of black parents of minor children. Black children were nine times more likely than white children to have a parent in prison. In part because of their conviction for drug offenses that carried mandatory minimum sentences the average term of incarceration was over 12 years in state prisons, and 10 years in federal prisons. With the prison population being predominately male, and disproportionately black, black fathers make up the majority of incarcerated parents (Mumola, 2000).

The limited existing literature indicates that children of incarcerated parents tend to experience many emotional and behavioral problems. The child, as well as the parent, suffers problems from lack of contact. The reintegration process for both parent and child is fraught with both emotional and economic issues, all of which impact more significantly on the black male and his children, given his over-representation in the criminal justice system.

The loss of a parental figure can have profound effects on a child. Children retain bonds and love for parents regardless of the label attached to these parents by society. However, once a parent is incarcerated, research has found that children experience feelings of shame, stigma, isolation, blame, guilt, and anger. They experience the shame of having a criminal for a parent. The parent's incarceration is often not talked about outside of the family for fear of stigma and further isolation. The child often feels as if he or she is to blame for the incarceration with the notion that there was something they could have done to prevent the imprisonment of their parent. This guilt often results in anger—anger at themselves, and anger at the parent for bringing the family into crisis (Child Welfare League, 1997; Friedman and Esselstyn, 1965). Fritsch and Burkhead (1981) found that children of incarcerated fathers were more likely to display acting-out behaviors such as running away, or truancy, while children of incarcerated mothers were more likely to exhibit "acting in behaviors" such as crying, or withdrawing.

The Osborne Association (1993) found that children of incarcerated parents were more likely to experience fear, anxiety, sadness, loneliness, and guilt. Their self-esteem was lower, they were more likely to be depressed, and to withdraw from remaining family and friends. This leads to a greater likelihood of problems at school, as well as other antisocial behaviors (Gabel, 1992). The Child Welfare League of America argues that, "as a result of parental incarceration, many of this population of children have experienced multiple placements, decreased quality of care, financial hardships and irreparable damage to family bonds. Because of these traumas, they are at risk for poor academic achievement, substance abuse, delinquency and criminal activity that can lead to their own incarceration" (Child Welfare League, 1997: 1). In that same report, it was projected that approximately 50 percent of the children of incarcerated parents will enter the juvenile justice system before their eighteenth birthday (Child Welfare League, 1997).

Contact between father and child is important to the well being of both, and to the maintaining of family ties, particularly given the rather lengthy sentences black men tend to face. Since their admission into state (80 percent) and federal (93 percent) prisons, most parents (figures not given by race and gender) report maintaining contact with their children through phone calls, letters, and personal visits (Mumola, 2000). Personal visits were the least frequent, and most problematic. For example, the majority of fathers (57 percent) in state prison reported never having a personal visit with their children since their incarceration. This is due in large part because of the geographical location of prisons, with the majority of parents being held in prisons located over 100 miles away from their home (Mumola, 2000).

This separation is likely to be disruptive and traumatic to the children involved. Maintaining social contacts is essential in preserving family ties. Contact with the outside world also aids in the continued family socialization process. The men who are incarcerated sustain at least some level their involvement with their families through these contacts. As in the case of fathers, the black male through his interactions with the his children (phone calls, letters, visitation) is able to maintain, albeit limited, his influence as a parental figure. To the extent that contact is cut off or limited, the socialization process moves from the family and into the prison setting. The behavioral/socialization patterns learned in the isolated realm of prison teaches one how to behave in prison not as a family member and father. This ultimately makes the reintegration process and responsible fatherhood more difficult. This is of course not surprising, since early on Holt and Miller (1972) found that those who consistently received visits from relatives tended to have a more favorable parole outcome. Prisoners with no visitors during their time of incarceration were six times more likely to violate their parole and return to prison, during their first year of parole. This is a finding that has been repeated throughout the research (Adams, and Fisher, 1976; Holt and Miller, 1972; Hostetter and Jinnah, 1993; Howser and McDonald, 1972; Leclair, 1978).

The incarceration of a parent not only affects the family while in prison, but also upon his or her release. The system further places the family in economic peril by sending prisoners to prison miles away from their home, limiting visitation days, and, perhaps most deplorable, double billing. Families that accept collect phone calls (the only calls that can be placed) from their incarcerated family member are billed a surcharge for the placement of the call and the collect fees at a long-distance rate. A phone placed inside a prison could earn as much as $15,000 per year in profits (Mergenhagen, 1996). Whether it is the geographical isolation of prison, or the gouging practices that prisons allow to occur, inmate families who are already in an economically untenable condition must chose between visiting or receiving phone calls from the incarcerated or meeting their other financial responsibilities. Once the inmate is released, the label of "convicted felon" follows them throughout their lives, making legitimate employment at a level sufficient to support a family difficult (Bernstein and Houston, 2000). Underemployment and unemployment in families that are economically strapped increases the likelihood of interpersonal violence, thus placing children and other family members at risk (Chasin, 1997). All of these are problems that are exacerbated in the black family, given his presence in the criminal justice system.

Mothers in Prison

The majority of research on incarcerated parents has focused on mothers, with little attention paid to the problems of inmate fathers, even though men are the most "imprisoned gender." The scholarly focus in recent years on women in prison has been at least two-fold: the hidden nature of women in the criminal justice system and the outdated patriarchal notion that mothers are solely responsible for the raising of children, and even this research is relatively recent, given that scholarly studies on women in prison were not conducted until the 1960s. Issues of isolation of these women and the issue of the physical geography of female prisons were not discussed until the 1970s (Pollock-Byrne, 1990). This stands in stark contrast to our long-standing interest in the subject of men and prison (Lawes, 1928; Clemmer, 1966; Clayton, 1970; Winning, 1933). With the rise of academic feminism in the 1970s, scholars turned their attention to the issues of women in prison (Burkhart, 1973; Van Wormer, 1978; Freedman, 1981; Rierden, 1997; Muraskin, 2000; Atwood, 2000). What had escaped our public and academic radar screens, although still marginalized, was now taking hold as a legitimate area of study. The emphasis of women and prison led to a more focused endeavor, that of study of incarcerated women and their children.

As researchers focused on the issues of women in prison and their children, it ironically reinforced the patriarchal notion that the ties that bind between parent and child are the ties between mother and child. It reinforced society's beliefs that parenting is primarily a "woman's job." While we continued to talk about men in prison, we ignored the fact that some of these men are fathers, and that their incarceration affected not only themselves but their children as well. The backlash on studying women in prison and their children is that with few exceptions (Gabel, 1992; Hairston, 1989; Lanier, 1993; Swan, 1981; Hairston, 1995) the academic community has reinforced the maybe not-so-outdated notion that women are solely responsible for the rearing of the children—or that it is a woman's job.

The studies of incarcerated women and their children can offer insights into how the criminal justice system can be instrumental in maintaining and restoring the kinship ties of black men and their children. Harm and Whompson (1997) after evaluating a 15-week parent education program for mothers, found that participants in these program experienced an increase in self-esteem, as well as the development of appropriate age-specific expectations of their children, an increased awareness of the needs of their children, a growing knowledge of the various alternatives to corporal punishment, and a wider understanding of acceptable family roles and responsibilities. Katz (1998) argued that to succeed (measured by not returning to crime) once released, mothers in jail need the collaborative efforts of both the criminal justice system and the child welfare system. It will, as she contends, require nothing less than drug and alcohol treatment for women in jail, and counselors and programs that can help children deal with the trauma of having an incarcerated mother and the issues that follow upon her release. Counseling and program staff that can provide continued support to the mother and her children both in jail and in the community is also needed. Similarly, Beckerman (1994) in assessing the long-term needs of the mother and her reunification with her children suggests developing a discharge plan, counseling, substance abuse treatment, and vocational and educational programs for the women. SnyderJoy and Carlo (1998) found that incarcerated women who participated in parenting classes coupled with a prison visitation program had positively affected interactions and communication between the mother and her child. Enhanced prison visitation programs offer a mechanism by which the mother-child relationship can be supported and aid in the reunification process upon release (Block and Potthast, 1998).

Completing the Family Picture: Wives, Girlfriends, and Other Family Members

L. Alex Swan (1981) in his book, *Families of Black Prisoners: Survival and Progress*, addressed the specific problems and needs of black families once the black male has been incarcerated. The focus of the study was on determining the nature and the extent of the problems that black families faced before and during the imprisonment of their family member. While conducted some 20 years prior to the initial Sentencing Project Report (1990) Swan found that the black men incarcerated in his study were young, between the ages of 21 to 30. The wives and girlfriends of these men reported that the men prior to their incarceration were involved in crime out of economic necessity versus a desire for a criminal life style. While not necessarily providing the majority of the family income, their contributions either through crime or through their often menial legitimate jobs added to the family budget. With the lack of income after the imprisonment the women worried about how they would survive financially. Help was provided for many of the women from extended families members—parents, grandparents, siblings and other family members. This came primarily in the forms of financial assistance, emotional support, and the provision of child care. The support network of family was often not enough to meet the financial and psychological needs of the women. Many of the women who sought financial assistance from various public and social service agencies were met with more obstacles than assistance. They often encountered a lack of caring and sensitivity from the professionals working in these agencies to their problems and needs. The stigma attached to being the wife or girl of an incarcerated inmate hampered in many cases their ability to receive assistance. In dealing with the prison system, the women discussed how the imprisonment of their loved one punished not only the men but the family as well, resulting in punishing not only the guilty but the innocent. Their visitations often suffered from a lack of privacy similarly their correspondences were intercepted and opened and read by prison officials before the men had an opportunity to read them. The women believed that these contacts, however restricted and limited, facilitated and enhanced the family's chances of staying together once he was released. The women overwhelmingly reported wanting their husbands/boyfriends back in their lives and looked forward to reuniting the family.

Restorative Justice

The latest paradigm shift to sweep through the criminal justice reform movement is the concept of restorative justice. While the concept is not new, in recent years it has been heralded as a revolution in criminal justice. The idea behind the concept is to restore or mend the relationship between the victim, the offender and the community. Restorative justice is a shift away from the notion that crime occurs in a vacuum. It acknowledges that there are victims, and their families who suffer not only from the criminal behavior that victimized them, but that the crime potentially has a lasting affect on them and their families economically and/or emotionally. The approach also recognizes (not excuses) the views and issues of the offenders, as to why they committed their crimes. Used in various restorative justice programs, the offender hears from the victim on how the crime has impacted his or her life and the lives of his or her family. The restorative justice concept is used only as an alternative to incarceration or other formal criminal justice processing, and is used only in non-violent, primarily first offense cases. The notion is that a more reflective, non-punitive approach, if it is to work, will work with non-violent, first offenders, who are given a glimpse into how their crimes have affected their victims and their families. The guiding principles that form the restorative justice model are: the nature of crime, the goal of justice, the role of victims, the role of the offenders, the role of the local community, and the role of the formal criminal justice system (for a full discussion, see Van Ness, 1990).

Taken from the broad philosophical notion that crime is not simply the breaking of laws, but indeed is a violation of one human being by another, the crime is synonymous with the violation—which, at its heart, affects the very essence of social relationships within the community. Thus, the goal of justice becomes repairing the damage caused by the crime to the victim of the family and the community. The victim's role in a restorative justice model is to seek validation for his or her pain. This validation, which at the very least means some form of participation in the process, occurs in a format that the victim may find comforting, and this participation can take the form of restitution, or perhaps mediation. The role of the offender in restoring the relationship is accepting his or her responsibility for the crime as well as his or her obligations for repairing the damage to the victim, the family and the community. To the extent that this can happen, it is incumbent on the local community to provide resources that can aid in the restoring process, as well as providing on-going prevention strategies for future criminal acts. Finally, in order for the restorative justice model to work it must be noncoercive. Each party must enter into the process willingly. The model rests on the assumption that changes in behavior, realization of personal wrongs, and culpability for those wrongs can occur only through a noncoercive environment (Van Ness, 1990).

The practical implementation of the six principles that shape the framework of the restorative justice model are being implemented to a greater or lesser extent in various programs throughout the country. While the programs vary, the goal is to "mend" the wrongs caused by the offender on the victim, without resulting to incarceration as the first and only resort. Restorative justice programs range from victim-offender mediation, and family group conferences, to victim-offender panels.

Victim-Offender mediation attempts to balance the needs of the offender with the victim. The offender meets with the victim in a safe supervised setting, where they can resolve their conflicts. Unlike a formal mediation process in which a third party hears both sides of the dispute and independently reaches a resolution, the victim-offender process relies on their resolution of the conflict. The victim's and offender's experiences are shared, the victim tells of the damage done to his or her life, while the offender discusses who he or she is, what led him or her to commit the crime and why. From this discovery process, the participants can then set about making things right, and restoring equity (for a full discussion see Brazemore and Griffiths, 1997). The two discuss how the offender might go about repairing the harm caused by their crime. While not limited to this, it often takes the form of financial restitution.

The family group conference is a more inclusive variation on the victim-offender mediation process. Conducted by a conference coordinator, the family group conference includes not only the victim and the offender but also the victim's family and friends, along with the offender's family and friends. The offender begins by telling his/her side of the story—why he/she committed the crime, why he/she chose that victim. The victim then tells the group how the crime has affected his/her life—or the damage it caused. The victim has the opportunity to ask the offender more direct questions, questions that perhaps were not answered in the offender's telling of the story. At this point the victim's family and friends talk about the damage caused by the crime, followed by the offender's family and friends having an opportunity to speak. After each side has aired its motivations, hurts, and pains the family group conference is directed towards (by the coordinator) solutions to remedying the injuries caused by the offender and the crime. Again, while not limited to this, the remedies reached are in the form of financial restitution.

While most restorative justice programs involve finding a solution or remedy where the person who is the offender is responding to the needs of his/her victim, offenders are not always brought to justice, and not all victims want to face their victimizer. But the need to face up to your crimes, or to be heard regarding your victimization, is not victim-offender specific. In other words, bringing together the offender and a group of victims who do not know each other, but who share a crime in common, is at the core of restorative justice. In the victim-offender panels, offenders who have engaged in, for example, the crime of theft, are brought together with victims of theft. Even though the offenders and victims are not matched, this type of panel gives the victims an opportunity to discuss the harm done to them by the crime, and a chance to find personal resolution and closure. Offenders get the chance to hear in general how their crimes affect a web of lives. This gives the offender a first-hand glance at the effects of the crimes they have committed, in a hope to change the offender's future attitudes and behaviors (for a full discussion of Victim Offender Panels, see Umbreit, Coats, and Kalanj, 1994).

The practical implementation of the six principles that shape the framework of the restorative justice model can be adapted and extended to the families of inmates. The victim-offender mediation process could be used to balance the needs of the offender with his family. In this mediation process, the family (wives, girlfriends, children, parents, siblings, grandparents and others) and the incarcerated man could come together and share how his crime and incarceration has affected their lives. From this discovery process, the participants can set about restoring the family. The family group conference could take a similar path—one where specific realistic remedies, for example counseling the family (including the inmate) to deal with the pains of imprisonment, can be sought. For inmates who are unwilling to participate with their families in such a process, the family offender panels could be used. Family members could be brought together with inmates not in their family, to discuss how crime and incarceration serve to alienate the innocent—the family. Such a process would also serve the offenders who did participate by giving them a first-hand look at how their behavior affects others. While by no means an exhaustive list of strategies that could be employed, the approach of including the inmate's family into a restorative model of justice has the potential of aiding in a successful reunification of the family (for a full discussion, see Brazemore and Griffiths, 1997).

In order for this to work, the criminal justice and social welfare systems must be willing to aid in this process. Prisons have to provide meaningful vocational and educational programs for the incarcerated, so upon their release they can pursue legitimate employment. Support from social service agencies are needed to meet the needs of the inmate's family while he is imprisoned and until he finds gainful employment once released. As indicated in Swan's (1981) study on the families of black prisoners, while not limited to, this support could take the form of temporary financial assistance to the families.

While not a panacea, restorative justice has a role to play in certain circumstances in restoring justice between the victim and the offender. A multifaceted, collaborative approach, such as the concept of restorative justice has implications for meeting the needs of the incarcerated—particularly the most "imprisoned gender" and racial group, black men. Debates over whether and to what extent the criminal justice system is racist (Wilbanks, 1987; Mann, 1993) aside, whether intentional or not, the system disproportionately affects the lives of black men and their families. It is thus incumbent upon the system to seek solutions and ways to reunite the black male offender and his family. Using a modified model of the principles of restorative justice the criminal justice system in conjunction with various social service agencies can mend and restore the kinship ties of incarcerated black men and their families.

Conclusion

The pains of the imprisonment are felt not only by the incarcerated but also by the inmate's family and kinship web. Research has shown that those pains include the isolation, stigma, uncertainty and loss of financial security for the family. With 2 million people incarcerated in the year 2000 the pains of imprisonment have far-reaching implications for a significant portion of American society. This is particularly the case with the black family, given the high numbers of incarcerated black men, the troubles that befall the families of incarcerated inmates are increasingly concentrated within the black community. Since the early work of E. Franklin Frazier (1939) that characterized the black family as deviant in part because of the criminality of the black male, and the now classic Moynihan Report (1965) which concluded that the black family was caught up in a tangle of pathology, academic discussions of the black family and the strategies which resulted have been largely "problem oriented." While both Frazier and Moynihan were neglectful in discussing structural impediments that affect the black family, their work, particularly Moynihan's, was instrumental in creating public controversy and establishing federal policy that has adversely affected the lives of the poor, blacks, and other minorities in this country. In this paper we argue that the emphasis in dealing with inmates and their families in general, and the families of incarcerated black men in particular (the most "imprisoned racial/gender") requires a "solution" oriented approach. One such approach is the restorative justice model, in which the offender and his family can work towards remedies in restoring and maintaining the family. As noted, for any such approach to work, it requires a structural approach, or one which is reliant upon the criminal and social welfare systems to aid in restoring and maintaining the ties between the inmate and his family.

References

Adams, D., and Fisher, J. (1976). The effects of prison residents' community contacts on recidivism rates. *Corrective and Social Psychiatry* 22, 21-27.

Atwood, J .E. (2000). *Too much time: Women in prison*. London: Phaidon Press.

Beck, A., and Karberg, J. (2001). *Prison and jail inmates at mid year 2000*. U.S. Department of Justice. Office of Justice Programs. Bureau of Justice Statistics. Washington, D.C. NCJ-185989.

Beckerman, A. (1994). Mothers in prison: Meeting the prerequisite conditions for permanency planning. *Social Work* 39: 9-14.

Bernstein, J., and Houston, E. (2000). *Crime and work: What we can learn from the low-wage labor market*. Washington, D.C.: Economic Policy Institute.

Block, K. J., and Potthast, M. J. (1998). Girl scouts beyond bars: Facilitating parent-child contact in correctional settings. *Child Welfare* 77, 5(Sept-Oct): 561-578.

Bonczar, T., and Beck, A. (1997). *Lifetime likelihood of going to state or federal prison*. U.S. Department of Justice. NCJ-160092.

Brazemore, G., and Griffiths, C. T. (1997). Conferences, circles, boards, and mediation: The 'new wave' of community justice decision-making. *Federal Probation* 61(2): 25-37.

Burkhart, K. W. (1973). *Women in prison*. Garden City, NY: Doubleday.

Chasin, B. H. (1997). *Inequality and violence in the United States: Casualties of capitalism*. Atlantic Highlands, NJ: Humanities Press.

Child Welfare League of America. (1997). *Parents in prison: Children in crisis*. October 2, 1997, News Release, Washington D.C.

Clayton, T. (1970). *Men in prison*. London: Hamilton Press.

Clemmer, D. (1966). *The prison community*. 2nd ed. New York: Holt, Rinehart and Winston.

Fellner, J., and Mauer, M. (1998). *Losing the vote: The impact of felony disenfranchisement laws in the United States*. New York: Human Rights Watch.

Fitsch, T., and Burkhead, J. (1981). Behavioral reactions of children to parental absence due to imprisonment. *Family Relations* (January): 83-88.

Frazier, E. F. (1939). *The negro in the United States*. New York: Macmillan Company.

Freedman, E. B. (1981). *Their sisters' keepers: Women's prison reform in America, 1830-1930*. Ann Arbor: University of Michigan Press.

Friedman, S., and Esselstyn, C. (1965). The adjustment of children and jail inmates. *Federal Probation* 29, 39-47.

Gabel, S. (1992). Children of incarcerated and criminal parents: Adjustment, behavior and prognosis. *Bulletin of the American Academy of Psychiatry and the Law* 20, 33-45.

Hairston, C. F. (1989). Men in prison: Family characteristics and parenting views. *Journal of Offender Counseling Services and Rehabilitation* 14(1): 23-30.

_____. (1995). Fathers in prison. In K. Gabel and D. Johnston (Eds.), *Children of incarcerated parents*. New York: Lexington Books.

Harm, N., and Whompson, P. J. (1997). Evaluating the effectiveness of parent education for incarcerated mothers. *Journal of Offender Rehabilitation* 24(3-4): 135-152.

Holt, N., and Miller, D. (1972). *Explorations in inmate-family relations*. Sacramento, CA: Department of Corrections Research Division.

Hostetter, E., and Jinnah, D. (1993). *Families of adult prisoners*. Washington, D.C.: Prison Fellowship Ministries.

Howser, J., and McDonald, D. (1972). Maintaining family ties. *Corrections Today* August, 11, 96-98.

Human Rights Watch: *World Report*. (2001). New York: Human Rights Watch.

Katz, P. C. (1998). Supporting families and children of mothers in jail: An integrated child welfare and criminal justice strategy. *Child Welfare* 77, 5(Sept-Oct): 579-592.

Lanier, C. S. (1993). Affective states of fathers in prison. *Justice Quarterly* 10, (1): 49-65.

Lawes, L. E. (1928). *Life and death in Sing Sing*. New York: Garden City Publishing Company, Inc.

Leclair, D. (1978). Home furlough program effects on rates of recidivism. *Criminal Justice and Behaviors* 5, 249-259.

Lusane, C. (1991). *Pipe dream blues: racism and the war on drugs*. Boston: South End Press.

Mann, C. R. (1993). *Unequal justice: A question of color*. Bloomington: Indiana University Press.

Mauer, M. (1990). *Young black men and the criminal justice system: A growing national problem*. The Sentencing Project, Washington, D.C.

_____. (1991). *Americans behind bars: A comparison of international rates of incarceration*. The Sentencing Project, Washington, D.C.

Mauer, M., and Huling, T. (1995). *Young black Americans and the criminal justice system: Five years later*. The Sentencing Project, Washington, D.C.

Mergenhagen, P. (1996). The prison population bomb. American Demographics, (Feb.): online.

Miller, J. (1996). *Search and destroy: African American males in the criminal justice system*. Cambridge: Cambridge University Press.

Moynihan, D. P. (1965). *The negro family: A case for national action*. Washington, D.C.: Government Printing Office.

Mumola, C. (2000). *Incarcerated parents and the children*. Bureau of Justice Statistics Special Report. U.S. Department of Justice, Office of Justice Programs. Washington, D.C. NCJ-182335.

Muraskin, R. (2000). *It's a crime: Women and justice*. Upper Saddle River, NJ: Prentice Hall.

The Osborne Association. (1993). How can I help? Working with children of incarcerated parents. *Serving Special Children* (Vol. 1) New York: The Osborne Association.

Pollock-Byrne, J. M. (1990). *Women, prison, and crime*. Pacific Grove, CA: Brooks/Cole.

Rierden, A. (1997). *The farm: Life inside a women's prison*. Amherst: University of Massachusetts Press.

Shapiro, A. (1997). The disenfranchised. *The American Prospect*. (Vol. 35 Nov-Dec), 60-62.

Shelden, R. (2001). *Controlling the dangerous classes: A critical introduction to the history of criminal justice*. Boston: Allyn and Bacon.

SnyderJoy, J,. and Carlo, T. A. (1998). Parenting through prison walls: Incarcerated mother and children's visitation programs. In S. Miller (Ed.), *Crime control and women: Feminist implications of criminal policy*. Thousand Oaks, CA: Sage.

Sykes, G. (1958). *The society of captives: A study of a maximum security prison*. Princeton, NJ: Princeton University Press.

Swan, L. A. (1981). Families of black prisoners: Survival and progress. Boston: G. K. Hall and Company.

Tonry, M. (1995). *Malign neglect: Race, crime, and punishment in America*. New York: Oxford University Press.

Umbreit, M. F., Coats, R. B., and Kalanj, B. (1994). *Victim meets offender: The impact of restorative justice and mediation*. Monsey, NY: Criminal Justice Press.

Uniform Crime Reports. (1999). *Crime in the United States*. Federal Bureau of Investigation. U.S. Department of Justice. Washington, D.C.

Van Ness, D. (1990). Toward restorative justice. In B. Galaway and J. Hudson (Eds.), *Criminal justice, restitution, and reconciliation*. Monsey, NY: Willow Tree Press.

Van Wormer, K. S. (1978). *Sex role behavior in a women's prison: An ethnological analysis*. San Francisco, CA: R. and E. Research Associates.

Wilbanks, W. (1987). The myth of a racist criminal justice system. Monterey, CA: Brooks/Cole Publishing.

Winning, J.R. (1933). *Behind these walls*. New York: Macmillan Company.

Part 2

The Importance of Fatherhood and the Social Significance of This Issue for African American Families

8

Behavioral Problems in Sons of Incarcerated or Otherwise Absent Fathers: The Issue of Separation

Stewart Gabel

According to the Bureau of Justice Statistics Bulletin (1989a), there were over 700,000 individuals in U.S. state and federal prisons at the end of 1989. This represents an increase of about 113 percent, or over 373,000 prisoners, from 1980 to 1990. The number of incarcerated individuals in local jails in 1988 was about 343,000 (Bureau of Justice Statistics Bulletin, 1990b), adding further to the overall number of incarcerated individuals in the United States at any one time. While the average number of children per incarcerated individual is not known, the above figures suggest that possibly millions of children in the United States either currently have a parent who is incarcerated or have had an incarcerated parent at some point in their lives.

Relatively little is known about the psychological reactions and behavior of children whose parents are incarcerated. Several investigators suggest that some children may experience a wide variety of problems due to separation from the parent, the stigma associated with parental incarceration, and the deception practiced on children about their parents' whereabouts and circumstances. The possibility that antisocial behavior in boys may follow directly on paternal incarceration has also been mentioned as a concern in the literature (Sack, 1977).

It is clear that boys are overrepresented in mental health samples and that boys are far more likely than girls to demonstrate aggressive and antisocial behavior (Gabel and Shindledecker, 1991a). Adult males are also more than ten times as likely as females to be incarcerated in federal or state prisons (Bureau of Justice Statistics Bulletin, 1990a). Because of these reasons and because most studies on the effects of parental incarceration deal with incarceration of fathers, this paper will focus on the behavioral and emotional reactions of children during paternal incarceration, emphasizing particularly the effects on boys. Studies that have evaluated the effects of separation on sons whose fathers are absent because of a variety of other reasons (for example, divorce, military service) also will be reviewed in order to examine whether it is separation as such that contributes to possibly adverse behavioral outcome in some offspring of incarcerated fathers, or whether poor outcome in these children is related to other factors. Most studies do not distinguish between male and female offspring reactions to the effects of paternal incarceration, however, and this paper will consider both sons' and daughters' reactions while emphasizing, when possible, the specific effects of paternal incarceration on boys. There will also be a brief mention of the literature on effects of maternal incarceration.

Literature Review

Morris (1965) studied the effects of incarceration on male prisoners and their families in England. Several hundred prisoners and their families were interviewed. About 5 percent of the prisoners' wives reported concerns about community hostility. Social stigma and shame were felt mainly by wives of first-time offenders, and this reaction seemed to occur early in the husband's incarceration. Overall, about 20 percent of the children were felt to have deteriorated behaviorally after the father's imprisonment.

Friedman and Esselstyn (1965) studied teacher ratings of children in California whose fathers had been incarcerated. These children were found to be rated below average on various social and psychological dimensions more commonly than were the children who were controls in the study. The control groups were not comparable to the experimental group, however, because more Mexican-American children were in the experimental group than in the control group.

Wilmer, Marks, and Pogue (1966), in a clinical/descriptive report, discuss the harmful effects of parental deception about the imprisonment of fathers on children. They argue that children's reactions of disobedience, temper outbursts, destructive or delinquent behavior are results of this deception. Deception is also emphasized as a particularly deleterious consequence for children of incarcerated parents by others such as Schwartz and Weintraub (1974). Hannon, Martin, and Martin (1984) argue that deception is practiced by the parents because of the social stigma of incarceration. They emphasize that this practice may make it impossible for children to discuss or work through their feelings about the incarceration.

Schneller (1978) did a survey study to assess changes that occurred in families of 93 incarcerated men who were black. He found that social stigma generally was not a major problem for these families since, in his view, these families thought of themselves as being a part of a subculture that viewed incarceration as a result of social prejudice against minorities. About two-thirds of the wives, however, did think that there had been negative family changes accompanying the incarceration.

Bakker, Morris, and Janus (1978) interviewed 7 wives of male prisoners to assess how incarceration had affected their lives. Only four of the wives had told the children that their father was in prison. Financial and housing problems, feelings of isolation, abandonment, and difficulties managing the children were reported by the women.

Fritsch and Burkhead (1991) reported on male and female prisoners' impressions of the behavior of their children in response to parental incarceration. Two-thirds of the prisoners felt that behavior problems had developed since their incarceration. The incarcerated men reported problems such as truancy, discipline, and delinquency. The incarcerated women reported problems such as fearfulness on the part of the child, poor school performance, and nightmares. The authors pointed out that the mothers and fathers reported problems in areas that are traditionally of most concern to them.

Swan (1981) studied 192 black male prisoners' families in Alabama and Tennessee. Most of the women reported that their children were aware of the father's imprisonment, but 15 percent did not know about it. For about one-half of the children, the imprisonment had had no or slight effect; for about 30 percent, there had reportedly been a major effect on the child. The mothers of about 11 percent of the children reported that remarks of other children in the community had been upsetting to the children because of their stigmatizing nature.

Lowenstein (1986), in a sample of first-time male Jewish offenders in Israel, studied a variety of factors that were hypothesized to relate to children's behavior. The wives of 118 prisoners completed interviews and questionnaires. Mothers reported that most of their children's problems were found in the areas of school work and in their reported physical health. Relationships, discipline, aggressive behavior, and withdrawal were other problems. The mothers' and families' coping resources as well as various imprisonment-related variables were important in determining outcome. Family solidarity and support networks were positive features. The kind of crime that the father had committed, the child's "preparedness" for the incarceration, and effects related to stigmatization were important. According to Lowenstein, social stigma of incarceration was especially difficult for children whose fathers had been convicted of white-collar crimes or because of sexual offenses since these children had had no prior contact with the criminal justice system.

As noted earlier, the effects of maternal incarceration have been studied less commonly than the effects of paternal incarceration (see Glick and Neto, 1977; Henriquez, 1982; Koban, 1983; McGowan and Blumenthal, 1978), although, with greater numbers of incarcerated females (Bureau of Justice

Statistics Bulletin, 1990a), this issue has become increasingly important. Studies of the effects of maternal incarceration emphasize problems due to rupture of the relationship in which mothers (unlike fathers) have been the primary caretakers of their children (Koban, 1983).

The studies noted above have mostly relied on parental reports about their children's behavioral reactions. Many of the children in these reports were quite young at the time of study. Since it is well known that boys of fathers with criminal backgrounds are at high risk for juvenile delinquency and/or adult criminal behavior themselves (Farrington, 1978; Glueck and Glueck, 1950; McCord, McCord, and Thurber, 1962; Robins, West, and Herjanic, 1975), a clinical report by Sack (1977) about the rapid emergence of antisocial behavior in a small group of pre- to early adolescent boys whose fathers recently were imprisoned merits attention.

Sack studied six families, seen at a health center in Boston, in whom a number of boys between the ages of 6 and 13 years had rather abrupt onset of aggressive or antisocial behavior problems within two months of their fathers' imprisonment. The families were lower middle class and white. Out of a total of 24 children in the 6 families, 12 showed behavioral disturbances. It was the male child, between the ages of 11 and 13, who seemed the most vulnerable to the effects of separation, although younger children did sometimes show separation anxiety of a temporary nature. Three of the 6 families were further disrupted through divorce, which seemed to have been precipitated by the imprisonment. These three families had had histories of prior separations, marital discord, and physical abuse. The boy's antisocial behavior was similar to the father's recent antisocial activity that had resulted in incarceration. On followup two years later, the boys in these three families showed significant disturbances as teenagers.

The boys in the three families in which the mother planned to continue the marriage after the father's imprisonment were somewhat younger than the boys in the other three families. They did not show the severity of antisocial behavior found in the first group, and also seemed to be doing better on later followup than the boys in the first group. Whether the lesser severity of symptoms was related to their younger age or to their possibly less chaotic and disturbed home environments prior to or during the imprisonment is not clear.

Sack and colleagues (1976, 1978) later studied nonclinical samples of children whose parents were incarcerated. Small samples of parents and children were interviewed. The findings were not as striking in descriptions of antisocial behavior as had been true in the clinical sample noted above (Sack, 1977). In one of these studies, Sack et al. (1976) found that about a third of the families practiced deception in some form around the issue of incarceration. Family attitudes, financial problems, social isolation, and social stigma were major problems confronting the families of the imprisoned parents. The wives of prisoners generally saw their children as being more disruptive, aggressive, and less obedient than prior to incarceration; the male prisoners felt their children's problems to be mild or not present at all.

Major Themes In the Literature

There are a number of major themes that emerge from the largely descriptive literature reviewed above:

1. Separation from a parental figure is likely to be traumatic to the child, disrupting personal and family bonds and worsening the family's social and financial condition.
2. Behavior problems do emerge in a sizeable minority of children; often these are nonspecific and relate to developmental stage, existing family supports, and coping mechanisms.
3. Stigma is an important problem for many children, although the degree of adjustment difficulty experienced may reflect the family's and subculture's view of the meaning of incarceration. Schneller (1978) argues that some black families feel that incarceration of blacks is the result of social prejudice against minorities, thereby not reflecting negatively on the incarcerated individual. In these cases, children may experience less stigma when their parents are incarcerated, although other problems related to the incarceration may be present.
4. Deception of the children by the remaining caretaker and incarcerated parent is commonly practiced. Some children are never told that their fathers (usually) have been incarcerated. Such deception is universally condemned in the literature as harmful to the child, and perhaps the cause of behavioral difficulties.
5. Most children do not show severe antisocial behavior at the time of their parents' incarceration. Boys at or near puberty may be at somewhat greater risk for antisocial behavior or conduct problems with the incarceration of their fathers. However, it appears that this behavior is more likely to emerge in the context of already existing family discord and dysfunctional family situations. Identification with the incarcerated parent, a process that might increase the likelihood of antisocial behavior on the part of the child, has not been adequately studied.
6. Maternal incarceration places additional burdens on children since they may lose their primary caretaker temporarily or permanently (for example, to foster care, to extended family). Children of imprisoned fathers generally continue to be cared for by their mothers. Such is not the case with children of incarcerated mothers who are rarely—10 percent in one study (Glick and Neto, 1977)—cared for by the incarcerated mother's husband.

Critique of the Literature

The literature reviewed above is heavily descriptive and anecdotal, with few empirical studies and significant methodological limitations. Selection of subjects for study has not been random. Often it seems that willing subjects are enrolled, with no comparison between subjects who enroll versus those who refuse to participate—a probably very different population. Control groups, for the most part, have not been used, making it difficult to determine if the children's behavioral difficulties are associated with parental incarceration or some other factor. The studies overall have not employed standardized assessment techniques or instruments, and there is almost no mention in the literature of the psychometric properties of the questionnaires employed. Parents are, in the main, the only informants about their children's behavior. As some reports indicate, depending on their perspective (being incarcerated or not), parents differ in their appraisal of whether problems have developed in their children. Teachers, children themselves, or mental health professionals would all offer different perspectives, and in some cases less biased ones.

Important preexisting behavioral, family, social, and legal data for the most part have been omitted from descriptions of the children and families. There are no longitudinal studies that have assessed these children and families over time or even at any two points, such as the periods prior to arrest, during the legal procedures leading to incarceration, during incarceration itself, or after release. This lack of longitudinal data, associated with a lack of appropriate control groups, make it impossible to say if behavioral change relates to incarceration itself, reactions around legal procedures, release and re-entry of the incarcerated parent into the family, or none of the above. Studies commonly have not described the kinds of criminal offenses of the parents, nor have they emphasized the duration of imprisonment as an important variable, especially as this might relate to the developmental stage of the child, the caretaker, or the family as a whole.

The literature also does not describe in any depth the relationship variables between the incarcerated parent and the child or other family members prior to the parent's incarceration. This omission in much of the literature makes it impossible to determine if, as seems likely, the child's relationship to the incarcerated parent and to the non-incarcerated parent (and siblings) determines how the incarceration is viewed psychologically and how the child will adjust. Except in a few cases, children's coping skills or resiliency, and the family's emotional assets have not been systematically studied as possible mitigating factors.

The studies have also generally neglected to mention in any detail whether other aspects of severe family dysfunction, such as parental substance abuse or child abuse/maltreatment, have been present. It seems likely that parental incarceration commonly is an index of severe family dysfunction that is associated with these other variables, as was found in a recent clinical sample of children attending a day hospital (Gabel and Shindledecker, 1991b).

In summary, the existing literature on children's reactions to parental incarceration provides clinical insights and possible directions for therapeutic work and for future research. At present, however, the literature's conclusions must be viewed cautiously, given the lack of an adequate empirical base to most of the reports cited. The following section, therefore, attempts to shed further light on the question of whether separation because of parental incarceration is harmful to the child by examining literature on the effects of other forms of paternal separation on the behavior of children.

Father-Absent Families

There is more empirical literature on the effects of other forms of father absence on the adjustment of children and adolescents, especially in the area of juvenile delinquency, than there is literature on the immediate effects of parental incarceration on the child's behavior, as reviewed in the preceding section. Accordingly, only several major studies and reviews will be discussed here. Rutter (1971) evaluated the effects of long-term separation on children who had been involved in two epidemiological studies. One group consisted of children (ages 9 to 12) in small towns on the Isle of Wight; the second group consisted of children living in an urban setting in London. Rutter studied the long-term effects of permanent or prolonged separations (for example, parental death, separation, or divorce) on children's behavior in relation to other variables such as family discord and poor family relationships. In homes not broken by divorce, separation, or death, antisocial behavior in boys increased significantly from 0 percent in good marriages, to 22 percent in fair marriages, to 39 percent in very poor marriages. In broken homes, separation seemed to have been a negligible factor contributing to delinquency and, in fact, appeared to have had little impact on the development of neurosis. It was the *duration* of the tension and discord in the child's home that seemed to be related to delinquent behavior. Furthermore, and optimistically, some of the effects of the previous home environment were reversible when the child was subsequently living in a better environment. In addition, while the rate of delinquent behavior in boys was significantly higher in homes with poor marital relationships that were filled with discord, compared to the rate of delinquent behavior in boys from homes with good marital relationships, a good relationship between one parent and the child was important in mitigating the effects of marital discord. These findings in relation to antisocial behavior and home environment applied almost wholly to boys. In girls, deviant behavior was not shown to increase significantly in situations where there was discordant parental relationship or parental personality disorder. Later studies by Rutter and colleagues (1978), with addition samples support these findings.

McCord, McCord, and Thurber (1962) studied the outcome of a group of 55 boys who were living with their biological mothers, but were from father-absent homes. These boys originally were part of a larger group of children specifically selected for study during the 1930s because they were thought to show signs of "incipient delinquency." The youngsters had had repeated assessments by staff of the Cambridge-Somerville Youth Study during a period of five years, between the ages of 10 and 15. The fathers of the boys McCord et al. (1962) studied had died, deserted, been in mental hospitals, been divorced or legally separated, and in 3 cases, were serving long prison terms. These father-absent boys were compared with a group of 150 boys whose natural parents were living together. McCord et al. did not find support for the view that paternal absence is associated with delinquent gang affiliation. Significantly, more boys from homes in which there were strong conflicts between parents who remained together were likely to be in delinquent gangs than was true in either father-absent or low parental-conflict families. Furthermore, significantly more boys with parent substitutes became gang delinquents than boys who lived in homes with two parents and little conflict. McCord et al. (1962) concluded that "the relationship between criminality and paternal absence appears to be largely a result of the general instability of broken homes rather than of paternal absence in itself" (p. 368).

Moerk (1973) addressed the question of whether emotional disturbance and delinquency are related to paternal absence due to imprisonment specifically. It will be recalled that the study of McCord et al., cited above, had only a few prolonged separations due to paternal imprisonment. Moerk compared 24 male children from father-imprisoned families with 24 male children from families in which fathers were absent due to divorce, matched on parameters such as socioeconomic status, parent educational level, ethnic group membership, and age at the time of separation from the father. The average length of paternal imprisonment was 1.8 years, with a range of less than 6 months to over 2 years. In every case, the father did not return to live with the family after his imprisonment, although there was some visitation in a few cases. Interestingly, on nearly all dimensions studied, including father/child relationship, mother/child relationship, self-concept, and problems with authority, there were no significant differences between the two groups, both of whom had father absence and low socioeconomic backgrounds.

While some studies, such as those of Rutter (1971, 1978) and McCord et al. (1962), have stressed the importance of the marital relationship, parental discord, and home instability in the development of children's antisocial behavior, other studies have highlighted the behavior and/or psychopathology of the mother (who is usually the parent remaining in the home) in preventing (or contributing to) antisocial behavior in children.

Goldstein (1984) studied the relationship between father-absent families, parental supervision, and conduct disorder in youth by examining Cycle III data of the Health Examination Survey that was conducted by the National Center for Health Statistics. This survey, conducted between 1966 and 1970, studied several thousand youths 12-17 years of age. The data collected were from youth report, parent report, and school report. Conduct problems were assessed on the basis of reported police contact, arrest, and disciplinary actions in school.

Goldstein's findings indicated that youths who were from father-absent families reportedly had been questioned by police significantly more often than youths from father-present families. Analysis by sex indicated that boys, and not girls, who were from father-absent families had significantly more contact with police. In terms of parental supervision as a possibly mediating variable, Goldstein found that in homes that had no supervision, boys but not girls, showed significantly greater likelihood of having had police contacts if they were from father-absent compared to father-present homes. Boys from father-absent homes with low supervision also showed a significantly greater likelihood of having had discipline problems in school than did boys from father-present homes. These findings are interesting in their suggestion that supervision by mothers may ameliorate the potential for antisocial behavior in father-absent homes in a general sample.

Patterson (1982, 1986) and Patterson and colleagues (1984, 1990) have worked extensively with aggressive and antisocial children. Their work with both clinical and nonclinical samples, in assessment and in treatment of antisocial children, has also emphasized the importance of parental monitoring and discipline in preventing antisocial and delinquent behavior in boys. Parental discord and parent psychopathology (for example, maternal depression) also have been linked to poor family management practices and to delinquent and antisocial behavior in boys.

Emery (1982) has reviewed the literature on the relationship between marital discord in divorced and nondivorced couples and childhood behavior problems. He concludes that it is conflict and hostile interactions between parents, not the separation through divorce, that is related to more deleterious outcomes in children's behavior. Behavioral undercontrol (conduct problems) is the most prominent childhood disorder resulting from such marital discord, and the response is greater in boys than in girls. The negative effects of interparental conflict can he mitigated partially by a good relationship between the child and one parent. Also, interparental conflict seems more important in producing childhood behavior disorder than a parent's individual psychopathology.

Wallerstein (1991) more recently has reviewed an extensive body of literature related to the effects of divorce on children. She has focused specifically on long-term effects and has reviewed the outcome of her own studies and those of others. Given the diverse projects she reviewed, the long-term nature of the studies, and the changing nature of the children and families involved over time, all of which make unqualified conclusions difficult, several points are noteworthy for the present paper. Children from divorced families generally fare less well than children from intact homes in a variety of social, behavioral, and academic areas. Family instability and inadequate parent-child relationships probably have been present in many families prior to actual divorce. The children in such families, therefore, are more vulnerable to new stresses at the time of actual divorce or separation. The impulsive and undercontrolled behavior of boys in post-divorce years often seems to be a continuation of their previous behavior in the family prior to divorce. Fathers in such families commonly have been disengaged and unreliable in their behavior toward their sons even prior to the divorce. Relationships between mothers and sons in unremarried groups of families remain particularly problematic, while sons seem gradually to improve in behavior in remarried situations. Biological fathers and their children commonly developed emotionally distant relationships after divorce, despite visitation. Few children had close bonds with both divorced parents. The crucial relationship for the child in the decade following divorce seems to be the relationship with the mother. Although differences between boys and girls may dissipate by young adulthood, boys earlier demonstrate more problems than girls, showing school difficulties, problems in peer relationships, and problems in managing aggression. Intense parental conflict around custody and visitation issues poses major threats to the psychological adjustment and stability of the child.

In her conclusion, Wallerstein (1991) states that "a frequent finding from these studies is the critical importance of the custodial parent-child relationship." But, "the characteristics of this relationship are not separate from the psychological condition or circumstance of either the parent or the child." Yet, "parental conflict, like the custodial parent-child relationship, does not stand alone. Often it derives from, and contributes to, severe psychopathology in one or sometimes both parents. The interpersonal conflict almost always spills into the parent child relationship in ways that are detrimental to the child" (p. 359).

Finally, while paternal absence due to imprisonment, death, or perhaps divorce may be considered nonnormative experiences for a child, other absences, such as father absence because of military service, may be expected and usual for certain groups. Jensen, Grogan, Xenakis, and Bain, (1989) studied a sample of children who had undergone this temporary, "normative" form of father absence. They evaluated the effects of father absence on military children whose father had been away during the previous year. Slightly over 200 families participated. Mothers, fathers, children, and teachers completed questionnaires. There were 92 boys and 88 girls, ages 6 to 11.9 years. Families in which the fathers had been away for more than one month during the last year (father-absent group) were compared with families in which the father, had not been away for more than one month in the preceding year (father-present group). Children in the father-absent group had significantly more reports of depressive and anxiety symptoms than children in the father-present group, but these effects did not persist on statistical analysis once family stress and maternal symptoms were controlled. Furthermore, the effects, while statistically significant, were rather small, suggesting that a generally healthy child and family would not experience major problems during father absence, at least as defined in this study.

In summary, the literature on other forms of parental absence in relation to childhood behavior problems focuses mainly on father absence. It is rather impressive, given the diversity of studies, differing methodologies, and different reasons for paternal separation from the family unit, that some consistency in findings can be discerned. The literature reports that the relationship between the remaining caretaker and the child, the adequacy of her parenting practices, and the individual characteristics (and psychopathology) of the remaining caretaker are major variables affecting the child's outcome behaviorally. Overall, boys may be more vulnerable to father absence than girls, at least in terms of the development of antisocial behavior and conduct problems.

Discussion

Children of incarcerated or otherwise absent parents are said to suffer greatly as a result of the separation from parental figures, a situation resulting in a variety of behavioral and emotional difficulties. Given the overwhelming majority of boys compared to girls who enter treatment in mental health facilities with problems of aggressive behavior and conduct disorder diagnoses (Gabel and Shindledecker, 1991a), and the more than 10:1 ratio of males to females in United States prisons (Bureau of Justice Statistics Bulletin, 1990a), this review has asked specifically whether separation through paternal incarceration contributes to the acknowledged high risk for antisocial, delinquent, and conduct disordered behavior found in sons of criminal or antisocial fathers (Farrington, 1978; Glueck and Glueck, 1950; McCord et al., 1962; Robins et al., 1975).

The literature that is available on the behavioral reactions of children whose parents are incarcerated provides little evidence empirically that separation itself is the most salient characteristic contributing to the behavior problems (aggressive, conduct-disordered, or otherwise) that a minority of children of incarcerated parents exhibit. While it may be that, for certain children, separation from parental figures or, specifically, separation from the father, does result in significant distress or in an exaggerated identification or modeling process that contributes to antisocial behavior, this is apparently not so for most youth. Behavioral disorder in children of incarcerated or otherwise absent fathers seems more closely related to factors such as psychopathology in the remaining caretaker (usually the mother), the caretaker-child relationship, the coping resources and social supports of the remaining family unit, and likely, too, the understanding of the incarceration for the child and family.

It is in this context that the clinical literature on parental incarceration can be understood and applied to therapeutic work with these children and families. Aid for the child in dealing with the stigma of parental incarceration, the meaning of the incarceration for the child and family, and avoidance of deception and unwarranted secrecy around the circumstances of the incarceration seem to be important. The remaining caretaker parent, the children in the family, and perhaps the incarcerated offender parent all may need therapeutic help around these issues.

I have found that, at least in one mental health sample of children attending a day-treatment program (Gabel and Shindledecker, 1991b), a history of parental incarceration was significantly associated with a history of parental substance abuse and reports of suspected abuse/maltreatment involving the child in treatment. In that sample, parental incarceration was viewed as an index of broader family dysfunction. Mental health involvement for the child and family (sometimes including the incarcerated parent) should be provided in addressing these and other family issues if they exist, as well as the more individual concerns of the child as he or she deals with the meaning of the incarceration.

The normative versus nonnormative characteristics of the separation also may be important, as this relates to issues of stigma, deception, positive compared to negative identification for the child and family, financial and social support for the remaining family members. Separations due to divorce (and probably even more when due to incarceration) are likely to have been preceded by family turmoil, conflict, and dysfunction in many cases relative to family functioning in intact families. This suggests that many of these families and children are vulnerable even more to further problems and behavioral disorders subsequent to the separation itself. The latter may increase social, financial, or personal difficulties with which already dysfunctional families cannot cope.

Separation then, as understood through the various studies encompassing incarceration, death, divorce, and military service of the father that have been referred to in this paper, presents a complex challenge to clinicians, researchers, and social policy planners. The context of the paternal separation must be addressed carefully from caretaker, child, individual, and relationship perspectives, as well as from normative versus nonnormative criteria, preexisting child and family coping mechanisms, and from a developmental context in which differing reactions would be expected from children at different stages along a life-span perspective. Despite the diverse and broad literature that has been covered in this review of the literature on separation, a finding that seems to be present nearly throughout, which relates to better versus worse outcome for the variety of children affected, involves the characteristics and psychological stability of the remaining caretaker parent and (usually) her relationship to the children at home.

Children of incarcerated parents merit additional mental health studies and public policy attention because they are an extremely high-risk group for later juvenile delinquency and substance abuse, a group that is increasing in number. The remaining members of the family unit merit mental health attention also around their individual issues as well as family interactive patterns and behavioral processes that apparently are often disordered and dysfunctional, an impression that I base in part on my own clinical experience.

Research that attempts to learn more about the characteristics and adjustment of children of incarcerated parents over a longitudinal course seems very much needed. Specific suggestions regarding methodological issues such as standardized assessment procedures, control groups, assessment at regular intervals have been provided earlier.

A more in-depth study of family interactive processes in such families with and without the incarcerated parent present also should yield a great deal of information about microsocial interactions in such families, and provide pointers for additional intervention from a family therapy perspective. A close relationship between mental health and judicial systems would be of enormous value in identifying children and families that would participate in longitudinal research and potentially would benefit from individual and family therapy intervention when parental incarceration occurs.

References

Bakker, L. J., Morris, B. A., and Janus, L. M. (1978). Hidden victims of crime. *Social Work* 23: 143-148.

Bureau of Justice Statistics Bulletin. (1990a). *Prisoners in 1989.* Washington D.C.: U.S. Department of Justice.

_____. (1990b). *Census of local jails, 1988.* Washington D.C.: U.S. Department of Justice.

Emery, R. E. (1982). Interparental conflict and the children of discord and divorce. *Psychological Bulletin* 92:310-330.

Farrington, D. P. (1978). The family backgrounds of aggressive youths. In L. A. Hersov, M. Flerger, and D. Sheller (Eds.), *Aggression and antisocial behavior in childhood and adolescence* (book supplement to the *Journal of Child Psychology and Psychiatry 1).* New York: Pergamon Press.

Friedman, S., and Esselstyn, T. C. (1965). The adjustment of children of jail inmates. *Federal Probation* 29:56-59.

Fritsch, T. A., and Burkhead, J. D. (1981). Behavioral reactions of children to parental absence due to imprisonment. *Family Relations* 30:83-88.

Gabel, S., and Shindledecker, R. (1991a). Aggressive behavior in youth: Characteristics, outcome, and psychiatric diagnoses. *Journal of the American Academy of Child and Adolescent Psychiatry* 30:982-988.

_____. (1991b). Children with parents who have been incarcerated. *Continuing Medical Education Syllabus and Scientific Proceedings* (144th Annual Meeting of the American Psychiatric Association). Washington D.C.: American Psychiatric Association.

Glick, R. M., and Neto V. V. (1977). *National study of women in correctional programs* (National Institute of Law Enforcement and Criminal Justice). Washington D.C.: U.S. Department of Justice.

Glueck, S., and Glueck, E. (1950). *Unraveling juvenile delinquency.* New York: Commonwealth Fund.

Goldstein, H. S. (1984). Parental composition, supervision, and conduct problems in youths 12 to 17 years old. *Journal of the American Academy of Child Psychiatry* 23:679-784.

Hannon, G., Martin, D., and Martin, M. (1984). Incarceration in the family: Adjustment to change. *Family Therapy* 11:253-260.

Henriquez, Z. W. (1982). *Imprisoned mothers and their children: A descriptive and analytic study.* Washington D.C.: University Press of America.

Jensen, P. S., Grogan, D., Xenakis. S. N., and Bain, M. W. (1989). Father absence: Effects on child and maternal psychopathology. *Journal of the American Academy of Child and Adolescent Psychiatry* 28:171-175.

Koban, L. A. (1983). Parents in prison: A comparative analysis of the effects of incarceration on the families of men and women. *Research in Law, Deviance and Social Control* 5:171-183.

Lowenstein, A. (1986). Temporary single parenthood—The case of prisoners' families. *Family Relations* 35:79-85.

McCord, J., McCord, W., and Thurber, E. (1962). Some effects of paternal absence on male children. *Journal of Abnormal and Social Psychology* 64:361-369.

McGowan, B. G., and Blumenthal, K. L. (1978). *Why punish the children? A study of children of women prisoners.* Hackensack, NJ: National Council on Crime and Delinquency.

Moerk, E. (1973). Like father like son: Imprisonment of fathers and the psychological adjustment of sons. *Journal of Youth and Adolescence* 2:303-312.

Morris, P. (1965). *Prisoners and their families.* New York: Hart.

Patterson, G. R. (1982). Coercive family process. Eugene, OR: Castalia Publishing Co.

_____. (1986). Performance models for antisocial boys. *American Psychologist* 41:432-444.

Patterson, G. R., and Forgatch, M. S. (1990). Initiation and maintenance of process disrupting single-mother families. In G. R. Patterson (Ed.), *Depression and aggression in family interaction.* Hillsdale NJ: Lawrence Erlbaum Associates.

Patterson, G. R., and Stouthamer-Loeber, M. (1984). The correlation of family management practices and delinquency. *Child Development* 55:1299-1307.

Robins, L. N., West, P. A., and Herjanic, B. L. (1975). Arrests and delinquency in two generations: A study of black urban families and their children. *Journal of Child Psychology and Psychiatry* 16:125-140.

Rutter, M. (1971). Parent-child separation: Psychological effects on the children. *Journal Child Psychology and Psychiatry* 12:233-260.

_____. (1978). Family, area and school influences in the genesis of conduct disorders. In L. A. Hersov, M. Berger, and D. Shaffer (Eds.), *Aggression and antisocial behavior in childhood and adolescence* (book supplement to the *Journal of Child Psychology and Psychiatry 1*). New York: Pergamon Press.

Sack, W. H. (1977). Children of imprisoned fathers. *Psychiatry* 40:163-174.

Sack, W. H., and Seidler, J. (1978). Should children visit their parents in prison? *Law and Human Behavior* 2:261-226.

Sack, W. H., Seidler, J., and Thomas, S. (1976). The children of imprisoned parents: A psychosocial exploration. *American Journal Orthopsychiatry* 46:618-628.

Schneller, D. P. (1978). *The prisoner's family: A study of the effect of imprisonment on the families of prisoners.* San Francisco: R and E Research Associates.

Schwartz, M. C., and Weintraub, J. (1974). The prisoner's wife: A study in crisis. *Federal Probation* 38:20-26.

Swan, A. (1981). *Families of black prisoners. Survival and progress.* Boston: G.K. Hill.

Wallerstein, J. S. (1991). The long-term effects of divorce on children: A review. *Journal of the American Academy of Child and Adolescent Psychiatry* 30:349-360.

Wilmer, H. A., Marks, I., and Pogue, B. (1966). Group treatment of prisoners and their families. *Mental Hygiene* 50:380-389.

9

The Effects of Negative Stereotypes on African American Male and Female Relationships

Micah L. McCreary and Richard C. Wright

Introduction

In July of 1994, we were invited to present a paper on "Spirituality and Sexuality: Healing Our Brokenness," to the Virginia Cluster for Pastoral Education. During preparation for that presentation we read a book entitled *The Sexual Mountain and Black Women Writers: Adventures in Sex, Literature, and Real Life*, by C. C. Hernton (1987). In this book, Hernton reviewed Lutie Johnson's story written in *The Street* by Ann Petry (1946). Hernton's chapter on *The Street*, showed that the novel provided several rich examples of the brokenness that has historically existed between African American couples and families. The book was thus used as a tool for discussing the current situation of African American relationships. After the presentation, audience reactions were mixed. Using the novel as a vehicle to discuss the brokenness between African American females and males was acceptable to some participants. Others, however, attacked the entire notion of using the novel, stating that the novel had no redeeming qualities whatsoever.

Since then, *The Street* has been revisited to examine the tensions that exist among the book's characters, and more importantly within current African American interpersonal relationships. It seems that the characters in the novel provide examples of the strong and direct correlation between the tensions in interpersonal relationships and racial, gender, and economic prejudices which affect past, present, and future human conduct. Thus, this chapter: (1) briefly reviews current research on the intersection of racism, sexism, and economic oppression; (2) explores origins of the Bad Man and Bad Woman stereotypes;

(3) analyzes the impact of the stereotypes on African American relationships; and (4) offers several recommendations for moving away from the brokenness that characterizes many current relationships and toward positive, nurturing interpersonal relationships with others.

Origins of Negative African American Stereotypes

African American scholars (Davis, 1983,1990; Hooks, 1992; Hernton, 1987; West, 1993a, 1993b) have suggested that mental health professionals consider the profound influences of racism, sexism, and economic oppression in their care and conceptualizations of African American men and women. Research on the persistent and pervasive effects of racial and gender prejudice on the lives of African American men and women supports this assertion (Bowman and Howard, 1985; Burlew, Banks, McAdoo, and Azibo, 1992; Jones, 1991). There is also convincing evidence that the systemic influences of sexism, racism, and economic oppression are pervasive and have existed throughout the history of Africans in America (Fanon, 1967; Thomas and Sillen, 1972).

One of the more powerful ways racial, economic, and gender prejudice have affected African Americans is through the use and maintenance of negative stereotypes. A stereotype is a relatively fixed, simplistic overgeneralization of something or someone that is not necessarily true or based on facts (Reber, 1985). Stereotyping is negative when the unfavorable characteristics of the target groups or things are emphasized. Stereotypes can change and can include positive and accurate characteristics. Historically, stereotypes held about African Americans have been negative, rigid, and inaccurate. For example, African Americans are consistently pictured by American society and media as criminals, drug users, drug sellers, absent fathers, and adolescent mothers.

Researchers, scholars, and counselors have lauded the connection between structural oppression and the internalization of negative stereotypes as a contributor to disenfranchising behavior and feelings (Comas-Diaz and Greene, 1994). McCreary and colleagues (1996) explored the role of negative stereotyping among 221 African American ninth- through twelfth-grade adolescents. They found African American adolescents who reported holding more negative stereotypes about African Americans tended to report more problem behavior and lower self-esteem than their counterparts. In an investigation of American women's responses to traditional ideals of their place in society, Chafe (1977) found that all women felt they were characterized, categorized, and controlled by various social systems. The effects of sexism and economic oppression were directly linked to the issue of social control.

In a keynote address to the Eleventh Annual Roundtable on Multicultural Psychotherapy and Counseling, Michele Fine (1994) mentioned that mental health professionals often blame women and minorities for their low social status and poor professional performances. She stressed the importance of crediting the oppressive systems for the institutional subjugation and restriction experienced by women and people of color. Both Fine and Chafe suggested that with women and people of color the spirit of individualism, value, worth, and desire to seek social justice are often curbed by the subtle oppression they experience from patriarchal, hierarchical, oppressive, and dictatorial systems. The cumulative effect of this barrage of oppressive forces can break the human spirit and destroy the group's coping mechanisms. The results of the internalization of negative social stereotypes are low self-worth, low self-respect, problem behaviors, and community stagnation.

The denial or inability of all Americans regardless of race, gender, or class, to successfully address the issues of sexism, racism, and economic oppression has resulted in an inordinate number of people experiencing disproportionate undereducation, underemployment, incarceration, economic disenfranchisement, and spatial isolation (Wilson, 1978, 1987; Johnson and Oliver 1990). The resulting sense of rage and/or helplessness has negatively impacted the African American community. Many African Americans accept the negative stereotypes as true. The stereotypes subsequently become self-fulfilling prophecies. Some African Americans, expecting to fail, exhibit criminal behaviors. Perceiving themselves as dangerous, they attack other African Americans at astronomical rates. Additionally, the old eugenic argument of African American inferiority in comparison to all other Americans continues to be affirmed. Herrnstein and Murray's (1994) book, *The Bell Curve: Intelligence and Class Structure in American Life*, is one example of literature and psychological theory that asserts the perspective that African Americans are less than all other human beings in intelligence, values and abilities.

According to Azibo (1996), Western culture has historically viewed human beings as inherently inadequate or deficient. This philosophical system serves as an interpretive heuristic for all people. Specifically, those who presume these theories true consider African Americans to be at the bottom of the human genetic pool, genetically predisposed to skill deficiencies, and evidencing greater psychopathology than Caucasians, who are perceived to be at the top of the genetic hierarchy. This deficit perspective, with its unstable and inaccurate stereotypes, only perpetuates the self-destructive behavior of the bad man and bad woman, which further verifies and substantiates the negative racial stereotypes held by whites about African Americans.

More than a Story

African American writers have long chronicled the struggles and heartaches of African American people. In, Ann Petry masterfully continues the tradition of African American writers when she connects the negative stereotypes of African Americans to the social difficulties of an African American family. Lutie Johnson, the heroine of the story, is an African American woman of strength and strong moral character. She epitomizes the hardworking, self-sacrificing, black woman. Her life, however, is intertwined with the lives of her father, husband, son, employer, and male friend.

Lutie offered unconditional support to her father when he was destitute, and he repaid her kindness with lies and deceit. Lutie worked to financially support her husband and son when her husband could not find work. Her husband repaid this commitment by not only cheating on her, but by also moving the other woman into her home. After this betrayal, Lutie goes back to school, gets a job as a clerk, and moves into an apartment. In the evening she works as a singer in a nightclub. At the club she is befriended by the band leader and it seems that things for Lutie will improve. Not so! She is betrayed once again, this time by her apartment superintendent, who tricks her son into stealing the neighbor's mail. When her son is incarcerated for stealing mail Lutie approaches her male friend, the band leader, for financial help. He, however, uses her vulnerability as an opportunity to sexually exploit her. Her friend devises a scheme to pimp her, or offer her sexually, to his boss in exchange for his own job security.

Hoping that she will be helped by her friend, Lutie arrives at his apartment only to learn that she has been manipulated. When his scheme fails, Lutie's friend attempts to rape her. Outraged at this betrayal, Lutie lashes out and strikes him with a candlestick holder, killing him. Hopeless and frightened, Lutie rides a bus headed to Chicago, abandoning her incarcerated son.

Origins of the "Bad Man" Stereotype

African Americans have a long and assorted relationship with negative racial and gender stereotypes. In the book, *All God's Children: The Bosket Family and the American Tradition of Violence*, Butterfield (1995) wrote about the family of Willie James Bosket, Jr., the youngest and most violent murderer in New York State history. In 1984, New York State convicted Willie of killing two men on the subway in Manhattan. Butterfield traced the Bosket family back to slavery, to the infamous town of Edgefield, South Carolina. Through the Bosket family, Butterfield (1995) introduces the reader to a culture of violence and an ethic of "primal honor" that the Scotch-Irish brought with them when they immigrated to the new world (pp. 9-10). According to Butterfield (1995), after losing the Civil War, white southern men's ethic of honor meant using violence to enforce their will on African Americans, to keep them separate and in their inferior place. They used their superior position to (a) swindle black sharecroppers, (b) disenfranchise black voters, (c) erect a new system of Jim Crow laws, (d) murder or lynch thousands of African Americans, and (e) rape African American women.

The results of this southern culture of honor and violence were increases in violence among both black and white populations. This code of honor dictated that men retaliate against the most minor offense. Some African American men, not immune to this southern culture of violence and ethic of honor, became violent, dangerous, and untrustworthy. White men used the actions of this small group of African American men to justify their own criminal behavior. It was the unspoken law of the South that African American men who opposed the oppressive forces of the master or boss had to be controlled. One way to control them was through stereotyping African Americans as not human and needing punishment and domination. Controlling African American men also meant excluding them from educational, economic, relational, and parental opportunities (Davis, 1990; West, 1993a, 1993b). In their characterization of the African American male, white society depicted African American men as rapists who wanted to use sexually and abuse Caucasian women. Over time, American society, particularly in the South, accepted this characterization of African American men as uncontrollable, sex-crazed thugs and expected African American men to behave accordingly.

As a consequence of being deprived of external sources of validation, some African American men find it necessary to rely solely on internal sources to affirm themselves in ways the larger society does not. That is, being deprived of economic and educational opportunities has had a negative impact on the relational and parental opportunities of African American men. Unable to affirm themselves through commitment to institutions, achievement or relationships, some African American men compensate for their low social status by overinflating the importance of concepts like respect and honor. Some African American men conclude that being respected and maintaining one's honor is more important than life itself. One such man was Pud Bosket, the great-grandfather of Willie Bosket.

Pud was a man who had a reputation as bold and tough. Unlike his father, Pud was not cautious, meek and humble, or accommodating to white supremacy. Pud was a sharecropper during the 1890s. One day when his white boss tried to whip him unjustifiably, Pud's "primal honor" and manhood dictated direct action. Refusing to be insulted, he grabbed the whip and snatched it away. Although Pud was in a situation that could emotionally overwhelm him, the consequences of his reaction were so great that he could not go outside the situation and hit back. Although the sharecropper was insulting Pud, the internalization of the role of African American men in that day prevented him from hitting the white boss. He walked away from the incident knowing that by snatching the whip away from a white man, he had gone as far as the system would allow (Butterfield, 1995: 59).

Pud's response to the violence, insult and degradation perpetrated by a white man was the beginning of his reputation as a "bad man" (pp. 58-67). This reputation positioned Pud as a black man who was to be both respected and feared for his fury, force and vengeance. Butterfield (1995) noted that the "bad man" reputation, created out of the fuzzy distinction between law and lawlessness, contained a critical self-destructive component. That is, the good of having a bad man reputation is in the "respect and fear" it engendered from both black and white people. The self-destructive component grows out of the fear that the "bad man" reputation engenders.

In the incident with the white man Pud responded in a way that most men would respect. The respect grows out of the male-based notion of "primal honor." That is, Pud "stood up for himself" and did not allow himself to be beaten. We suggest that black men projected onto Pud's behavior a personal and communal freedom that can lift spirits. An equally powerful rationale for respect arises from Pud's assertion of a basic human right: the right to freedom from unprovoked physical assault. In asserting a basic human right Pud was operating in the gray area between law and lawlessness. Although he had a legal right to defend himself, the moral and social law dictated that he not do so.

Pud's reaction also had the potential to engender fear in both blacks and whites. Pud's response was a direct challenge to the social and moral order. His willingness to go beyond the dictates of the social order made him someone to fear. Whites perceived Pud as a black man whom they could not control. Blacks feared him because his behavior caused them to face their own fears. Their fear was that of facing in themselves the emotional and psychological accommodations to which they committed in order to survive.

While African American men like Pud were acting to gain respect, southern Caucasian men were fearful that African American male honor would dictate retaliation against white people for all the evils perpetrated upon African American men and their families. Believing African American men deified white beauty in the same manner they did, white men worried that the bad black men would rape and victimize white women (Davis, 1990). This projection[1] was deadly for African American men, because it undergirded the stereotype of black men as white woman-lusting savages who needed to be controlled and kept in their places.

Over the years, African American men have had to contend with the realities and stereotypes that accompany the ascription of the bad man reputation. Butterfield suggested that the bad man stereotype is the origin of the modern day African American gangster. That is, being dishonored by economic, racial, and gender oppression has led African American men to lie, deceive, betray, and manipulate others in manners similar to the characters in the novel. This suggests that the behaviors of African American men are not always immature or stereotypical responses to their negative conditions. The Bosket story suggests that the acting out and immature behavior of some African American men occurs in response to their disenfranchised situations. More specifically, we think that the negative behaviors are, in part, a result of

Americans believing the lies about the inferiority and deficiencies of African American men (Haymes, 1995).

The "bad man" reputation also includes the burden of living up to the standard of the bad man via gambling, fighting, womanizing, and even committing murder. The bad man reputation has evolved. For instance, Pud Bosket did not have to hit or kill to establish himself as a bad man. His great grandson, Willie Bosket, did. It is our contention that to achieve and maintain the bad man reputation in today's society young black men believe they have to kill.

Current researchers (DeJarnett and Raven, 1981; Looney, 1988; Millham and Smith, 1981) suggest that both the history of oppression and the negative racial stereotypes severely affect African American men. Turner and Turner (1983) found African American women in their study viewed African American men as less responsible, reliable, and trustworthy than they viewed themselves. They also found that African American women in their study anticipated disappointment from the African American men they dated or married. An implication of this research is that African American women who internalize the negative stereotypes of African American men enter their relationships with presuppositions, such as that relationships with African American men are destined to be disastrous and problematic. This often becomes a self-fulfilling prophecy that results in failed relationships.

Researchers (DeJarnett and Raven, 1981; Looney, 1988; Millham and Smith, 1981) have also found that the consciousness-raising efforts of the civil rights and black power movements of the 1960s helped to raise the racial self-esteem of African American men but had little impact on their personal self-esteem. Furthermore, these researchers found that in spite of possessing egalitarian attitudes about gender, which should benefit interpersonal relationships, African American men have extremely unstable interpersonal relationships and the highest divorce rate in our nation. This finding is related to the fact that, in general, African American men hold very traditional conservative views about gender matters. Racism in America has also severely impeded their efforts to operate as traditional male providers (Burlew et al., 1992; Millham and Smith, 1981; Turner and Turner, 1983). As we will discuss shortly, Lutie's husband Jim is a good example of this phenomenon.

Origins of the Bad Woman Stereotype

Before, during, and after the period of slavery, southern Caucasian men sexually exploited African American women while deifying white female beauty. This victimization of African American women and glorification of Caucasian women has resulted in specific racial and gender stereotypes of African American women.

One stereotype that victimizes African American women is the view of African American women as sexually promiscuous, sexually aggressive, morally loose, strong, independent, and assertive in comparison to Caucasian American women. This "bad woman" stereotype has its roots in pre-colonial Africa. Prior to the slave trade, missionaries frequented Africa in an attempt to convert the African people to Christianity. The missionaries found a people who, unlike themselves, experienced no shame in the uncovering of their bodies and whose sexual practices lacked the secrecy and negative labeling commonly associated with European perspectives of sexuality. Moreover, they also encountered cultures that embraced polygamy. These polygamous relationships have as their correlate in European culture, the mistress or paramour relationship, which in European culture is common, yet taboo (Van Sertima, 1976).

According to the Judeo-Christian value system of America, monogamy is the preferred system of marriage and relationships. Relationships in which sexual liaisons were not monogamous were considered at worst adulterous, or at the very least concubinage. These differences were interpreted as indicative of a lack of moral constraint and a propensity toward nonselective uninhibited licentiousness (Mollenkott, 1992; Pagels, 1988). This perspective became European society's prevailing epistemology regarding African female sexuality. These early perceptions of African sexuality became myths. The myth or stereotype of the hyper-sexed African became the basis of a belief system and social practices that led to the sexual objectification of the African woman by Europeans.

The institution of American slavery continued the perpetuation of the hyper-sexed African female stereotype. During slavery, the African woman came to be utilized as a symbol of the utter dominance of African slaves by white males. As property, African slaves were routinely sexually exploited by slave owners (Brent, 1973; Gates, 1987). The sexual exploitation of female slaves was, for many slave owners, an economic necessity (Stampp, 1956). The African slave woman was, therefore, dually exploited as a woman for her desirability, and as an object for economic gain. Within this context the sexuality of the African female slave became a defining feature in terms of her value both as a person and as an economic asset to the slave owner. The white male character, Junto, in *The Street* clearly illustrates this point. In an attempt to sexually possess Lutie, Junto did not pay her when she sang in his club. He wanted to make her economically dependent on him and subsequently vulnerable to sexual exploitation. Because he also owned the house of ill repute he made a financial profit from the sexual exploitation of African American women.

African American slave women were used to maintain a double standard between white men and white women. White men were free to have sex while white women were severely restricted from having sex. To maintain the chastity of white females, black females were routinely raped and sexually exploited by white men.

In *The Street*, Lutie's character personifies the schizoid dimension of our image of African American women. Lutie is portrayed as both a positive and negative woman. On one hand, she is self-sacrificing, hard working, positive, independent, attractive, dignified, and classy—virtues that are highly valued in our society. However, Lutie is also characterized as vulnerable, needy, overbearing and socially isolated. She does not have any strong female or male friends. She is despised and rejected for getting a job and going to night school. Lutie is also the object of gender oppression. The superintendent of her apartment building attempts to rape her. Her male friend is coerced by his white boss to manipulate Lutie into having an affair with the white man. Her friend then tries to rape her when she maneuvers out of the trap. Lutie's character is the quintessential model of the "good and bad" woman. Her story chronicles the painful effects of negative stereotypes on the relationships and interactions between African American women and others.

Mrs. Hedges, another woman in the novel, is also affected by the bad woman stereotype. Mrs. Hedges operates a house of ill repute, and is a very powerful African American woman. She controls the sex act. She provides a place for men, black and white, to be bad. As the operator of the house of ill repute, Mrs. Hedges is an overseer or a woman in control (Comas-Diaz and Greene, 1994). She chooses to be a comfortable victim of racism and sexism and cooperates with her oppressor (Fanon, 1967). That is, a white man owns the house of ill repute and she makes sure he gets whichever woman he wants. In turn, he makes sure the house continues to operate and that she continues to be the operator.

Mrs. Hedges is making the best of a bad situation. She has to eat and wants to live comfortably. However, her position as the Madame fuels the negative stereotypes of African American women. People see her and her establishment, and it validates their presuppositions. That is, her establishment confirms the stereotype of African American women as only capable of being great sex partners and earning money for their master. As the Madame, she is also exploiting African American women by making a living off of their sexuality. As the overseer, Mrs. Hedges is also honoring men's perceptions that they have license to control the bodies and resources of women.

African American Interpersonal Relationships and Negative Stereotypes

The female and male characters in Petry's novel illustrate the intersection of race and gender and its consequence for African American relationships. Lutie is an African American woman who experiences feelings of vulnerability and victimization in her relationships with men. She bears the brunt of the bad man stereotype and as a result becomes a victim of male sexism. For example, Jim, her husband, attempted to operate as a healthy patriarch in an unhealthy patriarchal system. Jim is not a lazy man. He wants to work. Yet, he is unfairly fired from one job and is unsuccessful in obtaining another. He then falls into emotional and relational despair and falters in his responsibilities to his family. This affects Lutie, because when Jim is unable to adjust to his unemployment coupled with her absence and employment, he has an affair.

Lutie's father, Pop, also fails miserably in his relationship with her. Pop was evicted from his home and had to move in with Lutie and Jim. At the time of Pop's eviction, Lutie and Jim are foster parents. Lutie informed Pop that he could move in if he refrained from drinking, making moonshine, and having wild parties. She made this offer in spite of Jim's objections. Pop said he would honor her request; however, he does not uphold his end of the bargain. Once he moves in Pop continues his old behavior; as a result Lutie and Jim lose their income as foster parents. As a consequence of using her power, Lutie has to face Jim and her own disappointment.

Both Pop and Jim exemplify African American men who fail in their responsibilities to African American women and families. Both characters appear to be captives of the culture of slavery (Akbar, 1985). The situation between Pop and Lutie is tragic and illustrates some of the complications inherent in African American father-daughter relationships. By definition a father is a male parent, and a parent is any organism in relation to its offspring (Webster, 1989). Pop is an ineffective parent. Effective parents protect their offspring. Effective parents position themselves to provide emotionally and economically for their children. Pop's life circumstances have resulted in an empty life of one bad habit after another; these have made him undependable and dependent on his daughter. He is a negative role model and an ineffective teacher. Pop's behavior is immature and self-destructive. However, Pop's bad habits are molded by the scripts of the bad man. It is clear that racism, economic and educational disenfranchisement have prevented Pop from accomplishing more. Life's journey has made Pop weak and worn. Additionally, through historical and contemporary struggles, life for Pop is not family, but drinking, gambling, and self-deception. Also, by trying to help her father, Lutie creates conflict between herself and her husband. This conflict contributes to her problems and pushes Jim one step further toward behaving as a bad man.

Jim's character represents the African American male who, overwhelmed by economic oppression, reverts to the stereotype of the black man as a great lover and womanizer. By his behavior, Jim objectifies both Lutie and the other women; he treats them as if they were property, rather than people. Joblessness has made Jim feel powerless so he makes himself feel powerful by operating according to the standard stereotype of African American men. He acts like a stud, and does not realize that he is acting destructively. Through his behavior, Jim represents a poor model of manhood for his son. He is teaching his son how to objectify and oppress women, perpetuating the bad man stereotype. He is also teaching Bub that men handle their disappointments and setbacks with their sexual organs.

The "cool pose" conceptual frame (Majors and Billson, 1992) offers a helpful way of interpreting the behavior and emotional well-being of the men in *The Street*. The cool pose is a survival strategy adopted by many African American men. The cool pose is an internal and external posture that African American men assume when they are cut off from culturally sanctioned means of achieving manhood. The male characters in the novel either adopt a cool pose or move beyond cool to anger.

Cool pose is a matter of mind control. To be cool is to keep control of one's emotions and temper. The cool pose optimizes power, inasmuch as its intention is to show that the African American man has not been psychologically compromised by external pressures. According to Majors and Billson (1992), being cool is the only thing a black man can control. That is, in an environment where one is utterly controlled, the one place to exercise freedom is in one's psychological reactions. Jim was unable to control his employment status. He was unable to control the way in which he was treated by the police. He was unable to control the way he was treated by social services. However, he could control his cool. Pop was unable to control the social conditions that prevented him from owning property, but he could make the best moonshine and throw the best parties. By this "cool" behavior, Pop copes with his disenfranchisement and manages his despair.

The cool pose can, in many ways, be a positive coping strategy for African American men, but it can also be dangerous. Lutie encountered the dangerous aspect of the cool pose in her relationship with Boots. Boots is cool, and his cool is a part of his attractiveness. Lutie likes the fact that Boots is cool. Boots's coolness makes him seem strong and in control. Cool has helped Boots become friends with Lutie. Cool has helped him cope with his subservient status. Like Pud Bosket, Boots is a hired hand. He works for Junto, the white man who owns the bar and the house of ill repute. As mentioned, Junto tells Boots not to pay Lutie when she sings in his band. Junto tells him to set Lutie up so that she will come running to him. When Lutie resists his manipulation, he loses his cool, becomes full of rage, and sexually attacks her. Lutie's only defense against his violence is to become more violent.

In this post-World War 11 novel, Petry is telling a story about male castration, female rape, and violence against women. Her characters, Jones and Min, offer another example of the gender conflict manifested in African American interpersonal relationships. Jones is the apartment superintendent, who attempts to rape Lutie and who tricks her son into stealing mail. Min lives with Jones. Min is overweight and many of her teeth are missing. Min feels that no man has ever loved her or cared for her. She is afraid of Jones, but will not leave him because she believes she has nowhere else to go. Jones is a very mean, angry, and abusive man. He treats Min like "dirt." He disrespects and demeans her. He would like her to disappear, but he values having a woman around to cook and clean.

The relationships between these couples (e.g., Lutie and Boots, Jones and Min) are representative of the gender oppression that occurs every day. Some men exploit some women. Other men abuse power and subjugate women to menial roles. Many male partners are averse to dividing conjugal and familial tasks. Many African American men do not desire to share power or balance authority. In these relationships, the behavior of others is deemed good only when it is consistent with the dictates of the men.

The relationships between Jones-Min and Boots-Lutie are also based on misogynistic irresponsibility. Jones and Boots appeared to hate women, and they related to Lutie and Min accordingly. Convenience, rather than love and intimacy, appears to be the glue of these relationships. Min is not Jones's soul mate or life partner. They do not love each other. Lutie and Boots need each other, but Boots's hatred and low self-esteem overrides his need to love and be loved and his sense of commitment. As a result he acts maliciously and destructively toward Lutie.

Unfortunately, too many African American men relate to African American women out of a similar misogynistic pattern. Many men have internalized the "bad man" stereotype and unknowingly or unconsciously live and operate out of this sexist system without carefully examining the effects of the system on themselves or the women with whom they are in relationships (Hooks, 1995). They objectify African American women without recalling that these women are their allies in the struggle for equality. Too often, African American men relate to African American women in the same hierarchical, dictatorial, and oppressive fashions that have resulted in their own disenfranchisement.

Negative Stereotypes and Male Children

African American children have also suffered under the system of oppression that gave birth to the bad man stereotype. For example, from an early age African American children were expected to tend either cotton or the slave masters' children. Some children were the offspring of the conjugal relations between slave owners and slaves, and faced oppression from both Caucasian and African people. Most children were denied the simple joys of childhood and the opportunity to develop to their full potential (Gates, 1987; Van Sertima, 1976).

The ascription of the bad man stereotype has evolved to include not only adult African American males but also African American male youth. Lately, African American youth have been characterized as criminals, gang members, drug traffickers, and violent criminals (Haymes, 1995). The examples of Bub, Lutie, and Jim's son, will be used to further expand and elaborate on the effects of negative stereotypes on African American male children.

Bub loves his mother and father. He is affected by their separation. He was affected when his father lost his job. He was affected when his mother went to work as a domestic for a white family in upstate New York. He saw his grandfather drink, gamble, and cause the family to lose the income from the foster children. He saw his father bring another woman into their home, and he saw his mother's reaction when she found out. He watched his mother work her way through school and get a better job, recognizing that there were those who despised her because of her achievement. Bub is a child in a very challenging home environment.

Bub knows that his mother is having a hard time making ends meet. He knows that she cannot afford to buy him candy and expensive clothes. He is happy just to be with her and he does not want to disappoint her. He goes to school and does the best he can. He also asks Mr. Jones to help him make a shoeshine kit. He works hard on the kit that he is going to use to make a little extra money. He says to himself that the money will be a great help to his mother. He waits for his mother to come home. He wants to show her his kit. He is proud of his work and wants her to be proud also. Nonetheless, when Lutie sees the shoeshine kit she "hits the roof." She feels that her son is too good to shine shoes, and she has worked too hard for Bub to settle for such a lowly job. Thus, she slaps him in the face, knocks the kit out of his hands, smashes it, and throws it away. Bub is devastated. How could his mother do this to him?

By crushing the shoe shining idea and box, Lutie demoralizes Bub. She has not taken his needs into account. She has reacted to her own need for Bub to be different from his father and grandfather. She needs him to get a good education and a good job. It seems that Lutie is parenting Bub based on her tumultuous relationships with adult men, particularly her father and husband. Thus, she debases Bub. She belittles him and inadvertently communicates that the world, including their home, is not a safe place.

One might theorize that Lutie was attempting to socialize Bub toward success. She might also have been socializing Bub toward the ability to cope with oppressive societal pressures (Edward and Polite, 1992). Others might argue that Lutie was effectively parenting Bub. This position is supported by the fact that many African American parents use spanking and physical punishment to stress and promote the values of ambition and obedience in their children (Allen, 1985). Lutie might have been attempting to force Bub to set higher ambitions for himself. She wanted him to go to school and make something better of himself.

Lutie, more likely, was attempting to teach Bub about prejudice and racism. She wanted to help him become more emotionally and socially healthy and productive (Comer and Poussaint, 1992; Hopson and Hopson, 1990; Peters, 1988). However, her methods are questionable. Lutie slapped Bub. Now, parents do lose their tempers and hit children. Furthermore, a slap could be conceptualized as a form of spanking or punishment, and African American parents have been found to favor spanking (Knight, Cross, Giles-Sims, and Simpson, 1995; Straus, 1991). However, because of the timing and situation surrounding Lutie's slap, it was harsh and punitive. Researchers have found that many African American boys experience harsh punishment from their mothers (Dunier, 1992; Kotlowitz, 1991; Patterson, 1995). While parents must teach their children the values and behaviors of the majority culture, they must also counteract the negative stereotypes of African Americans. Additionally, they must help their children learn and respect their own cultural heritage. Nonetheless, some of the methods used by African American parents, and slapping is one of these methods, can be devastating to the child and have been consistently related to negative developmental outcomes (Knight, Cross, Giles-Sims, and Simpson, 1995; Straus, 1991).

Constructing a New Basis for African American Male and Female Relationships

The abuse of African Americans, justified by negative stereotype, existed before Petry wrote *The Street*, and continues. Among African Americans, negative stereotypes have resulted in an abundance of difficulties in interpersonal relationships. Thus, African Americans frequently believe and expect African American men to (a) be violent and abusive; (b) be noncommittal and irresponsible; and (c) refuse to be vulnerable, compassionate, and sympathetic.

While there are many African American men who rise above negative racist stereotypes, there are too many who live according to such dictates. That is, many African American men choose to be violent, abusive, and emotionally unresponsive to other men, women, and children. Men abuse power by using it against women in inhumane ways. The male characters in *The Street* were marginalized; they, in turn, used their power to abuse women.

More than fifty years after *The Street*, it seems that similar conditions exist between African American men and women. One would hope that following the Civil Rights and Black Power Movements of the 1960s and 1970s, desegregation, and entrance into the information era, the condition of African Americans would have improved. Yet, a simple walk through many urban center cities or a reading of the local newspaper quickly reminds Americans that the negative stereotypes and the disenfranchisement of African Americans continues.

No matter how discouraging the outlook, African Americans must never give up. African American men must re-empower themselves to be the partners, brothers, fathers, lovers, and sons that they were born to be. In an effort to contribute to the process of re-empowerment and the elimination and re-moval of the stereotypes, five relational-based recommendations are offered. The hope is that these recommendations will engender healthy discussions about the interaction of race and gender as well as discussions on the chang-ing responsibilities of the African American family.

Recommendation # 1: Work to eliminate self-hatred and self-contempt by building on the historical and ancestral strengths of African American man-hood. African Americans have historically been a people who live by the principles of justice, mercy, wisdom, reciprocity, and love. These principles must again become primary in personal and interpersonal relationships. When African American men return to the holistic communal mind set and behav-ioral patterns of the best in African people, they will overcome self-hatred. They must listen to fellow African American men, women, and children. They must value the scholarship, practical efforts and writings of African American intellectuals, poets, and musicians.

To eliminate self-hatred and self-contempt, African American men must strive for an awakening of consciousness (Comas-Diaz and Greene, 1994). Men must awaken and change their perceptions of situations and of them-selves. They must critically analyze their situation, actions, and relation-ships. This critical analysis is both a process of growth and the establishment of a new way of existing.

Recommendation # 2: Work to develop meaningful, constructive and criti-cal relationships among African American men. They must develop these relationships across social, psychological, economic and vocational bound-aries. No one understands the struggles and the "games" that African Ameri-can men play better than another African American man. Men must support each other in the struggle to become a "good" man, get a "good" education, develop a successful career, and maintain a happy home.

Healing the age-old wounds of oppression must also be an aspect of male-to-male relationships. African American men must work toward understand-ing one another. African American men must help each other understand the power of primal honor and the choice of many African American men of death rather than life. A better understanding of the man will lead to a better under-standing of both the existence and effects of negative racial stereotypes.

The elder black male holds a special and specific place of honor in male relationships. The wisdom and experiences of black elders are critical for healing the age-old wounds of oppression. African American elders can con-vey a sense of the history that has accompanied the struggle for freedom, justice, and equality.

The African American man must possess the skills to exist in two or three worlds. Many scholars laud education as the mechanism to obtain the variety of skills needed to exist in today's society. African American male relation-ships play a significant role regarding education. It takes both the relationship with African American men and the structural opportunities of education to advance the position of the black man in America.

We suggest that African American men must help themselves avoid taking the option of operating according to the negative stereotypes and negative aspects of cool. Black men can achieve this via an open, constructive, positive, and confrontative relationship with another black man.

Recommendation # 3: Work to respect women as valuable and equal. Society teaches most men that women are intellectually inferior and untrustworthy. We teach men that they are conquerors and leaders, and that women are sexual objects to be led and conquered. This mentality can lead to abusive behavior. Yet, men who respect women do not abuse them. They do not rape them. Rape is an act of aggression that asserts power by defaming and defiling the victim (Madhubuti, 1990, 1993). Rape is a result of men learning to solve problems by force. Men rape and abuse women because they glorify violence.

To respect women as valuable and equal will entail African American men cultivating healthy alliances with African American women. To develop such healthy alliances, African American men must work to view women as valuable partners. African American men must reject tendencies to dominate women and strive to become egalitarian partners. This entails African American men seeking out and respecting the independence, and self-reliance of African American women. It suggests that African American men will strive to give and to receive in their relationships with African American women, and that African American men will love, and accept love, from African American women. This recommendation infers that African American men will love a woman based on loving himself, while learning to love and accept love from his partner. This is a mature love that sometimes results in sexual relations, but also values other ways of expressing love. African American men must integrate into their lives an experience of love that merges choice, commitment, effort, behavior, and loving thoughts (Madhubuti, 1992; Pearsall, 1993).

To cultivate this healthy alliance with African American women, African American men must become men who are fair and treat women as equals. African American men must not behave as pimps or hustlers with the women and people who love them. Black men will accomplish this alliance by: (a) forcing themselves to become emotionally available to others; (b) taking risk, being vulnerable, and revealing their true thoughts and feelings; and (c) participating in all aspects of their intimate relationships (Madhubuti, 1990, 1993).

Recommendation # 4: Work to develop and maintain an active parental role. Many conflicts between men and women surround issues of household chores and child rearing tasks. If African American men equally share the responsibility for chores and child rearing, they will model for their daughters and sons that parents are equal. They will also teach their children to define themselves according to positive relationships rather than negative racist and sexist stereotypes and behaviors. As this understanding of equality takes root in the family, it will begin to manifest itself in relation to all people. When African American men teach their sons and daughters that they are, at times, vulnerable, nurturing, and compassionate they will also demonstrate that these virtues are not dishonorable and unmanly. If African American men become more active as parents, they will teach their families how men maturely handle the emotional stress of life.

Recommendation # 5: Work to be proactive and preventive about the problems in the African American community. It is not the way of the African American to wait until the family problem is so overwhelming that the family succumbs to helplessness. In being proactive and preventive, the African American man will recognize potential problems before they develop and/ or escalate. African American men must convey the urgency of the problems facing the black community and they must work together to alleviate the problems.

Conclusion

This chapter provided an analysis of the effects and influences of racism, sexism, and economic oppression on the lives of the characters in Petry's 1946 novel *The Street*. It was the thesis of this project that the negative stereotypes, created and maintained by a racist and sexist system, have influenced and divided African American male and female relationships. We thought that an examination of the origins of these negative stereotypes would shed light on current relational difficulties.

We have argued that by building on the historic and ancestral strengths of the African experience, African American men can work to create a new foundation on which to reestablish community and family. This new foundation will eliminate African American self-hatred and self-contempt. It will also eliminate patriarchy and male domination as we know it. Only when African American men once again love their bodies, love their women, and love their children will they find true freedom. We suggest that black men share love in vulnerability, nurturing, strength and protective power. This internal freedom will cause a renewed interaction between African American men, the women and children. It will again provide the context for African Americans to live out the Ashante African Proverb, "I am because you are, and because you are, therefore, I am."

Note

1. By definition, projection is the process of ascribing unwittingly one's beliefs, values, or other subjective processes to others (Reber, 1985).

References

Akbar, N. (1985). *The community of the self* (revised). Tallahassee, FL: Mind Productions.

Allen, W. R. (1985). Race, income and family dynamics: A study of adolescent male socialization processes and outcomes. In M. B. Spencer, G. K. Brookins, and W. R. Allen (Eds.), *Beginnings: The social and affective development of black children.* Hillsdale, NJ: Lawrence Erlbaum Associates.

Azibo, D. A. (1996). African psychology in historical perspective and related commentary. In D. A. Azibo (Ed.), *African psychology in historical perspective and related commentary.* Trenton, NJ: Africa World Press.

Bowman, P. J., and Howard, C. S. (1985). Race-related socialization, motivation and academic achievement: A study of black youth in three generation families. *Journal of the American Academy of Child Psychiatry* 24, 134-141.

Brent, L. (1973). In L. M. Child (Ed.), *Jacobs. H. A. 1813-1897: Incidents of a slave girl.* New York: Harcourt.

Burlew, A. K. H., Banks, W. C., McAdoo, H. R., and Azibo, D. A. (Eds.). (1992). *African American psychology: Theory, research, and practice.* Newbury Park, CA: Sage.

Butterfield, E. (1995). *All God's children: The Bosket family and the American tradition of violence.* New York: Alfred A. Knopf.

Chafe, W. H. (1977). *Women and equality: Changing patterns in American culture.* New York: Oxford University Press.

Comas-Diaz, L., and Greene, B. (Eds.). (1994). *Women of color: Integrating ethnic and gender identities in psychotherapy.* New York: Guilford.

Comer, J. P., and Poussaint, A. F. (1992). *Raising black children.* New York: Plume.

Davis, A. Y. (1990). *Women, culture and politics.* New York: Vintage Books.

_____. (1983). *Women, race and class.* New York: Vintage Books.

DeJarnett, S., and Raven, B. H. (1981). The balance, bases, and modes of interpersonal power in black couples: The role of sex and socioeconomic circumstances. *Journal of Black Psychology* 7, 51-66.

Dunier, M. (1992). *Slim's table: Race, responsibility, and masculinity.* Chicago: University of Chicago Press.

Edwards, A., Polite, C. K. (1992). *Children of the dream: The psychology of black success.* New York: Doubleday.

Fanon, F. (1967). *Black skin, white masks.* New York: Grove Weidenfeld.

Fine, M. (1994). Keynote address to the eleventh annual roundtable on multicultural psychotherapy and counseling. New York: Teachers College, Columbia University.

Gates, H. L., Jr. (Ed.). (1987). *The classic slave narratives.* New York: Mentor.

Guthrie, R. (1976). *Even the rat was white: A historical view of psychology.* New York: Harper and Row.

Haymes, S. N. (1995). *Race, culture, and the city: A pedagogy for black urban struggle.* New York: State University of New York.

Herrnstein, R. J., and Murray, C. (1994). *The bell curve: Intelligence and class structure in American life.* New York: Simon and Schuster.

Hernton, C. C. (1987). *The sexual mountain and black women writers: Adventures in sex, literature, and real life.* New York: Doubleday.

Hopson, D. P. and Hopson, D. S. (1990). *Different and wonderful: Raising black children in a race-conscious society.* New York: Fireside.

Hooks, b. (1995). *Killing rage: Ending racism.* New York: Henry Holt.

Hooks, b. (1992). *Black looks: Race and representation.* Boston: South End.

Johnson, J. H., Jr., and Oliver, M. L. (1990, June). Modeling urban underclass behavior: Theoretical considerations. Paper presented at the summer dissertation workshop for minority students engaged in the study of the urban underclass, Los Angeles.

Jones, R. L. (1991). *Black psychology* (3rd ed.). Berkeley, CA: Cobb and Henry.

Knight, D. K., Cross, D. R., Giles-Sims, J., and Simpson, D. D. (1995). Psychosocial functioning among adult drug users: The role of parental absence, support, and conflict. *International Journal of the Addictions* 30, 1271-1288.

Kotlowitz, A. (1991). *There are no children here*. New York: Doubleday.

Looney, J. (1988). Ego development and black identity. *Journal of Black Psychology* 5, 41-56.

Madhubuti, H. R. (1993). On becoming anti-rapist. In E. Buchwald, P. R. Fletcher, and M. Roth (Eds.), *Transforming a rape culture*. Minneapolis, MN: Milkweed Editions.

_____. (1990). *Black men: Obsolete, single, dangerous?* Chicago: Third World Press.

Majors, R., and Billson, J. M. (1992). *Cool pose: The dilemmas of black manhood in America*. New York: Touchstone.

McCreary, M. L., Slain, L. A., and Berry E. J. (1996). Predicting problem-behavior and self-esteem among African American adolescents. *Journal of Adolescent Research* 11, 217-236.

Millham, J., and Smith, L. E. (1981). Sex-role differentiation among black and white Americans: A comparative study. *Journal of Black Psychology* 7, 77-90.

Mollenkott, V. R. (1992). *Sensuous spirituality: Out from fundamentalism*. New York: Crossroad.

Pagels, E. (1988). *Adam, Eve, and the serpent*. New York: Vintage.

Patterson, O. (1995). The crisis of gender relations among African Americans. In A. E Hill and E. C. Jordan, *Race, gender and power in America: The legacy of the Hill-Thomas hearings*. New York: Oxford University Press.

Pearsall, P. (1993). Ten laws of lasting love. New York: Simon and Schuster.

Peters, M. E (1988). Parenting in black families with young children. In H. McAdoo (Ed.), *Black families*. Newbury Park, CA: Sage.

Petry, A. (1946). *The street*. Cambridge: Houghton Mifflin.

Reber, A. S. (1985). *The Penguin dictionary of psychology*. New York: Penguin.

Stampp, K. M. (1956). *The peculiar institution: Slavery in the ante-bellum south*. New York: Vintage.

Straus, M. A. (1991). New theory and old canards about family violence research. *Social Problems* 38, 180-197.

Thomas, A., and Sillen S. (1972). *Racism and psychiatry*. New York: Carol.

Turner, C. A., and Turner, B. E. (1983). Black families, social evaluations, and future marital relationships. In C. E. Obudho (Ed.), *Black marriage and family therapy*. Westport, CT: Greenwood Press.

Van Sertima, I. (1976). *They came before Columbus*. New York: Random House.

Webster's Dictionary of English Usage. (1989). Springfield, MA: Merriam-Webster.

Welsing, E. (1970). *The Cress theory of color confrontation and racism*. Washington, D.C.: Private Printing.

West, C. (1993a). *Prophetic reflections: Notes on race and power in America*. Common Monroe, ME: Courage Press.

_____. (1993b). *Race matters*. Boston: Beacon Press.

Wilson, W. J. (1987). *The truly disadvantaged*. Chicago: University of Chicago Press.

_____. (1978). *The declining significance of race*. Chicago: University of Chicago Press.

10

African American Fathers and Sons: Social, Historical, and Psychological Considerations

Jay C. Wade

The majority of studies on African American fathers focus on the patho-logical consequences of fathers' absence from the family or on the dysfunc-tional lower-class single-parent household and the "black matriarchy." Prior to the 1970s, fathers in general appeared only in research regarding boys' sex-role identity. Studies of delinquent boys in the 1950s and 1960s suggested that paternal absence, especially common in African American families, in-duced a type of hypermasculinity resulting in delinquent styles and behavior (Segal, 1990). Although studies in the 1970s contradicted these findings (e.g., Badaines, 1976; Davis, 1974; Hunt and Hunt, 1975; Longabaugh, 1973; Rubin, 1974; Wilkinson and O'Connor, 1977), it wasn't until the late 1970s and early 1980s that research on father-present, middle-class families focus-ing on the strengths of the African American family began to challenge the prevailing view of African American families as disorganized and unstable. Nevertheless, "absenteeism of males, combined with matrifocal homes, is suggested by the literature and accepted by society at large as the primary type of African American family household in the United States today" (Connor, 1988: 191).

In general, the research literature indicates that males in father-absent homes have problems with sex-role and gender identification, school perfor-mance, psychosocial development and adjustment, and controlling aggres-sion (Lamb, 1986). However, in reviewing the literature on African American father-absent families, Connor (1988) concluded that although depictions of the effects of father absence in some families may be accurate, they are not representative of African American families in general. Such portrayals fail to take into account factors such as socioeconomic status, the supportive extended-family network, and institutional racism and the effects of discrimination. These studies tend to be biased toward traditional Western family norms and values and lack a comparison group of African American families in which mother and father are present or in which the single-parent family is economically sufficient. More important, these studies are easily accepted as representative of African American male psychology because they fit well with stereotypes and myths cultivated by a historically racist and sexist society.

The purpose of this paper is to (1) present theory and research that question and refute the prevailing view of African American fathers and the impact of their role on the psychosocial development of male children and (2) explore the implications such theory and research have for counseling and psychotherapy with African American men and their families.

McAdoo (1993) advocated an ecological approach to the study of African American fathers in their various family roles. In this regard, the present article explores the role of fathers in European American culture from a sociohistorical perspective. How gender roles, power, and capitalism interconnect in a system of patriarchy is described in order to understand the larger social context influencing African American fathers. Following this, African American family patterns are discussed. From its historical roots in Africa to the present day, the role of the father in African American culture and how this role has been influenced by economic and social forces are explored. Theory and research pertaining to African American fathers as providers and in child rearing, with particular emphasis given to the father-son relationship, are also presented. A psychodynamic approach is used to discuss masculine identity development in order to understand the father-son relationship and the impact of father absence and father presence on the psychosocial development of male children. Finally, the ecological and psychodynamic perspectives are integrated to provide a conceptual framework for counseling and psychotherapy with African American men and their families.

Sociohistorical Context of Western Patriarchy

A few historians have reconceptualized the past by showing how gender has functioned in social, economic, and political developments in Western Europe and America. Rapid capitalist industrialization during the nineteenth century, in particular, is viewed as a period during which sexuality (Carrigan, Connell, and Lee, 1987; Foucault, 1978; Weeks, 1981), gender roles, and gender relations (Kimmel, 1987; Pleck and Pleck, 1980; Stearns, 1979) were dramatically redefined.

According to French philosopher and social historian Michel Foucault (1978), prior to the nineteenth century, blood relationships were an important element in the mechanisms of power. In Western Europe, political power was consolidated in monarchies, class order and castes, and lines of descent. The marriage system fixed kinship ties and the transmission of names and possessions. Explicit codes of canon law, the Christian pastoral authority, and civil law supported and ensured the existence of this system as well as regulated sexual relations. However, in the early 1800s, with the development of heavy industry and the need for a stable and competent labor force, the mechanisms of power increasingly addressed the proliferation and regeneration of life. Medical authorities undertook the management of sexual behavior, compartmentalizing it in an attempt to restrict sexual relations to the "legitimate" heterosexual couple. The marriage system directed sexual relations toward the reproductive function. This shift in the mechanism of power corresponded to a need for a labor force that would reproduce itself (in line with capitalist motives).

The "institutionalization of heterosexuality" (Carrigan et al., 1987) supported a patriarchal system in which the nuclear family was the dominant cultural norm; men were viewed as procreators and providers and women as childbearers and child rearers. Filene (1987) noted that "during the course of nineteenth-century industrial development in America, the split between work and home—his sphere and hers—increasingly defined child-rearing as a mother's responsibility" (p. 110). Gender roles became more rigidly defined (Stearns, 1979), and the "good provider" emerged as a specialized male role (Bernard, 1992).

Connell (1987) argued that the maintenance of (white) male authority and privilege, and the related notions of masculinity, can be attributed to an overarching, historically rooted system in which labor, power, and desire are the three main overlapping and interconnecting structures. The family, workplace, and state are the central institutions through which these structures operate. The dominant male and subordinated female roles are produced and supported by the division of labor in the family and work force. The maintenance of male power involves all of the institutions of authority, control, and coercion: the state and business hierarchies, sexual regulation and control, and domestic relationships. Connell (1987) further suggested that although the family institution seems less able now to provide a stable base for male authority, men's power in the family system is still upheld and partially reinforced by the state.

Both the ideological and coercive apparatuses of white male power are mediated by the system of patriarchy (Marable, 1983). The dominant ideology of a society is mirrored by the social relations of its members (Unger, 1989). There is no discontinuity between the family and society. The family serves its function if it falls in line with the overall strategy in society (i.e., patriarchal privilege). Conversely, no social strategy could achieve comprehensive effects if it were not propped and anchored by the family (Foucault,

1978). This continuity between the family and society is most obvious in the hierarchical structures of both. Whether it is the father of the family or the father of the country, priest as father or God as Father, culture and society invest authority in the symbolic figure of the father. Given the powerful symbiosis between family and society, any disruption in this union will have consequences. A nonpatriarchal family system and/or a redistribution of the power relationships within the family are likely to cause a rift in the social power structure—as was the case during the sexual revolution of the 1960s when the traditional family structure was challenged by the hippie, gay, and feminist movements. Conversely, changes in economic conditions and relationships of power in society can affect the structure of families in that society.

Sociohistorical Context of the African American Family

According to Madhubuti (1990), both monogynous and polygynous societies have always existed in Africa. Whether the African family pattern consisted of having one or many wives, marriage played an important role in African customs and traditions. Traditionally, the African father was intimately involved in raising his children, especially the male children. Fathers passed on skills such as food gathering and hunting, knowledge of medicine, building of houses and public dwellings, and military science to their sons. Young men were taught to be providers and protectors of their families and were instructed in the art of healthy love making. The elderly men in the society played a key role in introducing young African males to manhood.

Gutman's (1976) research on black families during slavery and after emancipation indicated that two-parent households predominated. Unions tended to be long lasting, except when broken prematurely by the sale of one or both partners. When blood relationships were broken, the kinship ideal was asserted through fictive kinship arrangements until a new pattern of blood ties could be developed. On plantations where slaves were sold infrequently and families were permitted to remain intact, relationships tended to be monogamous. Marital fidelity was highly regarded but prenuptial sex was tolerated and no stigma was attached to illegitimacy. Fathers played a significant and authoritative role in the family (Blassingame, 1979; Genovese, 1976). However, according to Frazier (1948), it wasn't until emancipation that the African American family developed a patriarchal form of social organization similar to the Anglo-American family. Emancipation brought new economic arrangements; as African American males acquired a measure of power and property, male authority in the family increased, leading to the economic subordination of women.

Between the years 1880 and 1925, two-parent families were the norm in poor black communities; black female-headed families were scarcely, if at all, more common than they were among comparable white families (Gutman, 1976). However, during the Great Migration, some African American families were torn apart as a result of urbanization and industrialization. Many African American men were unable to find work, whereas African American women found domestic work (Connor, 1988). Similarly, during World War II, when African American males migrated to large industrial areas in search of employment, an uneven ratio between the sexes was created that led to the disruption of families and family life (Connor, 1988). It was not until the late 1960s, when the cumulative effects of poverty, racism, and segregation peaked, the country's economic progress began to deteriorate, the economy began to shift away from unskilled labor, and the social programs of the Great Society began to have an impact on the poor (Murray, 1984), that the two-parent family structure among African Americans began to deteriorate (Connor, 1988). In 1950, 9 percent of African American homes were headed by one parent. By 1970, the number had grown to 33.3 percent, and by 1980, to 45.8 percent (Glick, 1981).

Consequently, the African American single-parent family can be viewed as an adaptation to the forces of racial oppression and economics—a byproduct of and response to modern capitalism. Wilson and Neckerman (cited in Connor, 1988) concluded that unemployment and underemployment of African American males and the resulting inability to provide for their families were directly related to the increase in African American female-headed homes. According to Eshleman (1985), black families have three distinct patterns. The matriarchal—matricentric family is usually headed by a single parent, although some include fathers who cannot support a family or who cannot exercise parental authority. Egalitarian two-parent families are primarily middle-class. Affluent families are usually patriarchal. In other words, the family's socioeconomic status affects its structure (Staples, 1988) and the role of the father.

The Father and Provider Roles

Madhubuti (1990) argued that fatherhood can increase a man's sense of failure and vulnerability if he knows or fears that he cannot provide for his wife and children. If African American men cannot negotiate a life for themselves and their family within the existing social structure, they may react negatively by withdrawing from the family or by abusing it, resort to a life of crime, develop outside relationships with other women, and/or resort to self-destructive acts of suicide and substance abuse.

Liebow's (1967) study of black "street" men indicated that some men did not associate with their families partly because they could not face the fact that they could not provide for their children. Campbell, Converse, and Rodgers (1976) and Voydanoff (1983) concluded that inability to provide for ones family is a great source of stress and contributes to a marginal position in the family. Unemployment has inhibited black men's attractiveness as a role model for their sons (Ray and McLoyd, 1986) and is related to fathers feeling less positively about their children (Sheldon and Fox, 1983). Although Ray and McLoyd (1986) pointed out that unemployment among lower-class African American fathers may result in fewer adverse effects because of the family's recognition of racial inequalities in society, Sullivan (1986) found that the African American community judges young fathers who do not attempt to provide care for their children.

Hendricks (1981) studied 20 African American adolescent fathers and found that these fathers were concerned primarily with financial responsibilities to their children, parenting skills, continuing their education, problems with the mother's parents, and their own future. Brown (1983) obtained similar results; the most frequent concern of 33 African American adolescent expectant fathers was financial responsibility for their family (this was not the most frequent concern for the expectant mothers). In a study of 50 African American teenage mothers, Massey (1991) found that 58 percent of the mothers reported receiving some marginal financial support from the father and 42 percent felt their baby's father was a good or an excellent provider.

Among African American families, as economic status rises, the father's active participation in his children's socialization increases (Cazenave, 1979; Davis and Havighurst, 1946; McAdoo, 1986). Cazenave (1984) found that when comparing African American men of lower and higher socioeconomic statuses, blue-collar men chose "provider" as the primary masculine role, whereas the provider role was the second choice among white-collar men. (Father was the first choice for married men and husband the first choice for unmarried men.) Thus, recent studies demonstrate that African American fathers are generally very concerned about being a "good" father and taking responsibility for and interest in the lives of their children and that an adequate and secure economic status facilitates the fathering role (McAdoo, 1986).

Father-Present Families

Allen's (1981) study of family interpersonal dynamics and adolescent male outcomes in 100 middle-class families revealed interesting differences between African American and white fathers. African American wives rated husband involvement in child care and child rearing slightly higher than did white wives, and 63 percent of the African American mothers versus 47 percent of white mothers perceived their husband as providing more help than the average husband in rearing the son. White fathers were least likely to reward their sons; material rewards were given to sons significantly more often by African American fathers than by African American and white mothers and more often by white mothers than white fathers.

According to the adolescents in Allen's (1981) study, African American mothers and white fathers shared significantly more activities with sons than did white mothers and African American fathers, even though African American parents apparently spent approximately the same amount of time in shared activities with the son. Sixty percent of African American adolescents claimed above-average closeness with their parents, whereas only 47 percent of white adolescents did. Strikingly, African American sons were significantly more likely than were white sons to identify more closely with the mother than with the father (which supported the findings of Kandel [1971]).

Connor's (1986) research on parenting attitudes of 136 young African American men revealed that the participants perceived themselves as being actively involved with their children. In a follow-up study, Donnor (1988) found that African American women ($n = 138$) also perceived African American men to be meaningfully involved with their children. Ninety-three percent of the fathers reported spending quality leisure time with their children. Hyde and Texidor (1988) found that African American fathers ($n = 135$) generally perceived the experience of fatherhood positively. The majority of fathers viewed child care as a responsibility to be shared by both the mother and father, including activities such as diapering, feeding, bathing, and dressing. These fathers were more likely than other fathers, who did not view child care as a shared responsibility, to have actually performed the tasks. Seventy-three percent believed that direct daily contact with their children was needed, and 90 percent indicated that they would like to spend more time with their children.

Although middle-class African American fathers tend to be more expressive and affectionate with their children than do their white counterparts, black and white fathers were more similar than dissimilar in their participation in and attitudes toward their role as fathers (Price-Bonham and Skeen, 1979). In general, middle-income African American fathers consider themselves effective, active participants in the care and upbringing of their children (Harrison, 1981) and exhibit the same range of attitudes, behaviors, and beliefs as do fathers from other ethnic groups in American culture (McAdoo, 1981).

Father-Absent Families

The highly valued role of father/provider has implications for absent fathers. A father who is unable to provide financial resources may feel, and therefore behave, as if he no longer has a role in the family. The frequency of contact with his children may be highly connected to his perception of usefulness as a provider. Isaacs and Leon (1987) interviewed 96 divorced mothers and found that the adaptive characteristics of the African American family historically, such as greater degree of self-sufficiency among women and strong ties with extended family, were related to visitation patterns. Additionally, establishing a regular visitation schedule, geographic distance separating the father from the children, discussing the children's needs after divorce, and the mother's living with her family of origin affected the frequency of visitations. Race and socioeconomic status were not related to visitation patterns.

Contrary to much of the literature, Earl and Lohmann (1978) found that many African American male children from father-absent homes saw their fathers frequently, and all of the boys in the study had access to an African American male who could serve potentially as a role model. When asked to whom the boys would go for advice that "only a man could help them with," 37 percent of the boys ($n = 53$) said they would go to their biological father. However, when the mothers were asked the same question about their sons, only 5 percent thought their son(s) would seek their father's help. Thus, the father-son relationship appeared to be more important to the boys than many of the mothers realized.

Increasingly, the African American family structure is reflected by a poor, single-parent, female-headed household. This type of family structure affects parental roles and child development, but does not necessarily lead to pathological or dysfunctional consequences. Father presence and absence can be viewed on a continuum. Cause, onset, duration, and degree of father absence, as well as the availability of father substitutes (including the mother), can result in a wide range of outcomes for children. Attention from parents appears to have the most significant impact on children (Shinn, 1978); other family and peer relationships may be able to compensate for the father's absence (Rubin, 1974).

In a study of 280 preadolescents, Rubin (1974) found no significant differences in any self-attitude measure among boys and girls from homes with no adult males present and boys and girls from homes with adult male figures. In Shinn's (1978) review of the literature on father absence and children's cognitive development, the effects of father absence varied less with race, age, or sex than with the reason for the absence. Divorce was among the more damaging causes when compared with death, desertion, or separation. No conclusive evidence regarding the effects of longer absences as opposed to shorter ones was found. Socioeconomic status appeared to be the most important moderating variable. Adams and Horovitz (1980) found that poverty exerted a leveling influence that overrode the differentiating characteristics of ethnic and age grouping, family structure, and father presence or absence in psychopathology in boys from poor homes. No positive association between the boys' psychopathology and their fatherlessness was found.

Masculine Identity Development

Historically, the father has been viewed as having a relatively insignificant role in early child development. His perceived role was as support to the mother to enable her to respond appropriately to her infant's needs. Leowald

(1951) recognized the father's role in freeing the infant from the early symbiotic relationship with the mother, and infant research has shown that infants become attached to both parents when both parents are involved (Lamb, 1980). Herzog coined the term "father hunger" to describe male infants' longing for their father (cited in Blos, 1985). Blos also referred to a preoedipal period during which the "dyadic father complex" appears. During this period, significant interactions occur between the child and the father; boys actively and persistently solicit their father's approval, recognition, and confirmation, thus establishing a profound and lasting libidinal bond.

> We have good cause to reason that these signals of approval and affirmation, transmitted by the father's presence (not necessarily verbalized), are received by the son during the early years of life and instill in him a modicum of self-possession and self-assertion—distilled, as it were, out of mutual sameness or shared maleness—which renders the wider world not only manageable and conquerable but infinitely alluring. (Blos, 1985: 11)

Thus, the father is idealized during early childhood. Although male children pull away from the father through a process of "deidealization" during early adolescence, father-son closeness is reestablished in a more mature form during late adolescence or early adulthood.

The close bond between sons and mothers in African American families (Allen, 1981; Kandel, 1971) does not negate the importance and influence of the father-son relationship. Taylor (1976) suggested that for the male youth, the mother may continue to function as an object of moral and emotional support, whereas the father and/or male significant others serve as models by which the boy discovers and cultivates his social and personal identity. Similarly, a father can serve as a negative role model, influencing the son to identify with models dissimilar to the father (Taylor, 1976).

Hetherington (1966) suggested that adequate masculine identification occurs by age six and that this identification can be maintained in the absence of the father. However, if the father leaves during the child's first four years, before this identification has been established, long-lasting disruption in sex-typed behaviors may result. Blos (1985) argued that, in the case of father absence, a boy's internal image and identification with the father are highly influenced by the mother's positive or negative attitudes toward the father, which may or may not become part of the boy's self-identity. The boy may also idealize the absent father, in which case the internal representation of the father is unchanging and identification is with the idealized image of the father (Herdt, 1989; Taylor, 1976).

Implications for Counseling and Psychotherapy

Cushman (1992) asserted that some family therapy theories, such as systems theory, treat families as if they were removed from the larger social context and do not take into account the influence of larger sociohistorical forces on the family. In this regard, psychodynamic and ecological perspectives need to be integrated to provide a conceptual framework for understanding and working with African American men and their families. From an ecological perspective, the sociohistorical forces that affect African American men as providers and fathers must be understood in order to counsel these men sufficiently. From a psychodynamic perspective, understanding the influence of the father on the psychosocial development of male children is primary.

Provider/Father Role Conflicts

Within the sociohistorical context of Western patriarchy, one can view African American fathers as being influenced by social norms that define masculine self-worth in terms of economic power and authority. Historically, however, social conditions have made it extremely difficult for African American men to achieve economic self-sufficiency and, therefore, to play an authoritative role within the family. As a result of their economic vulnerability, African American men may internalize beliefs that undermine their sense of self-worth. Their lack of authority in society is translated into lack of authority in the home or in some cases is overcompensated for by excessive and negative authoritative behavior in the home.

Practitioners should assess whether presenting problems of unemployed or underemployed African American men are related to their inability to fulfill societal and/or familial expectations as a provider. These men may suffer from a negative self-image and low self-esteem and may attribute their inability to secure gainful employment to some internalized deficiency of the self. A more realistic view would consider how a historically racist society and hostile environment have contributed to these men's predicament. Helping the client to determine the factors that he has control over and those he does not, as well as providing vocational assistance, may increase his sense of self-worth and value, regardless of his ability to provide for his family. For some men, employment-seeking skills can make a profound difference in their psychological well-being.

Fathers who are estranged from their children because of financial reasons and/or problems with their ex-wife may need to explore these issues in therapy. Divorced fathers who have little contact with their children manifest a higher incidence of psychiatric symptoms, particularly anxiety and depression (Feldman, 1990). Jacobs (1982) found that a divorced father's level of involvement with his children is a good predictor of his psychological adjustment after a divorce. Fathers may bury painful feelings associated with loss of their family and may need assistance in reestablishing a relationship with their children and in negotiating visitation rights with their ex-wives. Some men assume that their children have become attached to another male figure and thus give up hope for establishing a meaningful relationship with them. Although some fathers may not want to be involved with their children, practitioners should never assume that lack of contact or minimal contact means that the relationship is not important to the father and his children.

Nurturing Father and Male Child Development

Many studies indicate that children benefit from an involved and nurturing father (Pruett, 1987; Radin, 1982; Sagi, 1982). Blos's (1985) theory of masculine identity development suggests that during the infant-toddler years (birth to age four) and adolescent periods the father-son relationship is particularly important for the child.

In Western societies, many fathers believe that the mother should play the primary parenting role during infancy and early childhood. Practitioners should assess whether either parent would like the father to be more involved in child care. Fathers' perception of lack of support from the mother, feelings of incompetence with regard to child care, and work-related pressures are barriers that may contribute to fathers' lack of involvement with young children.

Strong father-son bonds during the early stages of a child's development make it easier for the father to deal with conflicts that may occur in later stages of development. During the oedipal period (ages three to five) boys become competitive and may exclude the father. However, if the father has been a nurturing parent during infancy, boys are less likely to experience the father as a competitive rival (Feldman, 1990). Similarly, during adolescence, boys' struggles with issues of autonomy, sexuality, and masculine identity may be less conflictual for nurturing fathers.

The mother-father relationship and the mother's attitude toward the father are critically important to the psychosocial development of male children. Although a son's closeness and identification with his mother do not obviate his identification with the father or other male figures, mothers play an instrumental role in this process. Mothers should be encouraged not to draw their children into their conflicts with the father or to denigrate the son's memory of his father. Practitioners can help couples deal with their anger and to separate behaviors that are within the father's control from circumstances that are beyond his control. Some fathers may withdraw from their children in order to avoid conflict with their wife or ex-wife (Feldman, 1990). Practitioners can help these fathers separate their feelings about the child's mother from their feelings about the child.

Adult Son-Father Relationships

Feldman (1990) suggested that fathers' feelings about their parental role should be a routine focus of assessment: "With all men, regardless of whether or not they are fathers, the crucial psychodynamic significance of their relationship with their own father should always be a major dimension of therapeutic exploration" (p. 104). According to Gordon's (1990) intergenerational model for working with men in therapy, therapy should help men obtain a fuller understanding of their own father and grandfather and thus help men come to terms with their own identity. Men with abusive or distant fathers should be helped to perceive their fathers as having human frailties as well as strengths.

> Realizing that one's own father was struggling with these roles rather than being all-knowing and omnipotent can allow one to struggle also, and to see that father's way was only his way, not the only way to be a father. (Gordon, 1990: 245)

The historical plight of African American men in the United States has had a profound effect on African American families. By helping African American men to connect with their heritage, gain a sense of continuity with their forefathers and those men's struggles, and view their situation within a sociohistorical context, practitioners can help African American men develop a positive sense of identity and realistic self-appraisal.

References

Adams, P. L., and Horovitz, J. H. (1980). Psychopathology and fatherlessness in poor boys. *Child Psychiatry and Human Development* 10(3), 135-143.

Allen, W. R. (1981). Moms, dads, and boys: Race and sex differences in the socialization of male children. In L. E. Gary (Ed.), *Black men*. Beverly Hills, CA: Sage Publications.

Badaines, J. (1976). Identification, imitation, and sex-role preference in father-present and father-absent black and Chicano boys. *Journal of Psychology* 92, 15-24.

Bernard, J. (1992). The good-provider role: Its rise and fall. In M. S. Kimmel and M. A. Messner (Eds.), *Men's lives*. New York: Macmillan.

Blassingame, J. W. (1979). *The slave community: Plantation life in the antebellum South*. New York: Oxford University Press.

Blos, P. (1985). *Son and father: Before and beyond the Oedipus complex*. New York: Free Press.

Brown, S. V. (1983). The commitment and concerns of black adolescent parents. *Social Work Research and Abstracts* 19(4), 27-34.

Campbell, A., Converse, P., and Rodgers, W. (1976). *The quality of American life*. New York: Russell Sage Foundation.

Carrigan, T., Connell, B., and Lee, J. (1987). Toward a new sociology of masculinity. In H. Brod (Ed.), *The making of masculinities: The new men's studies*. Boston: Allen and Unwin.

Cazenave, N. A. (1979). Middle-income black fathers: An analysis of the provider role. *Family Coordinator* 28, 583-592.

_____. (1984). Race, socioeconomic status, and age: The social context of American masculinity. *Sex Roles* 11, 639-656.

Connell, R. W. (1987). *Gender and power: Society, the person and sexual politics*. Stanford, CA: Stanford University Press.

Connor, M. E. (1986). Some parenting attitudes of young black fathers. In R. A. Lewis and R. E. Salt (Eds.), *Men in families*. Beverly Hills, CA: Sage Publications.

_____. (1988). Teenage fatherhood: Issues confronting young black males. In J. T. Gibbs (Ed.), *Young, black, and male in America: An endangered species*. New York: Auburn House.

Cushman, P. (1992). Psychotherapy to 1992: A historically situated interpretation. In D. K. Freedheim (Ed.), *History of psychotherapy: A century of change*. Washington, D.C: American Psychological Association.

Davis, A., and Havighurst, R. J. (1946). Social class and color differences in child rearing. *American Sociological Review* 11, 698-710.

Davis, J. A. (1974). Justification for no obligation: Views of black males toward crime and the criminal law. *Issues in Criminology* 9(2), 69-87.

Earl, L., and Lohmann, N. (1978). Absent fathers and black male children. *Social Work* 23, 413-415.

Eshleman, J. R. (1985). *The family: An introduction* (5th ed.). Boston: Allyn and Bacon.

Feldman, L. B. (1990). Fathers and fathering. In R. L. Meth and R. S. Pasick (Eds.), *Men in therapy: The challenge of change*. New York: Guilford.

Filene, P. (1987). The secrets of men's history. In H. Brad (Ed.), *The making of masculinities: The new men's studies*. Boston: Allen and Unwin.

Foucault, M. (1978). *The history of sexuality, volume 1: An introduction*. New York: Vintage Books.

Frazier, E. F. (1948). *The Negro family in the United States*. New York: Citadel Press.

Genovese, E. D. (1976). *Roil, Jordan, roil: The world the slaves made*. New York: Vintage Books.

Glick, P. C. (1981). A demographic picture of black families. In H. P. McAdoo (Ed.), *Black families*. Beverly Hills, CA: Sage Publications.

Gordon, B. (1990). Being a father. In R. L. Meth and R. S. Pasick (Eds.), *Men in therapy: The challenge of change*. New York: Guilford.

Gutman, H. G. (1976). *The black family in slavery and freedom, 1750-1925*. New York: Pantheon Books.

Harrison, A. (1981). Attitudes towards procreation among black adults. In H. P. McAdoo (Ed.), *Black families*. Beverly Hills, CA: Sage Publications.

Hendricks, L. E. (1981). Black unwed adolescent fathers. In L. E. Gary (Ed.), *Black men*. Beverly Hills, CA: Sage Publications.

Herdt, G. (1989). Father presence and ritual homosexuality: Paternal deprivation and masculine development in Melanesia reconsidered. *Ethos* 17, 326-370.

Hetherington, E. (1966). Effects of paternal absence on sex-typed behaviors in Negro and white preadolescent males. *Journal of Personality and Social Psychology* 4, 87-91.

Hunt, L. L., and Hunt, J. G. (1975). Race and the father-son correlation: The conditional relevance of father absence for the orientations and identities of adolescent boys. *Social Problems* 35-52.

Hyde, B. L., and Texidor, M. S. (1988). A description of the fathering experience among black fathers. *Journal of National Black Nurses' Association* 2, 67-78.

Isaacs, M. S., and Leon, G. H. (1987). Race, marital dissolution and visitation: An examination of adaptive family strategies. *Journal of Divorce* 11(2), 17-31.

Jacobs, J. W. (1982). The effect of divorce on fathers: An overview of the literature. *American Journal of Psychiatry* 139, 1235-1241.

Kandel, D. B. (1971). Race, maternal authority, and adolescent aspiration. *American Journal of Sociology* 76, 999-1020.

Kimmel, M. S. (1987). The contemporary "crisis" of masculinity in historical perspective. In H. Brod (Ed.), *The making of masculinities: The new men's studies*. Boston: Allen and Unwin.

Lamb, M. E. (1980). Observational studies in the family setting. In F. Pederson (Ed.), *The father-infant relationship*. New York: Praeger.

_____. (1986). *The father's role: Applied perspectives*. New York: Wiley Interscience.

Leowald, H. (1951). Ego and reality. *International Journal of Psycho-Analysis* 10-18.

Liebow, E. (1967). *Tally's corner.* Boston: Little, Brown.

Longabaugh, R. (1973). Mother behavior as a variable moderating the effects of father absence. *Ethos* 1, 456465.

Madhubuti, R. (1990). *Black men: Obsolete, single, dangerous?* Chicago: Third World Press.

Marable, M. (1983). *How capitalism underdeveloped black America.* Boston: South End Press.

Massey, G. (1991). The flip side of teen mothers: A look at teen fathers. In B. P. Bowser (Ed.), *Black male adolescents: Parenting and education in community context.* Lanham, MD: University Press of America.

McAdoo, J. L. (1981). Black father and child interactions. In L. E. Gary (Ed.), *Black men.* Beverly Hills, CA: Sage Publications.

_____. (1986). A black perspective on the father's role in child development. *Marriage and Family Review* 9, 117-133.

_____. (1993). The roles of African American fathers: An ecological perspective. *Families in Society* 74, 28-35.

Murray, C. (1984). *Losing ground: American social policy, 1950-1980.* New York: Basic Books.

Pleck, E. J., and Pleck, J. H. (Eds.). (1980). *The American man.* Englewood Cliffs, NJ: Prentice-Hall.

Price-Bonham, S., and Skeen, P. (1979). A comparison of black and white fathers with implications for parent education. *Family Coordinator* 28, 53-59.

Pruett, K. D. (1987). *The nurturing father.* New York: Warner.

Radin, N. (1982). Primary caregiving and role sharing fathers of preschoolers. In M. E. Lamb (Ed.), *Nontraditional families: Parenting and child development.* Hillsdale, NJ: Lawrence Erlbaum.

Ray, S. A., and McLoyd, V. C. (1986). Fathers in hard times: The impact of unemployment and poverty on paternal and marital relations. In M. E. Lamb (Ed.), *The father's role: Applied perspectives.* New York: John Wiley.

Rubin, R. H. (1974). Adult male absence and the self-attitudes of black children. *Child Study Journal* 4, 3346.

Sagi, A. (1982). Antecedents and consequences of various degrees of paternal involvement in child rearing: The Israeli project. In M. E. Lamb (Ed.), *Nontraditional families: Parenting and child development.* Hillsdale, NJ: Lawrence Erlbaum.

Segal, L. (1990). *Slow motion: Changing masculinities, changing men.* New Brunswick, NJ: Rutgers University Press.

Sheldon, A., and Fox, G. L. (1983). *The impact of economic uncertainty on children's roles within the family.* Paper presented at the meeting of the Society for Study of Social Problems, Detroit, Michigan.

Shinn, M. (1978). Father absence and children's cognitive development. *Psychological Bulletin* 85, 295-324.

Staples, R. (1988). The emerging majority: Resources for nonwhite families in the United States. *Family Relations* 37, 348-354.

Stearns, P. (1979). *Be a man! Males in modern society.* New York: Holmes and Meier.

Sullivan, M. L. (1986). *Ethnographic research on young fathers and parenting.* New York: Vera Institute.

Taylor, R. L. (1976). Black youth and psychosocial development. *Journal of Black Studies* 6, 353-371.

Unger, R. K. (1989). Sex, gender and epistemology. In M. Crawford and M. Gentry (Eds.), *Gender and thought: Psychological perspectives*. New York: Springer-Verlag.

Voydanoff, P. (1983). Unemployment and family stress. In H. Z. Lopata and I. H. Pleck (Eds.), *Research in the interweave of social roles: vol.3. Families and jobs*. Greenwich, CT: JAI Press.

Weeks, J. (1981). *Sex politics and society: The regulation of sexuality since 1800*. London: Longman.

Wilkinson, C. B., and O'Connor, W. A. (1977). Growing up male in a black single-parent family. *Psychiatric Annals* 7(7), 50-59.

11

The Contribution of Marriage to the Life Satisfaction of Black Adults

Ann Creighton Zollar and J. Sherwood Williams

Perhaps no topic generates more lively debate among students of the black community than the state of relationships between black males and females. At least one set of statistics, those that show the decline in the black marriage rate, indicates that the concern with the nature of these relationships is well founded. In 1970, 64 percent of blacks aged 18 years and over were married; by 1982 this figure had decreased to 49.9 percent. Even a cursory examination of the data reveals how dramatic the downturn in the proportion of married men and women has been since 1970 (U.S. Bureau of the Census, 1984). In 1970, for instance, almost 67 percent of black males were married, compared to 61.7 percent of black females. Since then, however, both groups have registered a persistent decline. By 1983, the proportion of married black males had dropped to just over one-half (52.2 percent), while that of black females had dropped below one-half (45.7 percent).[1]

Staples (1981a, 1981b, 1981c) has argued that in order to understand this decline in the black marriage rate, it is necessary to consider both structural and psychological factors, including how marriage patterns are affected by gender and socioeconomic status. First among the structural factors is an imbalanced sex ratio among blacks, in that there are fewer eligible males than eligible females. While the imbalanced sex ratio is primarily a reflection of higher mortality rates among young men, the pool of black male eligibles is further diminished by the large number of black men who are confined to prisons and mental hospitals and a smaller amount who prefer homosexual or interracial relationships. It is likely that many of the males who remain in the pool of eligibles may not be considered desirable for a variety of reasons (e.g., drug addicts or habitual criminals). It is also likely that most black men in the eligible pool are in different class groupings from those of single black women. Staples (1981a: 8) observes the paradox that many eligible black men do not have the opportunity to marry because of their low level of education and income, while the women fail to marry because of their high levels of education and income.

Staples argues that both black men and women hold antimarriage attitudes indicative of strong disaffection with the institution of marriage itself. Of black women he says, "There is a generalized discontentment with marriage among those who are married and an anticipation of unhappiness in the conjugal state among those who are not" (1981c: 186). Furthermore, Staples suggests that middle-class black men and women may be forgoing marriage because they have adopted the materialistic values of mainstream American culture and think that the shortest route to the "good life" is a trip for one rather than the sacrifices, compromises, and sharing with another person that characterize marriage.

Likewise, the decline in the marriage rate can be assumed to have both structural and psychological implications. The structural implications, such as the fact that the majority of black births are to single women and that more than half of the households headed by black women are poor, have even been discussed in the popular press. The psychological implications of marriage versus singlehood have, however, received less attention. It may very well be, for example, that single blacks are happier with their lives than those who are married. It may even be true, since black men have been described as "buyers in a buyers market," that marriage is more advantageous for them than it is for black women.

The goal of this study is to present evidence concerning the effects of marriage on black men and black women. We ask, is marriage more favorable for blacks than singlehood, and are the consequences of marriage more favorable for black husbands than for black wives?

The idea that marriage may not be a universally beneficial condition runs counter to common beliefs, yet it has been previously raised and examined. Bernard (1972) claimed that while marriage is distinctly beneficial to husbands, it is much less so for wives. In fact, she argued that a wide variety of emotional disorders in women can be attributed to marriage, and at least implicitly, she has suggested that until the institution of marriage has been reformed, away from its traditional pattern, it might be wiser for women not to marry at all.

Arguing that Bernard's assessment of the data was less than objective, Glenn (1975) set out to reexamine her thesis by testing three hypotheses. These hypotheses were:

1. Whereas married men, as an aggregate, will report substantially greater happiness than men who are widowed, divorced, separated, or never-mar-

ried, married women will report little or no greater global happiness than unmarried women.
2. Among married persons, men will report greater marital happiness than women.
3. Reported marital happiness will be more predictive of reported global happiness for men than for women.

Glenn's findings in regard to the first hypothesis were congruent with one of the most consistent findings in the literature on marital status and life satisfaction in the United States. Married persons of both sexes report higher levels of global happiness than any category of unmarried persons. Widowed and never-married persons report intermediate levels of personal happiness, while divorced and separated persons report the lowest levels of personal happiness (Bradburn, 1969; Bradburn and Caplovitz, 1965; Campbell, Converse, and Rogers, 1976; Clemente and Sauer, 1976; Glenn, 1975; Glenn and Weaver, 1979; Gurin, Veroff, and Field, 1960; Palmore and Luikert, 1972; Spreitzer and Snyder, 1974). Glenn's data also led him to reject the two additional hypotheses and to conclude that "American marriage, in spite of its many limitations, is typically beneficial to both husbands and wives" (1975: 599).

Glenn's analysis, however, answers none of these questions for marriage among black Americans. In his 1975 article Glenn suggested that patterns of reported happiness may differ substantially for blacks and whites. The small number of blacks in his sample, however, precluded a separate study. Glenn and Weaver (1981) did carry out separate and parallel analyses for blacks on the contribution of marital happiness to global happiness. While expressing concern about the relatively small number of blacks in their sample, they found that for all race-sex subpopulations, a "happy marriage seems virtually necessary for a high level of global happiness" (Glenn and Weaver, 1981: 163). Only in the case of black males does marital happiness fail to outrank work satisfaction as a positive predictor of global happiness.

There are few other analyses of subjective well-being among blacks. Campbell and associates (1976), analyzing data on adults of all ages, found that married and widowed blacks reported similar degrees of happiness and life satisfaction. Single and separated or divorced blacks reported much lower levels. Little difference in the satisfaction level of married and unmarried elderly blacks was found by Jackson, Bacon, and Peterson (1977-78). Ball (1983) found that, when age, health, social participation, education, and welfare ratio were controlled, there was no relationship between marital status and life satisfaction among black women. It seems imperative that the additional data now available for black adults of both sexes be analyzed. As a way of focusing our analysis we test the same hypotheses for blacks that Glenn (1975) tested for whites.

Methods

Data used for this study were collected by the National Opinion Research Center as part of its General Social Surveys. Surveys collected between 1972 and 1984 were combined and treated as a single data set. All surveys used national stratified multistage area probability sampling procedures. Modified-probability samples (with a quota procedure at the block level) were used from 1972 through 1974; full-probability samples were used from 1977 on; and the 1975 and 1976 samples were transitional, being half modified-probability and half full-probability. The combined data set consisted of face-to-face interviews with 2,228 black persons. The persons sampled were 18 years of age and older and lived in the continental United States. A more detailed explanation of the sampling design, interviewers' specifications, and general coding instructions can be found in Appendixes A, B, and C of the General Social Surveys, 1972-1984: Cumulative Codebook (Davis, 1984).

Our dependent variables, global happiness and marital happiness, were measured by single questions with three response options. Global happiness was determined by the respondent's answer to the question, "Taken all together, how would you say things are these days—would you say that you are very happy, pretty happy, or not too happy?" Marital happiness was determined by responses to, "Taking things all together, how would you describe your marriage? Would you say that your marriage is very happy, pretty happy, or not too happy?" (This was asked only of married persons.) The predictor variables, from the hypotheses, were marital status and sex. Nearly 47 percent of the sample was married and 41 percent was male. Three conditional variables were introduced on the basis of findings of past research and/or theoretical considerations. These variables included age, education, and the structure of the respondent's family of orientation up to the age of 16. Following Glenn (1975), we grouped age into three categories: 18-39 (49.5 percent), 40-59 (30.1 percent), and 60 or older (20.4 percent). Educational categories included those who had not completed high school (45.9 percent), high school graduates (42.5 percent), and those who had completed some college (11.6 percent). The nature of the respondent's family of orientation at age 16 was grouped into two categories: those raised by both parents (60.8 percent) and those raised by other than both parents (39.2 percent)

Contingency analyses were used to examine the basic hypotheses and multiple regression to estimate the combined effects of the variables on global happiness. Since the dependent variables and several of the predictors have a limited range, it is likely that the overall estimates will be lower than they would be with continuous data.

The Statistical Package for the Social Sciences (SPSSX) was used for all the analyses in this study (SPSS, Inc., 1986).

Findings

The data in Table 1 support the first part of Glenn's Hypothesis 1, that married men tend to be happier than unmarried men. The second part of the hypothesis, however, is not supported. Married women, in fact, are likely to report greater global happiness than are unmarried women. The percentage differences between the sexes on reported global happiness are not statistically significant. Thus, the data do not totally support the first hypothesis, and we must conclude that married black persons, regardless of gender, tend to be happier than unmarried black persons.

Under all conditions, married persons reported higher global happiness than did unmarried persons. For married males, global happiness was highest among persons 60 and over and those who had completed less than a high school education. Married females who were between the ages of 40 and 59, had attended college, and were raised by both parents reported higher global happiness than females in other conditions. The strongest associations between marital status and global happiness for males were found under the conditions of 40-59 years of age, high school graduates, and raised by both parents. For females, the strongest associations were among persons 40-59 years of age, having attended some college, and raised by other than both parents.

The data in Table 3 support the second hypothesis (that among married persons, men will report greater marital happiness than women). Although both sexes were more likely to claim that their marriages were very happy, females were significantly less likely to do so. It should also be noted, however, that this relationship is weak (C = .159).

Support is found for the second hypothesis regardless of age, education, or the constitution of the family of orientation at age 16. Table 4 indicates, however, that the difference between males and females on marital happiness increases as age increases. Similarly, as age increases, the proportion report-

Table 1
Percentage Reporting to be Globally "Very Happy" by Marital Status and Sex

	Male		Female	
Marital Status	%	N	%	N
Married	26.6	492	26.5	539
Widowed	22.6	62	21.4	201
Divorced/separated	15.9	144	13.3	307
Never married	14.6	199	16.7	257
Contingency coefficient.174	.179			
Significance level	.001		.001	

Table 2
Percentage Reporting Globally "Very Happy" by Marital Status, Sex, and Selected Characteristics

Controls	Married	N	Males Not Married	N	CB	Married	N	Females Not Married	N	C
Age										
18-39	19.7	193	12.6	223	.159*	19.4	272	14.3	398	.146*
40-59	27.2	195	12.9	101	.206*	34.4	186	15.3	176	.236*
60+	38.5	104	30.9	81	.096	32.1	81	22.4	192	.102
Education										
Less than high school	30.6	245	20.5	195	.151*	28.4	222	16.4	383	.148*
High school	23.5	187	12.4	177	.169*	23.2	246	16.9	307	.165*
College	20.8	53	13.8	29	.132	35.4	65	14.9	67	.238*
Reared by										
Both parents	25.8	302	17.8	213	.127*	28.0	325	18.3	393	.134*
Other	27.9	190	14.6	192	.191*	24.3	214	14.7	373	.170*

ac = contingency coefficient.

*Significant at or beyond the .05 level.

Table 3
Percentage Distribution of Marital Happiness by Sex

Marital Happiness	Males	Females	Male-Female % Difference
Very happy	54.6	48.9	5.7
Pretty happy	42.7	40.0	2.7
Not too happy	2.7	11.0	-8.3
N	405	462	

Note: Contingency coefficient = .159; level of significance = .0001.

Table 4
Percentage "Very Happily" Married by Sex and Selected Characteristics

Condition	Males	N	Females	N	Male-Female % Difference	C	p
Age							
18-39	49.4	168	47.5	238	1.9	.142	.016
40-59	54.2	153	47.8	159	6.4	.192	.003
60+	65.5	84	56.3	65	9.2	.139	ns
Education							
Less than high school graduate	55.6	198	47.0	181	8.6	.180	.002.
High school graduate	57.4	155	48.8	217	8.6	.164	.006
College	40.0	50	54.8	62	-14.8	.223	.054
Reared by							
Both parents	57.7	249	44.4	282	13.3	.184	.003
Other	52.6	156	51.8	180	.8	.160	.001

ing to be very happily married also increases for both sexes. In all age categories, females are at least three times more likely than males to report that their marriage is not too happy.

When education was controlled, the tendency for males to report greater marital happiness persisted, except among those respondents who had some college background. Among those with a college background, females were most likely to report that they were very happily married.

Males who were raised in a family with both parents to the age of 16 were 13.3 percent more likely than their female counterparts to report that they were very happily married. For those reared by other than both parents, there was little difference between the sexes in the percentage reporting that they were very happily married. The difference in this comparison is greatest between those reporting that their marriage was "not too happy." Females were 3.8 times more likely than males to report that their marriages were "not too happy."

Table 5 is presented to examine the hypothesized stronger association between marital happiness and global happiness among males than among females. It is clear that no support was found for the hypothesized relationship. In fact, regardless of conditions, marital happiness was a better predictor of global happiness for females than it was for males. Using the direction-of-differences-in-pairs interpretation for the Somers' d_{yx} coefficient, we can reduce our overall error in predicting global happiness from marital happiness by 11 percent more for females than for males.[2] In every condition the predictive value of marital happiness is greater for females than it is for males.

Table 5
Relationship between Global Happiness and Marital
Happiness by Sex and Selected Characteristics

Condition	Male	Sex N	Female	N	Male-Female Difference
Overall association	.365		.476		-.111
Age					
18-39	.324	167	.459	236	-.135
40-59	.360	153	.484	159	-.124
60+	.394	83	.563	65	-.169
Education					
Less than high school graduate	.381	198	.428	181	-.047
High school graduate	.323	153	.508	215	-.185
College	.490	50	.513	62	-.023
Reared by					
Both parents	.343	248	.503	281	-.160
Other	.401	155	.438	179	-.037

Note: The measure of association is Somers' d_{yx}. with global happiness as the dependent variable.

With five predictors we were able to explain 18 percent of the variance in global happiness. Only two predictors, age and marital happiness, were significant. The critical predictor, sex, was not statistically significant and added only .1 percent to the explained variance. The best predictor was marital happiness (beta = .397), which contributed over 85 percent of the explained variance. Age was also significant and added just over 2 percent to the explained variance. Relative to the issue at hand, sex is not a useful variable in predicting global happiness. (Sex and family of orientation were dummied, with "female" and "raised by other than both parents" equaling zero.)

Summary

Pooled data from national surveys conducted between 1972 and 1984 have been examined to uncover evidence concerning the effects of marriage on black men and black women. The questions we asked were (a) Do married black persons tend to be happier than unmarried black persons? and (b) Are the consequences of marriage more favorable for black husbands than for black wives? The data show that married black persons, regardless of gender,

Table 6
Regression of Global Happiness with Age, Orientation

Variable	R^2	R^2Change	Beta	F
Age	.023	.023	.128	11.526*
Marital happiness	.178	.155	.397	116.390*
Sex	.179	.001	-.024	.493
Education	.180	.001	.041	1.142
Family of orientation	.181	.001	-.016	.191

*Significant at or beyond the .01 level.

tend to be happier than unmarried black persons. In addition, the data show that among married black persons, men do tend to report greater marital happiness than women. The data also show, however, that reported marital happiness makes a greater contribution to the overall happiness of black wives than it does to the overall happiness of black husbands.

Notes

1. There has also been a decline in the percentage of persons in the white population who are married, but it has not been nearly so precipitous. In 1970, for example, 76.1 percent of white males and 69.3 percent of white females were married. In 1983 the percentages were 68.3 for white males and 63.3 for white females.
2. Somers' d_{yx} is an ordinal measure of association designed to attempt prediction when there are ties on the dependent variable (Somers, 1962). This measure has a proportional-reduction-in-error interpretation and will always be lower than Goodman and Kruskal's gamma coefficient when there are ties on the dependent variable. D_{yx} is generally, therefore, more conservative than gamma.

References

Ball, Richard E. (1983). Marital status, household structure, and life satisfaction of black women. *Social Problems* 30: 400-409.

Bernard, Jessie. (1972). *The future of marriage*. New York: Bantam Books.

Bradburn, Norman. (1969). *The structure of psychological well-being*. Chicago: Aldine.

Bradburn, Norman, and D. Caplovitz. (1965). *Reports on happiness*. Chicago: Aldine.

Campbell, Angus, P. Converse, and W. Rogers. (1976). *The quality of American life*. New York: Russell Sage.

Clemente, Frank, and W. Sauer. (1976). Life satisfaction in the United States. *Social Forces* 54: 621-631.

Davis, James A. (1984). *General social surveys, 1972-1984: Cumulative codebook*. Chicago: National Opinion Research Center, University of Chicago.

Glenn, Norval. (1975). The contribution of marriage to the psychological well-being of males and females. *Journal of Marriage and the Family* 37: 594-600.

Glenn, Norval, and C. Weaver. (1979). A note on family situation and global happiness. *Social Forces* 57 (March): 960-967.

Glenn, Norval, and C. Weaver. (1981). The contribution of marital happiness to global happiness. *Journal of Marriage and the Family* 43: 161-168.

Gurin, Gerald, J. Veroff, and S. Field. (1960). *Americans view their mental health.* New York: Basic Books.

Jackson, James, J. Bacon, and J. Peterson, Jr. (1977-78). Life satisfaction among black urban elderly. *Journal of Aging and Human Development* 8: 169-179.

Palmore, Endman C., and C. Luikert. (1972). Health and social factors related to life satisfaction. *Journal of Health and Social Behavior* 13: 68-80.

Somers, Robert H. (1962). A new asymmetric measure of association for ordinal variables. *American Sociological Review* 27: 799-811.

Spreitzer, Elmer, and E. Snyder. (1974). Correlates of life satisfaction among the aged. *Journal of Gerontology* 29: 454-458.

SPSS, Inc. (1986). *SPSSX user's guide* (2nd ed.). New York: McGraw-Hill.

Staples, Robert. (1981a). Black singles in America. In Peter J. Stein (Ed.), *Single life.* New York: St. Martin's Press.

_____. (1981b). Race and marital status: An overview. In H. McAdoo (Ed.), *Black families.* Beverly Hills, CA: Sage Publications.

_____. (1981c). *The world of black singles.* Westport, CT: Greenwood Press.

U.S. Bureau of the Census. (1984). *Statistical abstract of the United States, 1985.* Table No. 50. Washington, D.C.: Government Printing Office.

Part 3

Policy Initiatives

12

The Impact of Incarceration on African American Families: Implications for Practice

Anthony E. O. King

When a man is sentenced to prison, his entire family suffers, especially intimate companions, spouses, children, and extended-family members (Baker, Morris, and Janus, 1978; Brodsky, 1974; Hale, 1988; Morris, 1965; Newton, 1980; Sack, 1977; Showalter and Jones-Williams, 1980; Zalba, 1964). This sudden and involuntary separation from the family creates economic, psychological, and interpersonal problems similar to those experienced by divorced families and families who lose a significant adult because of death. In essence, the entire family system suffers when a family member is incarcerated.

The number of African American men in state prisons throughout the United States exceeds their proportion among the U.S. population. Imprisonment creates serious economic, emotional, and interpersonal problems for their families. Furthermore, these problems create excessive stress on family relationships at a time when the incarcerated African American male and his family most need each other's support. Social work, as well as other human service professions, has not responded to the needs of either the incarcerated African American male or his family. Unless social service agencies and professionals begin to address the problems incarceration creates for African American men and their families, imprisonment will become the most significant factor contributing to the dissolution and breakdown of African American families during the decade of the 1990s.

This chapter examines the disproportionate confinement of African American men in state prisons and how their imprisonment affects their families and family relationships. Five types of family-centered programs or services designed to help incarcerated African American males and their families survive the trauma of imprisonment are identified and described.

Disproportionate Incarceration

Since statistics on prison inmates in the United States have been recorded, African American men have constituted a disproportionate percentage of state inmate populations (Cahalan, 1979). In 1880, when African Americans were 13.1 percent of the United States population, 28.6 percent of all prisoners in state correctional institutions were African American men (Cahalan, 1979). By 1989, a year in which African Americans made up 12 percent of the U.S. population and African American men less than 6 percent of the population, African American men confined to state prisons had grown to 48 percent of the prisoner population (U.S. Department of Justice, 1989, 1991a). On the other hand, European American men comprise approximately 40 percent of the U.S. population but represent only 46 percent of the state prison population (U.S. Department of Justice, 1989, 1991a). In the northeastern and southern regions of the United States, African American men make up 50 percent and 58 percent, respectively, of state-prison inmates (U.S. Department of Justice, 1989, 1991a).

The disparity becomes even more apparent when one examines the incarceration rates for African American and European American men. In 1986, the combined state and federal incarceration rate for African American men was 342 per 100,000 African Americans, compared with 63 per 100,000 European American males (U.S. Department of Justice, 1991d). The male European American incarceration rate is comparable to rates in less punitive Western European nations, such as France, Italy, Spain, and Norway (Dunbaugh, 1979). African American males are incarcerated at a rate four *times* higher than indigenous African males in South Africa: 3,109 per 100,000 African Americans versus 729 per 100,000 indigenous Africans in South Africa (Brazaitis, 1991). Thus, the United States has the highest incarceration rate of Africans in the world (Brazaitis, 1991; Hawkins and Jones, 1989).

The African American male incarceration problem affects these men's representation in other social institutions such as colleges and universities. On any given day in 1990, approximately 525,000 African American men were confined to jails or state or federal prisons (U.S. Department of Justice, 1991b, 1991c). Similarly, on any given day, fewer than 480,000 African American men were enrolled in colleges or universities nationwide (Evangelauf, 1992). In other words, more African American men are in prison or jail than in college. Not surprisingly, therefore, more than 60 percent of all African American college students are female (Evangelauf, 1992). At the current pace of African American male incarceration, the year 2000 will see nearly 60 percent of the total U.S. prison population, or roughly 900,000 African American men, locked behind prison walls. Besides the human misery and family stress, the cost of incarcerating so many African American men is staggering. At an annual cost of $20,000 per inmate, the United

States spends approximately $7.6 billion per year to keep roughly 370,000 African American men behind bars (Brazaitis, 1991).

Why the Disproportionate Incarceration Rate?

Social scientists, particularly criminal justice scholars, have offered various explanations for the disproportionate incarceration of African American men. Some have argued that the uneven representation of African American men in state prisons is a consequence of the disproportionate percentage of serious crimes that African American men commit (*Furman v. Georgia*, 1972; Hagan, 1974; Blumstein, 1982). Others have suggested that race and class discrimination in arrest, conviction, and sentencing practices is responsible for this phenomenon (Adamson, 1983; Christianson, 1981; Christianson and Dehais, 1980; Dunbaugh, 1979; Hawkins and Jones, 1989; Lichtenstein and Kroll, 1990; Nagel, 1977; Petersilia, 1983; Zatz, 1987). Despite the conflicting and inconclusive research findings supporting both sides of this debate, African American men are convicted of serious crimes at a rate that is more than eight times the proportion of their representation in the U.S. population (U.S. Department of Justice, 1989, 1991a). It is also true, however, that institutional racism and discrimination continue to permeate every social, political, and economic institution in the United States. Thus, one can conclude that African American men are disproportionately incarcerated as a result of discrimination and a higher conviction rate for serious crimes.

Impact of Incarceration on Families

According to the U.S. Department of Justice (1989), 46 percent of the individuals incarcerated in state prisons were either married, widowed, divorced, or separated. Fifty-four percent were supporting someone at the time of conviction. Furthermore, more than 70 percent of these inmates were supporting two or more persons at the time of conviction. These data are not broken down according to race and gender. As a result, it is not possible to determine from these reports what percentage of African American male inmates were married or supporting other persons.

My experience as a clinical social work consultant with a state department of corrections has led me to conclude that a significant percentage of incarcerated African American males, regardless of marital status, were actively involved in the lives of nuclear, extended, or nonblood-related family members prior to confinement. Thus, marital status is not the only indicator of family involvement, particularly for African American men, whose cultural orientation embraces the extended and fictive family models. Nevertheless, social scientists have traditionally excluded unmarried inmates and their families from studies regarding the impact of imprisonment on families. The most notable exception to this trend as Zalba (1964), who conducted one of the first studies of incarcerated mothers and their children. Researchers' failure to include unmarried African American males in their samples is a salient oversight, given the hundreds of thousands of unmarried African American males in this nation's state prisons.

Financial Hardship

Studies focusing an families of incarcerated men have identified several general problems experienced by families. One of the most frequently cited problems is the loss of the incarcerated individual's income or earnings. After a male is imprisoned, he can no longer contribute to the financial maintenance of his family, which often plunges the family into a severe economic crisis resulting in eviction, loss of medical coverage, or insufficient funds to purchase adequate food or clothing (Schneller, 1976; Swan, 1981). Families of incarcerated African American men are at risk of extreme economic hardship because generally they come from the poorest strata of the African American community (Lichtenstein and Kroll, 1990; Swan, 1981). Sixty-nine percent of state prison inmates were employed prior to incarceration, and their incomes helped keep their families from financial ruin. Traditionally, the economic survival of African American families has depended upon the incomes of both spouses and, in some cases, the earnings of older children and other adults in the family as well (McAdoo, 1988; Staples, 1988). Thus, when the male's income is lost, the family may encounter a financial nightmare (Morris, 1965; Schneller, 1976).

The burden of replacing these financial resources frequently rests on the shoulders of the spouse or female partner. Unfortunately, wives and female partners often lack the education or skills required to obtain the type of employment needed to replace the earnings of their husband or male partner. According to the U.S. Department of Justice (1989), incarcerated individuals typically possess a tenth-grade education. It is likely that female partners of male inmates have similar educational backgrounds, due to the endogamous nature of dating and marital relationships in the United States. Therefore, spouses and partners find it difficult to upgrade their employment status. If the female partner *is* able to find a second job, she will have a difficult time assuming this additional burden, because the male absence reduces the number of child-care providers. Sixty percent of state inmates have children; approximately 36 percent have two or more children. Extended-family members often step up to provide economic support and personal assistance, but their resources are often scant. Consequently, families have to apply for public assistance benefits, which generally take months to receive and are rarely enough to replace the earnings of the absent male.

Emotional and Psychological Distress

When asked to identify the most negative changes encountered as a consequence of their husbands' incarceration, many women, after identifying financial problems, listed loneliness, depression, and nervousness or emotional problems (Schneller, 1976). The wife or female partner and the inmate's children may suffer depression, loneliness, anger, and feelings of abandonment (Brodsky, 1974; Friedman and Esselstyn, 1965; Sack, 1977; Schneller, 1976).

These problems make it even more difficult for individual family members to cope with the practical problems they face.

The children of incarcerated men are particularly vulnerable to emotional and psychological problems during the father's imprisonment (Sack, 1977; Schneller, 1976). Children whose fathers are incarcerated frequently feel abandoned, which often leads to problems such as difficulty sleeping, eating, and completing schoolwork These children are also at risk for acting out in school, including picking fights with other children (Sack, 1977).

The social stigma associated with having a parent or significant adult male incarcerated exacerbates the emotional difficulties that children experience. Dependent children also experience intense feelings of sadness and depression as a result of the male's incarceration. At least one clinical study has found that the psychosocial development of children, particularly boys, is adversely affected when the father or male caregiver is imprisoned (Sack, 1977). The anxieties male children experience also create conflicts in the mother-son relationship (Sack, 1977). These problems exacerbate the poverty, racism, community violence, and educational difficulties that African American children frequently encounter. The fact that many of these children become productive citizens is testimony to the resourcefulness of the female partners of these men.

African American men experience tremendous guilt over the hardships their families face as a result of their imprisonment. Their guilt leads them to discourage their children from identifying with them as role models out of fear that their children will also end up in prison.

Such messages are typically directed toward male children. In such instances, although the incarcerated father may try to teach his children a lesson based upon his experience with the criminal justice system, he also suggests to them that he doesn't deserve their respect and love because of the bad things he has done and the difficulties he has caused the family. This message is particularly damaging for adolescent African American males, because they need adult male role models at this stage of psychosocial development. By encouraging his son not to identify with or look up to him, the incarcerated father may unwittingly enhance the male child's sense of abandonment.

Strain on Family Relationships

The imprisonment of a father, male companion, or significant male family member places a great deal of stress on family relationships and structure. In many families, the structure of the family must be modified to compensate for the loss of this significant individual. The responsibilities of individual family members frequently change or increase. Incarcerated men are far more dependent on their families than they were before they were imprisoned. They are dependent on their families for money, clothing, and other personal articles, such as toiletries. In addition, incarcerated African American men are not able to exercise as much influence within their families as they did prior to incarceration. This situation further illuminates their dependent and "fallen" status within their families. This experience is particularly difficult for African American men, because many already have had difficulty fulfilling the roles of breadwinner and head of the household. Researchers have argued that the inability to cope with this role strain causes many African American men to withdraw from family responsibilities and committed relationships and to engage in risky behaviors such as criminal activity (Bowman, 1989; Cazenave, 1981).

Some incarcerated males harbor unrealistic expectations regarding their family's ability to meet the men's emotional and economic needs while they are imprisoned. When family members are unable or unwilling to meet these expectations, members feel guilty and the incarcerated individual feels abandoned. This problem increases emotional and psychological tension between the incarcerated male and his family. Correctional institutions and their staffs fail to appreciate the emotional pain and anxiety African American men and their families experience when they are unable to meet each other's expectations. I have facilitated groups in state correctional institutions that were designed to help inmates, especially African American inmates, cope with being separated from their families. During group discussions on the strategies inmates use to cope with being separated from their families, many inmates stated that as soon as the separation occurred they tried to create an emotional barrier between themselves and their families. The goal of this strategy is to reduce the pain and anguish of being separated from their families. To initiate this strategy, the inmate may stage an argument over the telephone or during a visit in order to legitimize his emotional and psychological alienation from the family or significant others. Mental health professionals within correctional institutions, as well as those who serve families of incarcerated men, need to acknowledge the extreme nature of such coping strategies among African American males and develop clinical services and programs that will help them manage their feelings in a more adaptive manner.

When incarcerated African American males are married or involved in serious monogamous relationships, those relationships are subjected to a great deal of stress. The sexual frustration of both partners increases the stress level. Questions of fidelity invariably arise during the period of separation and may cause conflict between the partners. Inmates, corrections staff, and social workers have stated that the easiest and quickest way to anger or arouse an inmate is to imply or question the fidelity of his spouse or partner. Too often, however, fidelity becomes a moot point, because the stress and anxiety associated with physical separation and various related problems lead to the dissolution of the marriage or relationship. This event adds to the emotional problems of both partners, their children, and other extended family members.

Unmarried African American Males

Little research examines the impact of incarceration on the families and family relationships of unmarried African American males. In my experience, however, inmates and their families experience profound emotional, psychological, and economic problems because many single African American males perform important roles in their nuclear, extended, and non-blood-related families. They may assume the roles of breadwinner, child-care provider, and big brother and confidant for younger siblings and relatives, while contributing economic, emotional, and psychological support to grandparents and older aunts and uncles. Their absence creates a void in the lives of elderly family members.

To summarize, the incarceration of African American men has profound economic, psychological, and interpersonal consequences for their nuclear and extended families. Imprisonment is a traumatic crisis with which few families are prepared to cope. In addition, most social service agencies and correctional institutions are unprepared or unwilling to help the families of incarcerated African American males. If these families are to survive the trauma of incarceration and remain supportive of the incarcerated male, community- and prison-based family-oriented programs and services must be made available to them.

Treatment Implications

During the past decade, a number of non-profit organizations and state correctional systems have begun to develop programs and services for families of incarcerated individuals (Fishman and Cassin, 1981). Various organizations provide services to families of incarcerated individuals, such as Friends Outside and the Service League of San Mateo County in California, Terrell House in Florida, Prison Families Anonymous in New York, and the Mental Health Unit of the Kansas State Penitentiary. Services include emotional support and family counseling, transportation to and from correctional institutions for family visits, child care during visiting hours, and financial assistance.

Although these programs and services are helpful they have not been offered consistently throughout the country. Moreover, funding for services is not a high priority for correctional institutions; therefore, the services that are available are often inadequate. Moreover, even if programs are available, they may not provide services culturally appropriate to the needs and circumstances of African American men and their families. African American men are the largest group of men in this nation's state correctional systems; therefore, it is imperative that social service agencies and correctional institutions develop and implement programs and services to meet their needs and those of their families. The following types of programs or services can help African-American men and their families cope with the effects of incarceration: (1) culturally appropriate family-support groups, (2) clinical services, (3) community-based family life education programs, (4) family life education programs in correctional institutions, and (5) family case-management services.

Culturally Appropriate Family-Support Groups

Incarcerated African American men and their families need support programs that are based upon the values, attitudes, and beliefs of their African and African American cultures. A support group developed from these cultural perspectives emphasizes the importance and strength of the extended-family system, the integration of non-blood-related individuals into the blood-related family system, role flexibility, and harmony, balance, and responsibility within the family and among family members. Moreover, Afrocentric family-support groups help families become more effective African American families, not caricatures of successful European American families.

Family-support groups also must acknowledge and build upon the spirituality of African American men and their families. Spirituality, or the belief in an omnipotent, omnipresent life force that governs the universe according to basic principles plays an integral role in the everyday lives of most African American people, regardless of their religious affiliation or lack thereof (Asante, 1987; Mbiti, 1990; Nobles, 1976; Richardson, 1989). Spirituality is and always has been a source of strength for African Americans during adversity (Bennett, 1970; Huggins, 1990; Lester, 1968; Mellon, 1988). Mental health professionals need to build family-support groups on this indigenous cultural characteristic in order to enhance the effectiveness of their helping efforts. This can be accomplished, in part, by allowing group participants to express their spirituality and concerns during sessions. Opening and closing group sessions with inspirational music or songs, prayers, and poems can be used to tap into African Americans' spirituality.

Culturally appropriate support groups should also be established for the children of incarcerated males. Their needs are often neglected, particularly if the father did not live with the child before he was imprisoned. African American males traditionally maintain contact with their children, even when they are no longer married to or romantically involved with the child's mother. Thus, the child and his or her relationship with the incarcerated father suffers when the father is imprisoned. Culturally appropriate family-support groups can be established in churches, recreation centers, community-based organizations, and as special programs within local social service agencies.

Clinical Services

African American men and their families also need clinical services that address their personal problems. Psychologists, social workers, and psychiatrists have documented the need for clinical services that address the special problems of African Americans (Acosta, Yamamoto, and Evans, 1982; Boyd-Franklin, 1989; Gordon, 1970; Harper, 1973; Jackson, 1976; Jones, 1979; Shannon, 1970, 1973; Taylor, Neighbors, and Broman, 1989). Services should acknowledge and build upon the indigenous cultural strengths identified above. Moreover, such services need to help both the incarcerated African American male and his family develop adaptive, proactive responses to institutional racism and discrimination (Boyd-Franklin, 1989; Gilbert, 1974; Gochroe, 1966; Houston, 1990; Shannon, 1973; Stikes, 1972).

Daily encounters with prejudice and institutionalized racism sap the emotional and practical resources of African American individuals and families, arousing anger and frustration that may lead to violent interpersonal conflicts between family members and other persons in the community. When a family encounters a crisis, such as the incarceration of a significant family member, members may lack the emotional and practical resources necessary for coping with this new crisis. Clinical services that fail to address these basic problems maintain the status quo rather than help African American men and their families develop adaptive coping strategies (Barnes, 1972).

Prison-based clinical programs need to focus on helping incarcerated African American males develop the following: (1) a positive social and cultural identity; (2) a culturally relevant belief system that will help them survive in a hostile and racist society; (3) a sense of compassion, responsibility, and respect for their community; and (4) social supports required to overcome pessimism, despair, and a sense of hopelessness. Cultural awareness programs such as the Manning Cultural Awareness Program (King, 1992) are designed to address these issues.

Community-Based Family Life Education Programs

Families of incarcerated African American males would benefit from community-based family life education programs. The imprisonment of a family member serves as an incentive for the family to seek and accept outside intervention (Golan, 1987).

Family life education programs and services also offer these families a chance to scrutinize their strengths and weaknesses in the light of present and past problems and crises. Moreover, this type of program helps families examine the various factors that played a role in the male family member's imprisonment (Rapoport, 1970). Lastly, such programs provide opportunities for underserved populations such as African American families to address other types of problems or issues that undermine their overall functioning.

Family Life Education Programs in Correctional Institutions

Family life education programs can be initiated inside correctional institutions, thereby affording the incarcerated male the opportunity to reflect on his family life with the support of trained mental health professionals. I have facilitated short-term family-relationship groups with many incarcerated African American men. Participants state that these groups help them reevaluate their family relationships as well as cope with the emotional difficulties associated with being separated from their loved ones. Prison-based family life education groups benefit unmarried African American males by providing them with an opportunity to discuss male-female relationship issues, parenting problems, and family issues with more mature and experienced men. Young, single, African American men rarely have the opportunity to engage in these types of group experiences.

Family Case Management

Families of incarcerated African American males need assistance locating and obtaining additional sources of income and other types of practical services. Without these services, the family and the incarcerated male suffer extreme hardships that undermine family relationships and cohesion. Help in locating these services can be provided through community-based case-management services offered under the auspices of churches, fraternities, sororities, and other types of local social organizations.

Professional Education and Service Delivery

Schools of social work must not only educate students about the plight of incarcerated African American males and their families, they must provide them with the knowledge and skills required to practice effectively with this population. Most schools and departments of social work offer little content on African Americans in general and little, if any, content on the economic, social, and psychological problems of African American males. Without such knowledge, practitioners are incapable of helping African American males and their families cope with their problems. Practitioners also need to be highly skilled group workers. Group work is an appropriate intervention method because of the importance of the group experience for African Americans.

Social service agencies need to help grassroots organizations in the African American community develop indigenous community-based support programs for the families of incarcerated African American males. Community-based programs such as the Community Reentry Program in Cleveland, Ohio, help former inmates make a smooth transition back into their communities by providing counseling, job placement, and cultural education services. Such programs need to be expanded and supported by professional social work associations and local social service agencies.

References

Acosta, F. X., Yamamoto, J., and Evans, L. A. (1982). *Effective psychotherapy for low-income and minority patients*. New York: Plenum Press.

Adamson, K. (1983). Punishment after slavery: Southern state penal systems. 1865-1890. *Social Problems* 30, 555-569.

Asante, M. K. (1987). *The Afrocentric idea*. Philadelphia: Temple University Press.

Baker, L. J., Morris. B. A., and Janus, L. M. (1978). Hidden victims of crime. *Social Work* 23, 143-148.

Barnes, E. (1972). Counseling and the black student: The need for a new view. In R. L. Jones (Ed.), *Black psychology*. New York: Harper and Row.

Bennett, L. (1970). *The black mood*. New York: Barnes and Noble.

Blumstein, A. (1982). On the racial disproportionality of United States' prison populations. *Journal of Criminal Law and Criminology* 73, 1259-1282.

Bowman, P. (1989). Research perspectives on black men: Role strain and adaptation across the adult life cycle. In R. L. Jones (Ed.), *Black adult development and aging*. Berkeley, CA: Cobb and Henry.

Boyd-Franklin, N. (1989). *Black families in therapy: A multisystems approach*. New York: Guilford Press.

Brazaitis, T. J. (1991, January 4). U.S. is the world's top jailer with high crime, tough laws. *Cleveland Plain Dealer*, 1A, 11A.

Brodsky, S. L. (1974). *Families and friends of men in prison: The uncertain relationship*. Lexington, MA: Lexington Books.

Cahalan, M. (1979). Trends in incarceration in the United States since 1880: A summary of reported rates and the distribution of offenses. *Crime and Delinquency* 23, 9-41.

Cazenave, N. A. (1981). Black men in America: The quest for 'manhood.' In H. P. McAdoo (Ed.), *Black families*. Beverly Hills, CA: Sage Publications.

Christianson, S. (1981). Our black prisons. *Crime and Delinquency* 25, 365-375.

Christianson, S., and Dehais, R. (1980). *The black incarceration rate in the United States: A nationwide problem.* State University of New York Training Program in Criminal Justice Education, Graduate School of Criminal Justice, Albany, NY.

Dunbaugh, B. M. (1979). Racially disproportionate rates of incarceration in the United States. *Prison Law Monitor* 1(9), 205, 219-222.

Evangelauf, J. (1992, January 22). Minority-group enrollment at colleges rose 10 percent from 1988 to 1990, reaching record levels. *Chronicle of Higher Education,* A33, A37.

Fishman, S. H., and Cassin, C. J. M. (1981). *Services for families of offenders.* Hartford, CT: Women in Crisis.

Friedman, S., and Esselstyn, T. C. (1965). The adjustment of children of jail inmates. *Federal Probation* 29(4), 55-59.

Furman v. Georgia, 408 U.S. 238, 399, 405. (1972). (Burger C. J. dissenting).

Gilbert, O. (1974). The role of social work in black liberation. *Black Scholar* 6(4), 16-23.

Gochroe, J. S. (1966). Recognition and use of anger in Negro clients. *Social Work* 11,28-34.

Golan, N. (1987). Crisis intervention. In *Encyclopedia of social work.* Silver Spring, MD: National Association of Social Workers.

Gordon, E. (1970). Perspectives on counseling and other approaches to guided behavioral changes. *Counseling Psychologist* 2, 105-114.

Grier, W., and Cobbs, P. (1971). *Jesus bag.* New York: McGraw-Hill.

Hagan, J. (1974). Extra-legal attributes and criminal sentencing. *Law and Society Review* 8, 357-383.

Hale, D. C. (1988). Impact of mother's incarceration on entire family system: Research and recommendations. In F. E. Hagan and M. B. Sussman (Eds.), *Deviance and the family.* New York: Haworth Press.

Harper, F. (1973). What counselors must know about the social sciences of black Americans. *Journal of Negro Education* 42(2), 109-116.

Hawkins, D. B., and Jones, N. E. (1989). Black adolescents and the criminal justice system. In R. L. Jones (Ed.), *Black Adolescents.* Berkeley, CA: Cobb and Henry.

Houston, L. N. (1990). *Psychological principles and the black experience.* Lanham, MD: University Press of America.

Huggins, N. I. (1990). *Black odyssey: The African American ordeal in slavery.* New York: Vantage Books.

Jackson, G. G. (1976). The African genesis of the black perspective an helping. *Professional Psychology* 7, 292-308.

Jones, D. L. (1979). African American clients: Clinical practice issues. *Social Work* 24, 112-118.

King, A. L. O. (1992). *Reducing youth violence: An Africentric approach for correctional settings.* Paper presented at the University of Pittsburgh Public Health Social Work Institute, Pittsburgh, PA.

Lester, J. (1968). *To be a slave.* New York: Dell Publishing.

Lichtenstein, A. C., and Kroll, M. A. (1990). *The fortress economy: The economic role of the U.S. prison system.* Philadelphia: American Friends Service Committee.

Mbiti, J. S. (1990). *African religions and philosophy* (2nd ed.). Portsmouth, NH: Heinemann Educational Books.

McAdoo, H. P. (1988). Transgenerational patterns of upward mobility in African American families. In H. P. McAdoo (Ed.). *Black families* (2nd ed.). Newbury Park, CA: Sage Publications.

Mellon, J. (Ed.). (1988). *Bulwhip days: The slaves remember: An oral history.* New York: Avon Books.

Morris, P. (1965). *Prisoners and their families.* London: George Allen and Unwin.

Nagel, W. G. (1977). On behalf of a moratorium on prison construction. *Crime and Delinquency* 23, 154-172.

Newton, A. (1980). The effects of imprisonment. *Criminal Justice Abstracts* 12(1), 134-151.

Nobles, W. W. (1976). Black people in white insanity: An issue for black community mental health. *Journal of Afro-American Issues* 4(1). 21-27.

Petersilia, J. (1983). *Racial disparities in the criminal justice system.* Santa Monica, CA: Rand Corp.

Rapoport, L. (1970). Crisis intervention as a model of brief treatment. In K. W. Roberts and R. H. Nee (Eds.), *Theories of social casework.* Chicago: University of Chicago Press.

Richardson, D. M. (1989). *Let the circle be unbroken: The implications of African spirituality in the diaspora.* Trenton, NJ: The Red Sea Press.

Sack, W. H. (1977). Children of imprisoned fathers. *Psychiatry* 40,163-174.

Schneller, D. P. (1976). *The prisoners family: A study of the effects of imprisonment on the families of prisoners.* San Francisco: R and E Research Associates.

Shannon, B. (1970). Implications of white racism for social work practice. *Social Casework* 51, 270-276.

_____. (1973). The impact of racism on personality development. *Social Casework* 54, 519-525.

Showalter, D., and Jones-Williams, C. (1980). Marital and family counseling in prisons. *Social Work* 25, 224-228.

Staples, R. (1988). The black American family. In C. Mendel, W. Habenstein, and J. Wright (Eds.). *Ethnic families in America: Patterns and variations* (3rd ed.). New York: Elsevier.

Stikes, C. (1972). Culturally specific counseling: The black client. *Journal of Non-White Concerns* 1, 15-23.

Swan, L. A. (1981). *Families of black prisoners: Survival and progress.* Boston: G. K. Hall.

Taylor, R. J., Neighbors, H. W., and Broman, C. L. (1989). Evaluation by black Americans of the social service encounter during a serious personal problem. *Social Work* 34, 205-211

U.S. Department of Justice. (1989). *Correctional populations in the United Stares, 1986.* Office of Justice Programs, Bureau of Justice Statistics (NCJ-111611). Washington, D.C.: U.S. Government Printing Office.

_____. (1991a). *Correctional populations in the United States, 1989.* Office of Justice Programs, Bureau of Justice Statistics (NCJ-130-445). Washington, D.C.: U.S. Government Printing Office.

_____. (1991b). *Jail inmates, 1990.* Office of Justice Statistics Bulletin (NCJ-129756). Washington, D.C.: U.S. Government Printing Office.

_____. (1991c). *Prisoners in 1990.* Office of Justice Programs, Bureau of Justice Statistics Bulletin (NCJ-129198). Washington, D.C.: U.S. Government Printing Office.

_____. (1991d). *Race of prisoners admitted to state and federal institutions, 1926-1986.* Office of Justice Programs, Bureau of Justice Statistics (NCJ-125618). Washington, D.C.: U.S. Government Printing Office.

Zalba, S. R. (1964). *Women offenders and their families.* Los Angeles. Delmar Publishing.

Zatz, M. S. (1987). The changing forms of racial/ethnic biases an sentencing. *Journal of Research in Crime and Delinquency* 24(1), 69-92.

13

Parents in Prison: New Directions for Social Services

Creasie Finney Hairston and Patricia W. Lockett

The problems parents who are in prison face in maintaining meaningful and constructive relationships with their children and other family members have been largely ignored by social service agencies and organizations. This situation exists despite a general social services commitment to the preservation of family bonds and to the strengthening of family support systems and despite research that indicates that strong inmate-family relationships are beneficial to all parties concerned.[1]

Most parents want a better life for their children, and parents who are incarcerated are no exception. They face obstacles, however, that other parents do not typically face in seeking to achieve this goal. Incarceration is disruptive to families.[2] Prolonged absence of a parent from the home not only threatens family cohesion but also puts excessive strain on parent-child relationships. Participation in family living on release from prison, a stressful situation even under ideal conditions, is even more difficult when there has been little contact between the prisoner and his or her family during the prison term. When these factors are combined with an absence of effective approaches for helping inmates fulfill their parental roles and commitments and a steadily increasing prison population, it is obvious that large numbers of children and families are at risk.

Developing Parental Skills

In recognition of the problems created by the separation of parent and child by prison walls and in recognition of the desire of many inmates to be involved in a positive way in their children's upbringing, residents of the

Tennessee State Penitentiary submitted a proposal to the prison administration for a program to teach parenting skills relevant for the prison population. As a result, in 1981, a program offering family support services was started at the prison. Known as "Parenting in Prison," this program has developed into an innovative and unique approach for strengthening families and developing parental skills and commitments during a father's imprisonment.

The major purpose of Parents in Prison is to help inmates work toward ensuring better lives for their children and themselves. Through a series of educational activities and special events, the program seeks to increase participants' knowledge of child development, effective parenting styles and techniques, and family communication patterns; to strengthen inmate-family relationships during and following incarceration; and to increase inmates' understanding of the impact of incarceration and absence from the family on children and other family members.

In addition to objectives directed toward the program's participants, the program seeks to develop community awareness of the needs of incarcerated persons and their families during and following the incarceration period and to develop community support for efforts that address these needs.

Structure

Parents in Prison is an inmate organization officially sanctioned by the Tennessee Department of Correction. Leadership is provided by a 15- to 20-member Central Coordinating Committee. The committee, composed of inmates, is formally structured with officers and subcommittees, all of which have specific duties

The committee initiates, plans, coordinates, and implements all program activities; recruits volunteers and program participants; disseminates program information; develops resource materials; identifies new service needs; and evaluates program activities. Primary planning takes place at weekly meetings of the committee, and ongoing planning and program implementation are carried out through the subcommittee structure.

An advisory board consisting of interested individuals and representatives of community agencies serves as the community sponsor for the program. The board's primary function is to promote the Parents in Prison mission outside the prison walls. To accomplish this, the board meets with "free world" (i.e., non-inmate) groups and Department of Correction administration staff on behalf of the organization and identifies and obtains from the community the resources needed to carry out programs. Board members also provide consultation and technical assistance to the committee in priority setting and program planning and are involved, as appropriate, in program implementation.

The institutional sponsor, a Department of Correction staff person, has major responsibility for the coordination and facilitation of all matters internal to the prison. For example, the sponsor assists the committee in processing requests to the prison administration, handling organizational funds, obtaining prison resources needed to carry out activities, and facilitating volunteer visits and correspondence.

Program Components

Four major components make up the program: home study courses, structured classroom courses, a monthly special event/rap session, and special projects.

The home study courses are four correspondence courses that are offered sequentially on an ongoing basis. Inmates who enroll in the courses are sent weekly lessons—reading materials and related questions—by messenger mail. The content of the courses, "Children: One to Ten," "Teenagers Today," "Raising an Emotionally Mature Child," and "Childhood Comes First," focuses on ways to better understand and deal with children. Each of the home study courses is available to men in administrative segregation, including those on death row, and to inmates in the general prison population.

Three structured classroom courses of nine weeks each: "Understanding Your Child," "Workshop on Stress," and "Communicating with Your Child" are offered several times per year to men who are preparing to leave the institution and return to their families. These courses use a small discussion group and an experiential learning format. The focus is on the effects of long separation on the child and immediate family, ways fathers can become involved in a positive manner in their children's lives, and recognition and positive management of problems related to reentering family life after a period of incarceration.

Participants who successfully complete the courses are awarded certificates. A copy of each inmate's certificate is placed in his institutional file as an indication of participation in constructive and meaningful activities and is usually presented to him at one of the monthly special events.

A monthly special event/rap session featuring guest speakers is provided for the general prison population. The speakers are community volunteers whose services and programs are relevant to the Parents in Prison mission. A variety of family and parental topics are addressed and discussed during this two-hour event. Topics such as self-defeating behavior, domestic violence, labeling, and stress management are presented. These events are publicized by the distribution of flyers to the entire population and through posters placed in areas such as the dining hall and library.

The rap sessions are follow-ups to the monthly event. They provide an opportunity for inmates to discuss their own experiences in relationship to the special event presentation. Attention is directed toward helping inmates identify the impact that these experiences have on their attitudes, expectations, and behavior as parents and the impact that their behavior has on their wives and children.

Throughout the year, the program sponsors special projects that emphasize family cohesion and support and the prevention of child abuse and neglect. These include, but are not limited to, displays in the prison library of books on child abuse and families, distribution of free pamphlets on parenting to inmates and their families, and repair and upkeep of visiting-area playground equipment. A Christmas banquet and summer picnic for program participants, participants' families, and community volunteers provide opportunities for family interactions in a more informal setting.

Innovative Features

Parents in Prison builds on existing knowledge and techniques but is unique in several respects. The following list illustrates the innovative features of the program:

1. The target population is fathers. Although the majority of parents who are in prison are fathers, the few programs that exist for parents who are incarcerated usually focus on mothers.
2. The major thrust is the strengthening of families rather than the reason for incarceration. Emphasis is placed on how inmates, despite their incarceration, can become better fathers and enable their children to lead better lives.
3. The program is a collaborative community, institutional, and inmate effort that takes place within the prison.
4. The program is open to the entire prison population. Diverse activities and a flexible format allow widespread participation that would not ordinarily be possible in a prison setting.
5. The program enables inmates to develop and utilize leadership skills that can be used for successful functioning in the community. This is particularly true with respect to Coordinating Committee members, who provide leadership for the program. Responsible participation by inmates in program activities also supports their development of general skills that can strengthen responsible action as parents and as family members.
6. The program uses a time-tested adult education model, home study courses, to teach parent education. The unique factor, however, is that it has developed this model, including procedures for recruitment, dissemination, and evaluation, for use within the prison setting.
7. The program utilizes community volunteers in traditional and nontraditional capacities. Volunteers teach courses, conduct seminars, prepare public relations materials, develop proposals, develop courses, and obtain resources. In contrast to traditional volunteer-led activity in prisons, the volunteers work with the inmates, often under their direction.
8. The program is cost-effective. Inmate and community volunteers carry out most activities, thereby negating the need for a large number of paid

staff. The Parents in Prison program model can, in other words, be implemented by inmates working with community groups and can be carried out with a small budget.

Implications

Several indicators point to the fact that Parents in Prison is a successful program and that it has implications of national importance. The program, for example, has expanded from its beginning as one minicourse on parenting skills in 1981 to the diverse program elements described here. This growth has occurred despite changes in the prison administration, turnover in inmate residents, and the closing of the community agency that served as the first community sponsor.

At the time of writing, over 400 inmates had successfully completed home study or classroom courses or both and had demonstrated, through formal course evaluation procedures, increased knowledge of child development and positive parenting techniques Two-thirds of the participants said that they shared the course materials with family members and other inmates and over 90 percent stated, in postcourse evaluations, that the courses had been beneficial to them. Several inmates reported increased and improved contact with their children and families.

An inmate provided an illustration of the direct benefits of the program when he said,

> Being an incarcerated parent, I have long wondered about questions concerning my child, such as what to tell my son when he asks why I am in prison and when will I be coming home. These questions and answers are being addressed in this program.

Further evidence of Parents in Prison's potential as a major new service delivery model is the recognition that the program has received from local, state, and national organizations, groups, and individuals. Among these are Ray Helfer, a pioneer in child abuse prevention; Yale University's Bush Center for Child Development; and the National Committee for Child Abuse.[3]

In summary, Parents in Prison represents an important new program direction in the area of family support services. The service delivery model provides a challenging opportunity for social workers to work with and in behalf of a long-neglected population on its commitment to strengthening families.

Notes

1. For studies in this area, see N. Holt and D. Miller. *Explorations of Inmate-Family Relationships* (Sacramento: California Department of Corrections, 1972); S. L. Brodsky, *Families and Friends of Men in Prison* (Toronto, Canada: D. C. Heath &

Company, 1975); A. Peck and M. E. Edwards. "Father-Children Groups in Prison Settings." *Probation and Parole* 9 (Fall 1977): 31-38; K. Nash. "Family Interventions: Implications for Corrections." *Corrective and Social Psychiatry and Journal of Behavior Technology, Methods, and Therapy* 27, No. 4 (1981): 158-166; and A. Swan. *Families of Black Prisoners: Survival and Progress* (Boston: G. K. Hall & Co., 1981).

2.   For studies in this area, see D. P. Schneller. *The Prisoner's Family: A Study of the Effects of Imprisonment on the Families of Prisoners* (San Francisco: R. and E. Research Associates, 1978); L. J. Bakker, B. A. Morris, and L. M. Janus. "Hidden Victims of Crime." *Social Work* 23 (March 1978): 143-148; S. Sutherland-Fox. "Families in Crisis: Reflections on the Children and Families of the Offender and the Offended." *International Journal of Offender Therapy and Comparative Criminology* 25, No. 3 (1982): 83-88; and Swan, *Families of Black Prisoners.*

3.   The following are publications in which Parents in Prison has been featured: "Termination of Parental Rights: The Incarcerated Parent." *Legal Responses: Child Advocacy and Protection* 3 (Summer 1982); "Helping Parents in Prison." *National Committee for Prevention of Child Abuse, 1982 Annual Report* (Chicago: NCPCA, 1982); *Working Papers #1: Family and Corrections Network* (Waynesboro, VA: FCN, November 1983); "Parents in Prison Project." *Programs to Strengthen Families* (New Haven, CT: Yale University and Family Resource Coalition, 1984); and C. Bartholomew, "Inmate Fathers Are Still Parents." *Nashville Banner,* January 8, 1983, Sec. B, p. 2.

14

The Endangerment of African American Men: An Appeal for Social Work Action

Paula Allen-Meares and Sondra Burman

We live in a nation strained by racism, hostility, and hatred. Our communities and neighborhoods are overcome by violence, fear, and apathy. Our homes, which were once considered safe havens, have now become the sites of increasing acting out of frustration and anger. Due to inequities, oppressive conditions, and uncontrollable stresses, individuals are turning against themselves, their loved ones, and others to vent their feelings of helplessness and hopelessness. Many African American men are especially caught up in this cycle of violent behaviors and victimization and consequently are becoming an endangered species (Gibbs, 1984, 1988; Staples, 1987). The adverse consequences of this cycle—including major injury and death—will affect the future of African American men, their families, and generations to come. Society's level of concern says much about us as a nation.

Many studies have reported on the extent of violence in the African American community, citing alarming statistics and predictions. Relatively high victimization rates of violent crimes have been reported for individuals who are African American, male, poor, young, or single. According to the Bureau of Justice Statistics (1985), African American men have an unusually high likelihood of being murdered; African Americans are more than five times as likely to be the victims of homicide as white people (Hawkins, 1986). Homicide is the leading cause of death of African American men between ages 15 and 34, and since 1960, the suicide rate for African American men between ages 15 and 24 has tripled (Gibbs, 1988). In 1992, of the 23,760 homicide victims reported, 50 percent were African American and 48 percent were white, a disproportionate amount considering that African Americans are only 11 percent of the population.

Eighty-four percent of violent crimes perpetrated against African Americans were by African Americans (Bureau of Justice Statistics, 1990). Ninety percent of those arrested for homicide were men; 55 percent (10,728) were African American, and 43 percent (8,466) were white (U.S. Department of Justice, 1993). In 1990, African Americans were 35.7 percent of the prison population, compared with 50 percent for white people (Criminal Justice Institute, 1991). These figures are startling but do not examine the structural forces that engender crime: inadequate education and job training, unemployment and underemployment, and the inequitable distribution of wealth and power (Seidman and Rappaport, 1986).

Because the justice system places a higher value on white men than on African American men, the latter have had disproportionately higher incarceration and death penalty rates (Poussaint, 1983). Investigations of crimes against African Americans are given low priority. Crimes against white people are more stringently punished. Excessive force, police brutality, harassment, and false arrests against African Americans are widespread (Feagin, 1986). As Radelet and Vandiver (1986) pointed out, "Equality for blacks has not yet been achieved in American society, least of all in the criminal justice system. The idea that all of us are born with an equal chance of eventually dying in the electric chair remains a myth" (p. 189).

Despite the risks of school failure, family estrangement, homicidal violence, and stress-related illnesses that beset African American men from the vulnerable underclass, there is a growing number of middle-class African Americans who excel in family, community, and national leadership roles (Bowman, 1989). Since 1970, the number of African Americans earning over $35,000 a year has risen by almost one-third. Yet there was also a general decline in middle-class incomes between 1970 and 1984, resulting in an increase in lower-income families (Malveaux, 1988). Thus, the gap between economically disadvantaged and middle-class African Americans is growing. A vast majority of African Americans are excluded from the economic and political participation that would improve their standard of living. This loss of human resources and talents to the economy is the high cost of racism (Tidwell, 1991).

Despite the growth in the African American middle class, there continues to be a marked differential in the incomes and poverty levels of African Americans and white people in this country. According to the U.S. Department of Commerce (1992), African American families had a median income of $21,550, whereas the median income of white families was $37,780. Thirty-three percent of African Americans were living in poverty, compared with 11 percent of white people; and African Americans were more than twice as likely as white people to be among the working poor.

Why should the profession of social work be concerned by these staggering data? Is there cause for alarm and justification for taking action to alleviate the conditions and circumstances that contribute to the high-risk status and demise of people in our midst? This chapter attempts to answer these questions by presenting a history of events that led to the current crisis for African American men who have underachieved and lack the opportunities, skills, and power to rise above their places in society.

Institutional Racism

Despite equal opportunity laws and affirmative action policies, many African Americans are struggling on a day-to-day basis. Unemployment in the African American community continues to rise, female-headed families on public welfare live at bare' subsistence levels, and children are being victimized as the poorest of the poor, with little hope of surmounting their essentially predetermined destinies. These conditions arose from years of deprivation, oppression, and bias, exacerbated by institutional racism that goes unrecognized by the dominant forces at large; contemporary racism is much more subtle than the blatant exclusionary practices of the past (Tidwell, 1991).

Institutional racism is a product of the societal arrangements and structures that exclude African Americans and other people of color from necessary resources and power that would establish the determination to change their oppressed conditions (Pinderhughes, 1989). Public schools fail to provide them with satisfactory educations and marketable skills (Staples, 1987). The discrimination that exists in jobs, housing, and the availability of health and social services undermines the ability to gain control of self and community (Morales, 1981). Inequality and economic stagnation, inflamed by an enduring history of oppression and institutional racism, have fueled a sense of outrage at a system that promises, but does not deliver, opportunity for all.

According to Feagin (1986), "The end of slavery as a legal condition did not end the subordination of black Americans" (p. 180). Although almost 130 years have passed since the 13th Amendment to the Constitution abolished slavery, discriminatory practices and oppressive conditions have continued to relegate a vast majority of African Americans to a form of imposed submission through extreme poverty, exclusion from job opportunities that would provide security and stability, and the denigration of pride in self and the African American culture. African Americans are still attempting to obtain *basic* human and civil rights that were legally but immorally confiscated with the infamous Dred Scott decision of 1857. These elements have contributed to the devaluation of African American lives both outside of and within the African American community.

Scholars have argued that the devaluation of African Americans and their culture has resulted in psychological scarring, violence, and victimization. In reporting on black-on-black homicide, Poussaint (1983) remarked, "Institutional racist practices place a positive value on whiteness and a negative one on Blackness.... Many of the problems in the Black community are related to institutional racism, which fosters a chronic lack of Black self-respect, predisposing many poor Blacks to 'behave self-destructively and with uncontrollable rage" (pp. 163, 166). Despair, low self-esteem, and rage become forces of destruction, homicide, and suicide. An adolescent who lives in poverty and sees his father unemployed and the family suffer, and who is surrounded by destitution, disparagement, murder, and crime, is vulnerable to striking out against others and himself. Survival and optimistic life chances are not part of his destiny without major endemic and societal changes. And these are not in his foreseeable future.

A devalued status, racial stereotypes, and high crime rates have led to the societal perception of violence as "normal" in African American communities and families (Hawkins, 1987). Yet this image belies the historical facts of close-knit and protective kin that have survived despite forced separations and intolerable circumstances.

The African American Family

Franklin (1988) poignantly stated, "The family is one of the strongest and most important traditions in the black community" (p. 23). This family strength was continually demonstrated by the mutual support provided by early slaves to rise above excessive abuses and cruelties. Freed slaves searched frantically for their divided loved ones. Although migration to the urban North temporarily separated families, many were reunited to maintain the strong bonds of nuclear and extended kinships. Even through the Great Depression of the 1930s, the typical family was cared for by two parents (Gutman, 1976). As late as the 1960s, 75 percent of African American families were headed by a husband and wife.

But through the years, the forces of racial practices, policies, and attitudes weakened the family fabric (Franklin, 1988). By the 1980s, there were more than 1.5 million African American female-headed families in the United States, resulting in poverty for these families (Baker, 1988). Nevertheless, there has been an ongoing debate about the causative factors of the problems and disintegration of these families. Thirty years ago, Moynihan (1965) perceived a matriarchal structure that was destructive; however, Bell, Bland, Houston, and Jones (1983) argued against the position that female-dominated families led to inadequate, irresponsible, and absent fathers. Actually, most African American families were egalitarian, and spouses shared in decision making, negating the myth of the black matriarchal family system (Staples, 1982).

Policy Issues

In a caustic report on the social welfare system, Murray (1984) blamed the deteriorating conditions of African Americans and poor people on expanded federal policies of the 1960s. His solution was scrap existing assistance programs such as Aid to Families with Dependent Children, Medicaid, food stamps, unemployment insurance, worker's compensation, subsidized housing, and disability insurance. His solution was to put working-age people to work. The supposition was that without these subsidies, people would become more responsible and motivated to seek employment. Yet several researchers challenged these concepts and reform measures. Sampson (1987) reported that family disruption was created by exceedingly high African American poverty levels and male joblessness rather than liberal welfare policies. Stoesz and Karger (1990) commented, "If workers are unable to earn enough to be economically self-sufficient, how can welfare recipients be expected to become economically independent of public assistance?" (p. 147).

Murray's (1984) assumptions do not fit the reality of many African American experiences. He stated,

> Our schools know how to educate students who want to be educated. Our industries know how to find productive people and reward them. Our police know how to protect people who are ready to cooperate in their own protection. Our system of justice knows how to protect the rights of individuals who know what their rights are.... In short, American society is very good at reinforcing the investment of an individual in himself. (p. 234)

For those who realize the poor quality of many urban public schools, the severe lack of jobs, and the discriminatory practices of many police officers, it is difficult to comprehend that ours is a system of justice protecting the rights of all citizens. Unless equitable and fair practices materialize, and sufficient training and employment are readily available, federal welfare policies should not be made the scapegoat for the harsh conditions and corresponding behaviors experienced by the disenfranchised. Pessimism and feelings of powerlessness and hopelessness are the consequences of generational deprivation and bias that culminate in the destruction of the individual, families, and society at large. These factors have been especially devastating for African American men.

The Dilemma of the African American Man

What happens to an individual who perceives the larger society as hostile, intolerant, and uncaring; opportunities for survival and advancement as limited; and little hope of rising above the status quo? There can be little doubt that depression, frustration, anger, and pessimism can result. Self-esteem and self-worth are violated, and feelings of powerlessness and helplessness to combat a society where one does not "fit in" can play havoc on thought processes and emotional states. The consequences of deleterious and demeaning experiences can create a climate for alienation, unrestrained rage, physical assaults, homicides, and suicides. Lives that could have been productive are lost.

According to Sampson (1987), "[Historically] there is nothing inherent in black culture that is conducive to crime" (p. 348). It is the feelings of powerlessness to alter the economic deprivation and isolation that create the negative behaviors evidenced in many African American men. Unemployment and the lack of marketable skills and adequate incomes can lead to crime and imprisonment; alcohol and drugs are a means of escape from the awareness of "their superfluous existence in a country that devalues and fears them" (Staples, 1987: 10). Williams (1984) summed up the results most succinctly: "poverty, in addition to racial inequality, provides 'fertile soil' for criminal violence" (p. 289).

The ultimate tragedy is that African Americans who experience these conditions feel trapped in an unalterable life situation (Hendin, 1978). As Harvey (1986) expressed, "There is a definite relationship between the inability of young Black men to find employment; the increasing number of female-headed households in the Black community; the economic and psychological trauma endured by the Black poor; and the high rates of homicidal activity among young, impoverished Black males" (p. 164). The results are the endangerment of a people, a culture, and the constructive search for a better quality of life. Actions that convey racism and discrimination create apprehensions in the African American community. Parents fear that their sons will not be respected, will be feared because of the color of their skin, and will be "beaten down" (Boyd-Franklin, 1992). Their children often fail in schools and drop out, reacting to a sense of failure with disruptive, violent, and self-destructive behaviors (Allen-Meares, 1990; Comer, 1985). These stark realities sow the seeds of disillusionment and projections of hostility and animosity toward an unrelenting society that restricts upward mobility and success. Certainly, the availability of guns and other lethal weapons and media coverage of violence in various forms can cause emulation of aggressive behaviors that counteract frustration and anger.

Social workers, policymakers, and other professionals must heed the warnings of the disruptiveness engendered by years of subjugation, prejudice, and inequities. Already these factors have produced an alarming rate of destruction to individuals, families, communities, and the society at large.

Social Work's Role

Social work interventions have focused on problems in living based on a person-in-environment paradigm. Our historical mission has been to care and advocate for the disadvantaged, disenfranchised, and oppressed—those who are left behind and face an alien world and daily struggle. Our goals have been to enhance functioning and coping, to provide services and resources, and to act as a bridge between the individual and organizational systems. It behooves us to take action to right unfairness and injustice and to seek to improve the quality of life of those in need.

Yet when viewing the inequities and social conditions that afflict many African American men and their families, there appears to be a discomforting silence from the social work profession. Interventions focus on individual pathology and antisocial activities, rather than the unfair and intolerable practices of larger systems and institutions that create dissension and corresponding malfunctioning. It is for this reason that social workers are thought to be agents of social control instead of advocates for social change.

In acknowledging the high-risk status and problems of African American men, social work must address stresses in the environment. Discriminatory practices and economic disparity reveal the plight of many families who are victims of their consequences. Inequities based on race and socioeconomic status, which limit economic, social, and political power, resources, and opportunities, spawn division and despair, ultimately creating a society of chaos and decline. If we look the other way, this trend will persist.

Implications for Practice

The profession needs to develop program strategies that strengthen social support networks and resources in the community. The church, which has been a mainstay in the lives of African Americans, should be included in an integral role of support and assistance (Gary and Leashore, 1982). The church has taken on responsibility for helping teenage parents, fighting alcohol and drug abuse, and providing aid to indigent and ill people (Lincoln, 1989).

Outreach services that assist with financial and legal aid, housing, health care, job training, and employment possibilities will alleviate intolerable pressures and concerns. And policies ensuring gainful educational and employment opportunities, satisfactory wage scales, adequate benefits, and the elimination of discrimination and harassment are mandatory to deter pent-up aggression and restrictive and deteriorating lifestyles.

Society's discriminatory practices and negative valuations that reflect inferiority and inadequacy often yield a pervasive powerlessness in taking charge and directing one's own life (Solomon, 1976). To rectify this, emphasis must be placed on empowerment and personal control and the recognition of innate and cultural strengths. Thomas (1987) reported how many African Americans have found solutions to their enforced conditions that can be instructive to practitioners who seek to alter perspectives, attitudes, and motivation toward self-help and community interventions. Elements of these solutions include

- Believing that one is a worthy, useful human being with a place of dignity in society.
- Developing a sense of Afrocentric solidarity…strong bonds to deal with stress and a variety of environmental events.
- Eliminating pervasive helplessness, racial inferiority, and other victimizing social liabilities…a shift in social focus to what blacks can do for themselves (pp. 159-160).

To provide impetus for change, factors that affect self-esteem, self-image, and self-worth must be addressed. Pride in self and heritage is necessary for healthy functioning. Active supports from role models, caregivers, and policymakers can make a difference for young and adult males and their families who are trying to persevere under extreme duress.

Proposed Model for Activism

The authors' proposed model for activism derives many of its concepts and strategies from the work of other social work scholars, researchers, and practitioners. It is basically a model that is attuned to the history, culture, and values of African Americans and particularly to the current state of social and economic affairs.

Morales (1981) described a form of activist practice that takes into consideration an awareness of racial, ethnic, and political factors in providing services to assist with social problems in Third World communities. This type of practice entails the active recruitment of bicultural and bilingual students and faculty in schools of social work and practitioners in social services agencies and the development of proactive intervention strategies such as advocacy, empowerment, and class action social work. The latter requires close, interdisciplinary collaboration (for example, between schools and the legal and health professions) on behalf of client welfare.

Trader (1977) reminded us that we must not ignore the realities of external environments of oppressed groups. Historical and current societal conditions must be taken into account when deriving theoretical frameworks and models to guide practice. Rather than concentrating on pathology and internal, psychic change, it is necessary to seek changes in the outer society. The goals of treatment are to learn the skills of independent and productive control of self through obtaining essential resources and eliminating external constraints. Therefore, the practitioner acts as the mediator between systems to promote individual and environmental change.

Devore and Schlesinger (1991) remarked, "The interface between private troubles and public issues is an intrinsic aspect of most approaches to social work practice" (p. 175). Their model of ethnically sensitive practice calls for attention to both micro and macro issues and their consequences, including the results of racism, discrimination, and poverty. Knowledge of the community—its power structure, available resources, services, and networks—and an understanding of the culture and responses to traumas, conflicts, and tensions from an "insider" perspective are important to setting the stage for both micro and macro interventions.

Professional activism initially requires a firm foundation in schools of social work that can enlighten the future practitioner about its relevance and importance. Courses in ethnic diversity that focus on the historical and current context of cultures, problems, and concerns should be a part of both policy and intervention studies. A greater emphasis on the need for activism on behalf of oppressed and disadvantaged people should be incorporated into the curriculum. This information will provide basic knowledge and understanding of conditions alien to most students. Educational systems do have the power and influence to shape ideas, activities, and practice directions.

Social workers should seek strategies to address policies and practices that promote advocacy, social justice, social change, and knowledge and education for empowerment while activating change at macro and micro levels. The profession must raise awareness at the national and local (community) levels of the severity of the problems that African American men and their families face. Active leadership is needed to correct economic and social inequities and deprivations. When employment is so critical to survival and a sense of usefulness, more efforts must be made for equitable hiring practices in multiethnic communities. Local high schools, trade schools, and community colleges need more outreach in communities to help residents recognize what is available to improve education and job skills. Social workers must have greater participation in illuminating discrimination and harassment in the workplace and all institutions and agencies that serve people. Community organizing to fight crime and vulnerability to alcohol and drug abuse is necessary. Helping people obtain adequate health care, including providing transportation and reducing the waiting and red tape involved, will save and improve lives.

A primary function of the activist role will be working closely with the African American community as a team member to gain an in-depth understanding of indigenous support networks and strengths, actions that must be taken to resolve specific problems, and the approachable target systems that will be the focus of change. The numerous roles will include facilitating, mediating, and instructing at all levels to tie together the goals of the community and the individuals who are an integral part of its stability. In many cases, community programs will need to be developed and those in place will need to be expanded to provide additional resources and services. Programs such as Head Start and aid to the elderly population and ill people should reach more individuals. Key mediating institutions, such as the church and voluntary associations, that have had positive influences on African Americans should be provided more supportive, collaborative interventions from the social work profession. But at all levels, active participation of community members will be commensurate with achieving empowerment and ownership of the ventures.

The aim of the activist is to provide hope for constructive change so that optimism can replace despair and concrete solutions can alleviate daily struggles. Change will provide the motivation for individual striving and accomplishment and will reduce what Gary and Leashore (1982) called "the high-risk status of African-American males in this society" (p. 57) that endangers them and their families in the present and future. Activism at the community, state, and national levels is the key to successful functioning and the promise of equality for all. And we, as social workers, can make a difference through a vision, a dedication, and a commitment.

References

Allen-Meares, P. (1990). Educating black youths: The unfulfilled promise of equality. *Social Work* 35, 283-286.

Baker, F. M. (1988). Afro-Americans. In L. Comas-Diaz and E. H. Griffith (Eds.), *Clinical guidelines in cross-cultural mental health*. New York: John Wiley and Sons.

Bell, C. C., Bland, I. J., Houston, E., and Jones, B. B. (1983). Enhancement of knowledge and skills for the psychiatric treatment of black populations. In J. C. Chunn, P. J. Dunston, and F. Ross-Sheriff (Eds.), *Mental health and people of color: Curriculum development and change*. Washington, D.C.: Howard University Press.

Bowman, P. J. (1989). Research perspectives on black men: Role strain and adaptation across the life cycle. In R. L. Jones (Ed.), *Black adult development and aging*. Berkeley, CA: Cobb and Henry.

Boyd-Franklin, N. (1992, July). *African-American families in therapy*. Paper presented at a workshop sponsored by the National Association of Social Workers, Springfield, Illinois.

Bureau of Justice Statistics. (1985). *Risk of violent crime* (U.S. Department of Justice Special Report). Washington, D.C.: U.S. Government Printing Office.

_____. (1990). *Criminal victimization in the United States, 1990* (U.S. Department of Justice Special Report). Washington, D.C.: U.S. Government Printing Office.

Comer, J. P. (1985). Black violence and public policy. In L A. Curtis (Ed.), *American violence and public policy*. New Haven, CT: Yale University Press.

Criminal Justice Institute. (1991). *The correctional yearbook, 1990*. Washington, D.C.: U.S. Government Printing Office.

Devore, W., and Schlesinger, E. G. (1991). *Ethnic-sensitive social work practice* (3rd ed.). New York: Macmillan.

Feagin, J. (1986). Slavery unwilling to die: The background of black oppression in the 1980s. *Journal of Black Studies* 17,173-200.

Franklin, J. H. (1988). A historical note on black families. In H. P. McAdoo (Ed.), *Black families* (2nd ed.). Newbury Park, CA: Sage Publications.

Gary, L. E., and Leashore, B. R. (1982). High-risk status of black men. *Social Work* 27, 54-58.

Gibbs, J. T. (1984). Black adolescents and youth: An endangered species. *American Journal of Orthopsychiatry* 54, 6-21.

_____. (1988). *Young, black, and male in America: An endangered species.* Dover, MA: Auburn House.

Gutman, H. (1976). *The black family in slavery and freedom.* New York: Pantheon.

Harvey, W. B. (1986). Homicide among young black adults: Life in the subculture of exasperation. In D. F. Hawkins (Ed.), *Homicide among black Americans.* Lanham, MD: University Press of America.

Hawkins, D. F. (Ed.). (1986). *Homicide among black Americans.* Lanham, MD: University Press of America.

_____. (1987). Devalued lives and racial stereotypes: Ideological barriers to the prevention of family violence among blacks. In R. L. Hampton (Ed.), *Violence in the black family.* Lexington, MA: Lexington Books/D.C. Heath.

Hendin, H. (1978). Suicide: The psychosocial dimension. *Suicide and Life-Threatening Behavior* 8, 99-117.

Lincoln, C. E. (1989). Knowing the black church: What it is and why. In J. Dewart (Ed.), *State of black America 1989.* New York: National Urban League.

Malveaux, J. (1988). The economic statuses of black families. In H. P. McAdoo (Ed.), *Black families* (2nd ed.). Newbury Park, CA: Sage Publications.

Morales, A. (1981). Social work with third-world people. *Social Work* 26, 45-51.

Moynihan, D. (1965). *The Negro family: The case for national action.* Washington, D.C.: U.S. Department of Labor.

Murray, C. (1984). *Losing ground.* New York: Basic Books.

Pinderhughes, E. (1989). *Understanding race, ethnicity, and power.* New York: Free Press.

Poussaint, A. F. (1983). Black-on-black homicide: A psychological—political perspective. *Victimology* 8, 161-169.

Radelet, M. L., and Vandiver, M. (1986). Race and capital punishment: An overview of the issues. In D. F. Hawkins (Ed.), *Homicide among black Americans.* Lanham, MD: University Press of America.

Sampson, R. J. (1987). Urban black violence: The effect of male joblessness and family disruption. *American Journal of Sociology* 93, 348-382.

Seidman, E., and Rappaport, J. (Eds.). (1986). *Redefining social problems.* New York: Plenum Press.

Solomon, B. B. (1976). *Black empowerment: Social work in oppressed communities.* New York: Columbia University Press.

Staples, R. (1982). *Black masculinity: The black male's role in American society.* San Francisco: Black Scholar Press.

_____. (1987). Black male genocide: A final solution to the race problem in America. *Black Scholar* 18(3), 2-11.

Stoesz, D., and Karger, H. J. (1990). Welfare reform: From illusion to reality. *Social Work* 35, 141-147.

Thomas, C. W. (1987). Pride and purpose as antidotes to black homicidal violence. *Journal of the National Medical Association* 79, 155-160.

Tidwell, B. J. (1991). More than a moral issue: The costs of American racism in the 1990s. *Urban League Review* 14(2), 9-28.

Trader, H. P. (1977). Survival strategies for oppressed minorities. *Social Work* 22, 10-13.

U.S. Department of Commerce. (1992). *The black population in the United States.* Washington, D.C.: Economics and Statistics Administration.

U.S. Department of Justice. (1993). *Crime in the U.S. 1992.* Washington, D.C.: Federal Bureau of Investigation.

Williams, K. R. (1984). Economic sources of homicide: Reestimating the effects of poverty and inequality. *American Sociological Review* 49, 283-289.

15

The Crisis of the Young African American Male and the Criminal Justice System[1]

Marc Mauer

Introduction

In recent years policy attention regarding the crisis of the African American male has focused on a variety of areas in which African American males have suffered disproportionately from social ills. These have included education, housing, employment, and health care, among others. Perhaps in no other area, though, have these problems been displayed as prominently as in the realm of crime and the criminal justice system.

African Americans have been affected in this area in two significant regards. First, African Americans are more likely to be victimized by crime than are other groups. This creates a set of individual and community problems that impede upon other areas of productive activity. Second, the dramatic rates at which African American males have come under some form of criminal justice supervision has created a complex set of consequences that affect not only individual victims and offenders, but families and communities as well.

This chapter will explore the current status of African American males within the criminal justice system and consider projections for the future should current policies continue. It will also assess the factors that have created such high levels of criminal justice control. Finally, it will provide a set of recommendations for public policy that would help to alleviate the disastrous circumstances that currently prevail while having a more constructive impact on public safety.

Overview of the Status of African American
Males and the Criminal Justice System

A wealth of statistical information is now available to document what a walk through virtually any urban courthouse or state prison displays quite graphically. A courtroom observer in New York, Detroit, Atlanta, Los Angeles or any other major city will witness a sea of black and brown faces sitting at the defense table or shackled together on the bus transporting prisoners from the jail for court hearings. In the prison visiting room, mothers, wives, and girlfriends who have often traveled several hours by bus or car wait to see their loved ones in stuffy and noisy atmospheres with little privacy.

Living conditions within the prison system have never been pleasant or comfortable, but a harsher political climate now threatens to undo many of the reforms achieved through litigation and political advocacy over the past several decades. Congressional action in 1994 prohibited inmates from receiving Pell grants to continue higher education studies, while many states have passed their own legislation denying inmates access to various forms of recreation or cultural activities. Much of this legislation has been not only mean-spirited but counterproductive as well, by limiting prisoners' access to the acquisition of skills that might be used constructively upon their return to the community.

These conditions now disproportionately affect African American males and other minorities due to their overwhelming numbers within the criminal justice system. The state of these disproportions can be seen in the following:

- 46 percent of prison inmates nationally are African American, compared to their 12 percent share of the overall population.[2]
- Nearly one in three (32 percent) black males in the age group 20-29 is under some form of criminal justice supervision on any given day—either in prison or jail, or on probation or parole.[3]
- As of 1995, one in fourteen (7 percent) adult black males was incarcerated in prison or jail on any given day, representing a doubling of this rate from 1985. The 1995 figure for white males was 1 percent.
- A black male born in 1991 has a 29 percent chance of spending time in prison at some point in his life. The figure for white males is 4 percent, and for Hispanics, 16 percent.

While African American males have been the most severely affected demographic group within the criminal justice system, other minorities have also been disproportionately affected. Hispanics now constitute 16 percent of the prison population nationally, compared to their 13 percent share of the total population. The number of Hispanic inmates increased by 67 percent in the period 1990-2000. Women, and particularly minority women, while incarcerated in smaller numbers than men, have also experienced dramatic growth in recent years. The number of women in the prison system increased by 418 percent from 1980 to 1995, compared to a rise of 236 percent for men. Black women are now incarcerated at a rate six times that of white women.

Toward an Understanding of the Over-representation of African American Males in the Criminal Justice System

In 1954, at the time of the historic *Brown v. Board of Education* decision, African Americans constituted about 30 percent of persons admitted to state and federal prisons. That figure should have been disturbing since it was substantially higher than the black share of the national population. But that proportion has now increased still more dramatically, to the point where blacks represent half of all prison admissions.

This development would seem to be rather odd considering the changes that have taken place in American society over the past half-century. The nation has experienced the civil rights movement and economic opportunities have opened up for many historically disadvantaged groups. Within the criminal justice system, minorities have moved into positions of leadership in many jurisdictions, so it is now common to see blacks as police chiefs, judges, and prison wardens, perhaps not in proportion to their share of the population, but nonetheless considerably more prominently than in former times.

Given these positive changes, how has the situation of black males within the criminal justice system worsened so considerably to the point where it threatens the viability of an entire generation? Some have argued that these outcomes may be unfortunate, but are inevitable given high black rates of crime. Others suggest that a new generation of "superpredators" unlike any cohort of the past has been created. In the following sections we analyze the statistical evidence and research findings that enable us to understand these developments. These can be divided into four areas of inquiry: (1) crime rates; (2) race and class effects; (3) bias within the criminal justice system; and (4) drug policies.

Crime Rates

All things being equal, the degree to which members of a demographic group engage in crime should be related to the extent to which members of that group are incarcerated. In addition, among those individuals who commit crimes, the extent of an individual's criminal history is a critical factor that influences whether an offender will be sentenced to prison. Thus, if African Americans exhibit higher rates of serious offending and/or have lengthier criminal histories than other groups, we could expect this to be reflected in the composition of the prison population.

For property offenses, African Americans constituted 28 percent of arrests in 2000[4], disproportionate to their 12 percent share of the national population. (While arrest rates may not correlate precisely with crime rates, they are generally the best approximation of the degree of offending.) For violent crimes, though, black offending rates are considerably higher than for other groups, accounting for 38 percent of those arrests in 2000.

The high black proportion of violent crime clearly explains some of the disparity that we see in the prison population, but not to the extent that is often portrayed in popular media. Two issues in particular stand out in this regard:

- While the black proportion of violent arrests is high, it remained essentially unchanged for twenty years. From 1976 to 1996, this proportion fluctuated in a narrow range of 42-47 percent, and by 2000, had declined to 38 percent. Even during the upsurge of black juvenile homicides in the late 1980s, a declining rate of homicide among black adults resulted in a stable rate overall for African Americans.
- Explanations of black juvenile homicides in the 1980s that focus on the "superpredator" theory have no basis in fact. Justice Department data show that the entire rise in such homicides for the period 1984-1994 was related to firearms, as has been the decline in homicides beginning in 1995. Thus, the *lethality* of young offenders increased by having access to guns, rather than there being a new "breed" of young killers. Further, if the 15-19-year olds who were committing violent crimes in the late 1980s were actually "superpredators," then they should have displayed these tendencies in the early 1980s as well, when they were in the 10-14 age range. Data for this period, though, show no such trends, with that group's rate of violence similar to other periods of time.[5] This therefore lends support to the explanation that the greater availability of firearms, much of it related to the drug trade, was the primary source of the increase in violence.

Prominent analyses of the overall racial composition of the prison population have been conducted by criminologist Alfred Blumstein. In an examination of the 1991 state prison population, he concluded that 76 percent of the higher black rate of imprisonment could be accounted for by higher rates of arrest for serious offenses.[6] While this held true for most crimes, the critical exception in this regard was drug offenses, which will be detailed further below. The remaining 24 percent of disparity might be explained by criminal histories, racial bias, or other factors.

A related examination of incarceration data by sociologists Robert Crutchfield, George Bridges, and Susan Pitchford found that while national level data seemed to show a high correlation between arrest rates and incarceration for African Americans, the variation in this relationship at the state level was quite significant.[7] In the northeast states, only 69 percent of racial disparity was explained by arrest, while in the north central states, fewer blacks were actually incarcerated than one would have predicted by just using arrest data. Overall, this suggests that a variety of factors, which include crime rates, law enforcement practices, and sentencing legislation, may play a role in the degree of racial disparity in incarceration.

A second factor that may explain higher rates of incarceration is the criminal history of an offender. The more serious a prior criminal record, the greater the likelihood of receiving a prison term for a new offense. Whether one acquires a criminal record is clearly in part related to the level of criminal activity, but it is also often a function of race, geographical location, and other factors.

Many African Americans, for example, have experienced the crime known as "Driving While Black." In different parts of the country, there is strong evidence regarding the propensity of police to stop black males while driving for alleged traffic violations. Often the justification offered for these actions is that they are necessary for the purpose of apprehending alleged drug traffickers, with the aid of drug courier "profiles." In Volusia County in central Florida, researchers documenting traffic stops made by local police in the late 1980s found that more than 70 percent of the drivers stopped were either African American or Hispanic. This compared to data showing that blacks constituted 12 percent of the state's driving age population and 15 percent of drivers convicted of traffic violations. Blacks and Hispanics were also stopped for longer periods than whites, and represented 80 percent of the cars that were searched following a stop.[8] These types of discretionary law enforcement practices may lead to African Americans acquiring a criminal record more rapidly than whites, later resulting in a greater chance of receiving a prison sentence. In addition, given that most drivers stopped in "profile" checks are in fact not drug traffickers, these practices often contribute to African American distrust of law enforcement.

Race and Class Effects

As the trials of O. J. Simpson illustrated so clearly, discussions of race and the criminal justice system are often heavily overlaid with considerations of class as well. Racial disparities are related in part to the volume of crime committed by various groups, but they are also a function of differing forms of treatment that relate to the background and resources of the offender.

Criminologist Delbert Elliott has conducted analyses of youthful offending and its relation to race and class.[9] In longitudinal studies of data from the National Youth Survey he has found several intriguing patterns:

- Self-reported rates of offending behavior by young males are high across all racial groups, with 42 percent of males reporting that they have engaged in some form of violent offending—aggravated assault, robbery, or rape—by the age of 27.

- Black males engage in serious violent offending at higher rates than white males, but not dramatically so. By age 27, 48 percent of black males have reported at least one instance of such behavior, compared to 38 percent of white males, a ratio of about 5:4. For lower class males, the differences are even smaller, about 7:6 black to white.

- Offenses by blacks are more likely to lead to arrest than those of whites. While the self-reported involvement of adolescent males represents a 3:2 black/white differential, the arrest ratio is 4:1.

- While there are no dramatic differences in the degree to which blacks and whites become involved in offending *at some point*, blacks are nearly twice as likely to *continue* offending into their twenties. The key variable in this regard is the adoption of adult roles. Thus, among young adults who are employed or living in a stable relationship there are no significant differences in the persistence of offending by race.

Overall, these studies suggest that while criminal behavior cuts across race and class lines, the societal response to these behaviors may significantly influence the course of a potential criminal career. Decisions regarding the most effective balance of responses by law enforcement, social services, and community intervention are critical in determining many of these outcomes.

Racial Bias in the Criminal Justice System

The criminal justice system has historically served as a focal point of much of societal racism. A long legacy of practices such as the convict leasing system, extra-judicial lynchings, and police brutality have shaped the history of African Americans and the criminal justice system. Over the past thirty years, though, significant change has occurred in some aspects of the system. In many jurisdictions minorities have moved into positions of leadership within law enforcement, the courts, and corrections systems. Supreme Court decisions have placed restrictions on such practices as prosecutorial bias in jury selection. Despite these constructive changes, though, racial disproportions have worsened over this period of time.

In assessing the extent to which racial bias within the criminal justice system has contributed to these disparities, there is mixed research evidence. Imposition of the death penalty provides the most compelling evidence for ongoing racial disparity. A series of studies has demonstrated that, controlling for a wide range of variables, the race of both victim and offender has a significant impact on the determination of a sentence of death as opposed to life in prison. David Baldus and colleagues, for example, found that murder defendants charged with killing whites faced a 4.3 times greater chance of receiving death than those charged with killing blacks.[10]

In looking at sentencing outcomes for other offenses, the research evidence is less clear regarding whether minorities receive harsher sentences than whites. A number of studies have found little difference in sentences imposed when controlling for relevant variables, particularly the severity of the offense and the offender's prior record. A 1990 Rand study, for example, concluded that offenders in California generally received comparable sentences regardless of race for most offenses.[11] The one exception was in the area of drug sentences, a distinction that we will explore below.

Other research illuminates the complexity of these findings. A review of prosecutorial decisionmaking conducted by John Hagan and Ruth Peterson suggests that prosecutors stereotype cases according to case-specific characteristics, by making racially biased assessments of the credibility of the victim and offender as witnesses. Nonwhite victims tend to be considered less credible witnesses, while white victims, especially of nonwhite defendants, are considered highly credible.[12] Since most crime is intraracial, committed against victims of the same race, these dynamics may actually benefit black defendants but penalize black victims in some cases. Thus, studies that conclude that no racial bias can be detected at sentencing may actually be overlooking more complex victim-offender racial dynamics.

Research on sentencing in a number of jurisdictions has concluded that disparity based on race does in fact occur. One of the more sophisticated such studies examined case processing and sentencing outcomes for persons arrested for a felony offense in New York State for the years 1990-92. Controlling for factors including prior criminal history, gender and county, the researchers found that for the more serious offenses, there was relatively little difference in sentencing, although it was estimated that 300 black and Hispanic offenders who received prison terms would not have had they been white. For property offenses and misdemeanors, though, minorities were considerably more likely to receive jail terms, resulting in an additional 4,000 sentences a years for minorities statewide.[13] Similar results regarding sentencing in less serious cases have been found in other studies.

The key issue in this regard appears to lie in the use of discretion by the courts when sentencing offenders. Violent offenders, regardless of their race or ethnicity, are quite likely to be sentenced to prison. But for less serious offenders where there is an option, but no *obligation*, to sentence an offender to prison, prosecutors and judges are making decisions in each case about whether an offender will receive six months in jail, for example, or be required to enter a treatment program and make restitution to a victim.

It would be a mistake simply to attribute the results of such studies to prosecutorial and judicial racist beliefs; in some jurisdictions a significant number of prosecutors and judges are minorities prosecuting and sentencing other minorities to terms of incarceration. The results instead may reflect the degree to which offenders bring different sets of resources with them to the court system. For example, do white offenders have greater access to private defense attorneys who can devote more time to their cases to try to convince prosecutors and judges that a jail or prison term is not warranted? Do they have greater access to expert psychiatric testimony or can they afford to subsidize placement in a substance abuse treatment program? Or, is unconscious racism at play: do whites speak in a language and manner that is more comfortable to the decisionmakers in the courtroom?

These questions have important implications for developing remedies for the racial disparities that are so prominent in the criminal justice system. While some might advocate that a solution to minority overrepresentation in the prison system would be to sentence more white offenders to prison, such an approach would be extremely costly and would not alleviate any of the harms suffered by minority communities.

The alternative approach is to examine the factors that enable white, or middle-class, offenders to be sentenced to non-prison terms more frequently and to replicate those conditions for low-income people. For example, if middle-class offenders have greater access to drug treatment resources, courts and communities could expand such services to make them accessible to a broader range of offenders. Additionally, greater resources could be devoted to indigent defense services, a proposal to which former Attorney General Janet Reno frequently called attention.

Drug Policies and Racial Disparity

Since 1980, the "war on drugs" has been the most significant factor contributing to the rise of prison and jail populations. Drug policies have also had a disproportionate impact on African Americans and have exacerbated the racial disparities that already existed within the criminal justice system. This has come about in two ways: first, drug offenses overall have increased as a proportion of the criminal justice population and, second, the proportion of African Americans among drug offenders has been increasing.

From 1980 to 2000, drug arrests nationally nearly tripled from 581,000 to 1.6 million, thus bringing a million additional drug cases to the court system each year. Over the course of this period, drug cases came to be treated much more harshly. Primarily as a result of mandatory sentencing policies adopted by all fifty states and the federal government, convicted drug offenders are now far more likely to be sentenced to prison than in the past. Justice Department data reveal that the chances of a drug arrestee being sentenced to prison rose by 447 percent between 1980 and 1992.

The combined impact of increased drug arrests along with harsher sentencing policies has led to a vast expansion of drug offenders in the nation's prisons and jails. Whereas in 1980, one of every sixteen state prison inmates was incarcerated for a drug offense, by 1999, one of every five prisoners was a drug offender. The increase from 19,000 drug offenders in 1980 to 251,200 in 1999 represented more than a 1200 percent increase in this nineteen-year period.

While the numbers of inmates in the federal prison system are smaller overall, the scale of the increase has been similar. The 4,900 federal drug offenders in 1980 represented 25 percent of the inmate population. This grew to 68,360, or 61 percent, by 1999. Looking at prisons and jails combined, there are now an estimated 450,000 inmates either awaiting trial or serving time for a drug offense, out of a total inmate population of 1.9 million.

As these policies have been implemented, they have increasingly affected African American and Hispanic communities. The African American proportion of drug arrests has risen from 25 percent in 1980 to 35 percent in 2000. Hispanic and African American inmates are more likely than non-Hispanic whites to be incarcerated for a drug offense, with 26 percent of each group's inmates being imprisoned for a drug offense in 1999, compared to 13 percent for non-Hispanic whites. Between 1990 and 1999, drugs accounted for 27 percent of the total growth among black inmates, 15 percent among Hispanics, and 14 percent among whites.

In recent years much attention has also been devoted to discussion of the federal crack/cocaine sentencing disparities. As a result of mandatory sentencing legislation passed by Congress in 1986 and 1988, crack cocaine offenses are punished far more harshly than powder cocaine crimes. Whereas the sale of 500 grams of powder cocaine results in a mandatory five-year prison term, only 5 grams of crack cocaine is required to trigger the same mandatory penalty. Since crack cocaine is manufactured from powder cocaine these sentencing policies create a set of odd consequences. For example, a major dealer in powder cocaine who is apprehended with 499 grams of the drug will receive at most one year in federal prison. But when those 499 grams are converted to crack and distributed at the street level, someone possessing just five grams will receive a mandatory five years in prison.

The racial disparities created by these policies have been dramatic, and have resulted both from the sentencing legislation and law enforcement practices. In 1999-2000, for example, 84 percent of persons charged with crack trafficking offenses in the federal system were African American, while blacks represented just 30 percent of persons charged with powder cocaine offenses.[14] Federal prosecutors have often contended that the high numbers of black crack prosecutions reflect the proportions of large-scale traffickers in crack, who qualify for federal prosecution because of their substantial role in the drug trade. Data analyzed by the U.S. Sentencing Commission, though, cast doubt on this contention. In the Commission's analysis of crack defendants in 1992, only 5.5 percent of the defendants were classified as high-level dealers, while 63.7 percent were considered street-level dealers or couriers, and 30.8 percent were mid-level dealers.[15]

The ways in which the racial disparities in the prosecution of drug offenses come about are complex. Overall drug use by African Americans is not substantially different than for other demographic groups. Household surveys conducted by the Substance Abuse and Mental Health Services Administration have found that blacks represent 15 percent of monthly drug users, roughly comparable to their 12 percent share of the national population. For drug selling, there is no means of estimating precisely whether African Americans are more engaged in these activities than other groups, although a National Institute of Justice analysis of drug transactions in six cities found that "respondents were most likely to report using a main source who was of their own racial or ethnic background.[16]

A report issued by the Wisconsin Policy Research Institute, for example, assessed differences in the white suburban drug markets and inner-city black and Hispanic neighborhoods of Milwaukee.[17] While drug dealing was prevalent in each of the communities, the inner-city sales tended to be neighborhood-based, often taking place on street corners. In contrast, the suburban distribution of cocaine and other drugs took place by word of mouth through contacts at work, bars, athletic leagues, and alternative cultural events such as "raves." Suburban sales locations were more hidden from law enforcement than were those in the inner city neighborhoods, but they were "not very difficult to locate," in the words of the author.

Most criminal justice observers believe that these disparities have emerged as a result of the underlying assumptions behind the "war on drugs." Unlike crimes such as murder or armed robbery where it is clear that a strong law enforcement response is immediately necessary, drug crimes offer a range of policy options by which to respond, with increased law enforcement representing just one choice

A justification that is often presented for the heavy law enforcement presence in low-income communities is that these communities have distinguishing characteristics in regard to drug sales. In many such communities drug sales are more likely to take place in open air drug markets, in contrast to middle-income communities where they are more commonly conducted behind closed doors. Thus, in the low-income communities, drug use is both more disruptive to community life as well as providing an easier target for law enforcement.

From this point of view, the disproportionate impact of the "war on drugs" on minority communities might appear somewhat reasonable. The problem with this assumption, though, is that the available policy options are *not* to just make drug arrests or to do nothing. Rather, a whole range of family and community interventions could plausibly address substance abuse problems. These would include support for pre-school families, job creation, community-based policing, expanded treatment options, and other services. A consistent body of research has demonstrated that treatment interventions for substance abuse are far more cost-effective than continued reliance on an expanded prison system. The Rand Corporation, for example, has estimated that investing an additional $1 million in drug treatment programs would reduce fifteen times more serious crime than expanding the use of mandatory prison sentences for drug offenders.[18]

Despite these and similar findings federal drug spending through both Republican and Democratic administrations since the early 1980s has emphasized the back-end responses of law enforcement and incarceration over the front-end approaches of prevention and treatment. Approximately two-thirds of the current $18 billion federal allocation for anti-drug spending is designated for law enforcement purposes, a proportion that has held steady for twenty years.

By choosing to focus primarily on law enforcement and incarceration, therefore, policymakers have implicitly chosen an approach that both worsens racial disparities in the criminal justice system and is demonstrably less effective in responding to the problem of drug abuse than other options. This approach has not necessarily been consciously adopted with the intent of locking up more black males, but in the failure to anticipate its likely consequences, policymakers have contributed to such an outcome.

Intended and Unintended Consequences

The stated intent of policies that result in large-scale incarceration is to respond to and control crime. While the decline of crime in recent years has been cited by some as due in part to the rising number of people in prison, the evidence in this regard is ambiguous at best. Proponents of greater incarceration point to the 22 percent decline in crime since 1991, at a time when the prison population rose by 75 percent, as evidence that prisons reduce crime. But in the seven years just preceding this, the prison population rose by 79 percent, yet crime rates *increased* by 17 percent. Looking over a broader time frame, the nearly 700 percent increase in the prison population from 200,000 in 1973 to 1.4 million in 2000 has not had any dramatic impact on crime overall. In a 1993 analysis, the National Research Council asked what impact the tripling of time served for violent crime had between 1975 and 1989, and answered, "Apparently, very little."[19] Other factors in recent years that have been coincident with the increased prison population—a decline in the drug trade, efforts to remove guns from juveniles, the expansion of community policing, a growing economy—are much more likely explanations for recent drops in crime.

While much attention has been focused on the relationship between incarceration and crime, comparatively little analysis has been conducted on what might be termed the unintended consequences of large-scale incarceration of the sort that is now quite prevalent in many African American communities.

That is, are there family and community dynamics that come into play once the scale of incarceration reaches a certain threshold?

One area of inquiry relates to the effect of imprisonment on deterring crime. It is generally assumed that since people fear the prospect of going to prison, some may refrain from crime as a result. But what happens to that deterrent effect as the experience of prison becomes quite pervasive in a community? Since going to prison is now a commonplace event in some neighborhoods, the prison experience may come to be seen almost as an inevitable part of growing up for many black males and one over which many individuals believe they have little control.

While the impact of imprisonment on individual offenders is direct, there are also a set of consequences for the families and communities of offenders. These will vary significantly depending on the individual and the offense. Removal of a violent offender who is terrorizing a neighborhood brings some level of public safety to a community. But what about removing large numbers of property or drug offenders? Some modest reductions in crime may be achieved but negative consequences may ensue as well.

One effect of the high rate of incarceration of African American males has been to contribute to the declining number of marriageable men in the African American community. Along with high rates of homicide, AIDS-related deaths and other factors, this has created a substantial imbalance in the male-female ratio among adult African Americans. Whereas gender ratios for African Americans at birth are about 102-103 males for every 100 females, by the age range 40-44, this declines to 86 males per 100 females, whereas white rates are 100:100 for this group.[20] Further, men who have been imprisoned or are likely to be so are hardly strong marriage prospects.

The large-scale reach of the criminal justice system also may interfere with the informal mechanisms of crime control that exist in varying degrees in all communities. This dynamic involves the influence of families, schools, religious bodies, and other institutions to transmit values and promote positive role models. Neighborhoods with high levels of joblessness and social disorganization may be less able to have parents and neighborhood leaders assert the type of influence that would bring greater social cohesion in more well-off neighborhoods.

The negative consequences of high rates of incarceration may well extend to the next generation of children. Children whose parents are imprisoned may develop feelings of shame, humiliation, and a loss of social status. This may lead to acting out in school and a distrust of authority figures. The changing economic circumstances of families experiencing imprisonment may also lead to greater housing relocation and transitory populations, resulting in less cohesive neighborhoods. In far too many cases, these children may come to represent the next generation of offenders.

The impact of the criminal justice system on communities goes beyond issues of well-being and family stabilization, but to issues of political influence as well. One of the most significant areas in which this emerges regards voting rights. As a result of laws that disenfranchise felons and ex-felons in various states, an estimated 1.4 million African American males, or 13 percent of the black male adult population, is either currently or permanently disenfranchised as a result of a felony conviction.[21] In thirteen states, a felony conviction can result in lifetime disenfranchisement, and in seven of these states, an estimated one in four black males is permanently disenfranchised. Thus, not only are criminal justice policies contributing to the disproportionate incarceration of African Americans, but imprisonment itself then reduces the collective political ability to influence these policies.

Projections for the Future

With crime rates having declined for the past nine years, one might think that prison populations also would begin to decline. Common sense would suggest that with fewer crimes being committed, there would be fewer offenders to be locked up. In fact, though, nothing of the sort has happened, with both the total national prison population as well as the number of incarcerated African American males having risen by 59 percent during this nine-year period.

The primary reason why these institutional populations continue to increase is due to increasingly harsh federal and state sentencing policies. The establishment of these policies also suggests that absent any change, the number and proportion of African American males under the supervision of the criminal justice system is likely to increase over the next ten years and that racial disparities will grow even wider. These increases can be anticipated for several reasons.

First, prison populations may continue to grow in coming years. Despite falling crime rates, a variety of sentencing policies adopted in the past twenty years have contributed to the burgeoning of the prison population. These include the mandatory sentencing laws now in effect in all fifty states and the federal system, the "three strikes and you're out" laws in nearly half the states, and newly adopted "truth in sentencing" policies that will increase the time served in prison for many offenders by requiring that they serve 85 percent of their sentence. Preliminary indications of this trend are already evident in research by the Bureau of Justice Statistics, which show that the percentage of sentence served prior to release increased from 38 percent in 1990 to 44 percent in 1996.[22]

With African Americans representing half the national prison population, any increase will clearly affect them in a substantial way. It is likely, though, that the racial disparities we observe today will actually worsen as prison populations rise, primarily due to the impact of drug policies. As we have seen, drug arrests and prosecutions represent the most significant change in the criminal justice system since the early 1980s. These policies have disproportionately affected minorities. To the extent that drug offenders continue to comprise a substantial portion of the inmate population it is likely that the African American share of the prison population will grow as well.

None of these developments are preordained, of course. Most criminal justice officials now recognize that prison populations represent public policy choices as much as they do crime rates. Thus, decisions regarding which types of offenses should represent priorities for prosecution, what sentencing options exist for judges, and legislative policies regarding sentencing and time served in prison will all play a significant role in determining the size and composition of the prison population.

In assessing future trends in crime and the criminal justice system it is critical to engage in a broad and proactive perspective. As we have seen, the contention that there is a coming wave of "superpredators" on the horizon has little basis in reality. Even if this were true, though, one can consider the policy options that it presents. The predicted coming generation of hard-core criminals would be composed primarily of boys who are five years old today but who would be believed to develop into high-rate offenders ten years from now. A society that anticipated these developments has one of two means by which to respond. It could begin a massive prison construction program designed to have sufficient space to house these high-rate offenders when they unleash their projected crime wave. Or it could invest in a variety of family, community, and school-based programs designed to reduce the prospects that this crime wave would take place. It would seem that only a society with an extremely bleak view of the future would choose the former course in public policy.

Approaches to Reducing Racial Disparities in the Criminal Justice System

Since racial disparities in the criminal justice system arise from a complex set of circumstances, there are no "quick fix" solutions to the problem. Only a multifaceted approach can respond to many of the underlying social and economic social and economic forces that have contributed to the current situation. Nevertheless, within the criminal justice system, there are a variety of policy and programmatic changes that could have a direct impact on the scale of incarceration and the degree of racial disparity within the prison system. In order to accomplish this, it is first necessary to establish a framework for such change. This would include the following:

- *Jurisdictional commitment to reducing disparity.* Efforts to reduce disparity will only succeed if there is a jurisdiction-wide commitment to address the problem. Otherwise, efforts to reduce disparity at one point in the system may be offset by countervailing actions within other components of the system.

- *Coordinated efforts by relevant actors.* Approaches to reducing disparity require a coordinated effort by all the relevant actors in the system, including law enforcement, prosecution, defense, judiciary, corrections, probation and parole.
- *Public safety focus.* Approaches to reducing racial disparity should not be inconsistent with improving public safety and, in fact, generally represent rational public policy on crime control. Thus, any proposals to reduce disparities should also assess the crime control impact of the proposed changes.

Specific recommendations for change can be considered in the areas of legislative change, criminal justice officials' initiatives, and criminal justice/community partnerships. The following is a suggested means of promoting efforts to reduce racial disparities.

1. Legislative Actions

Reconsider Mandatory Sentencing Policies. Mandatory sentencing policies, particularly for drug offenses, have contributed to the escalating number of minorities in prison. While these policies have proved to be politically popular, they have also resulted in the incarceration of many low-level offenders at great expense. A vast body of research, as well as practitioner perspectives, suggest that mandatory sentences are unnecessary for crime control purposes and have a variety of negative consequences. Repeal of mandatory sentencing laws would thus provide one of the most significant steps that could be immediately undertaken in this regard.

In the current absence of political will to repeal mandatory sentencing, several interim reforms can be considered by policymakers to lessen the negative impact of these policies:

- *"Safety valve" provisions.* Recognizing the impact of mandatory sentencing on low-level federal offenders, in 1994 Congress adopted a "safety valve" that grants judges wider discretion for offenders who have limited criminal history and no involvement with violence. This has resulted in 4,000 offenders a year being sentenced to a shorter prison term than would otherwise have been possible. Congress could now consider an expansion of the "safety valve" to a broader category of offenders, as could state legislatures.
- *Restore practitioner discretion.* Criminal justice leaders in a number of jurisdictions have utilized their discretion to avoid some of the excesses of mandatory sentencing while providing effective responses to offenders. The Drug Treatment Alternative to Prison program developed by Brook-

lyn, N.Y., District Attorney Charles Hynes, for example, diverts drug offenders facing mandatory prison terms into long-term residential treatment programs. Recidivism rates for offenders completing the program are considerably below those of comparable offenders sentenced to prison.

- *Sunset legislation.* Given the controversy regarding the effectiveness of mandatory sentencing, legislatures could adopt sunset provisions that would result in the laws expiring after a set period of time unless renewed. Such a provision would thus require a legislative review of the effectiveness of any legislation and would permit appropriate modifications.

Equalize Penalties for Crack and Powder Cocaine. The racial disparities that have resulted from the federal sentencing distinctions for crack and powder cocaine offenses have been well documented. The 100:1 quantity disparity has contributed to the disproportionate number of African Americans in prison as well as causing great resentment in the black community. Equalizing penalties for the two drugs at the level of cocaine offenses would reduce some of the racial disparities in incarceration as well as some of the inappropriately lengthy sentences for lower-level offenders.

Develop Racial/Ethnic Impact Statements for Sentencing Policy. In recent years some jurisdictions have required that fiscal impact statements be prepared for any proposed legislative changes in sentencing policy. Similarly, legislatures could require that projections be developed to estimate the racial/ethnic impact of sentencing legislation prior to its adoption. Such a policy would not prohibit legislatures from adopting new sentencing legislation, but would allow policymakers to assess whether any unwarranted disparities might result. This would aid in consideration of alternative crime control measures that could produce effective results without undue disparities.

Establish a Goal of Reducing the Non-Violent Offender Population by 50 percent over Ten Years. Non-violent property and drug offenders now constitute 52 percent of state prison inmates, an increase from 45.5 percent of the total in 1986. Nationally, this represents more than a half million inmates and a total cost of incarceration of more than $10 billion. Legislatures could adopt a policy goal of reducing this population by 5 percent a year for ten years, using the funds saved on imprisonment for community-based supervision and treatment programs.

Increase Funding for Indigent Defense and Sentencing Advocacy. To the extent that minorities in the criminal justice system are disproportionately low-income, they do not obtain the advantages that wealthier defendants bring to the system. These include access to attorneys with reasonable caseloads, sentencing consultants, and diagnostic services. Greater provision of these services would aid courts in fashioning more appropriate sentencing options for many low-income offenders and would likely result in diversion from prison for some minority offenders.

2. Criminal Justice Officials' Initiatives

Expand Drug Policy Options. Criminal justice officials are increasingly recognizing the importance of providing drug treatment as a component of effective sentencing and corrections policy. Drug treatment might reduce the number of minorities and others in prison in one of two ways: by diverting offenders to treatment programs rather than incarceration and, by reducing drug addiction and therefore, recidivism. Options in this area include drug courts, prosecutorial diversion programs, in-prison residential treatment, and other approaches.

Expand the Use of Alternative Sentencing. A variety of alternative sentencing programs have been developed in recent years. These programs include community service, day reporting centers, victim-offender mediation, and a variety of substance abuse treatment programs. While the experience of these programs in reducing prison populations is mixed, they hold the potential to divert offenders from a prison sentence while addressing both offender and victim needs in an effective manner.

Monitor Alternative Sentencing Programs to Assess Racial Balance. In many jurisdictions, white offenders are more likely to be sentenced to probation and alternative sanctions than are minority offenders. This may be due to relevant factors such as crime severity and criminal record or to system bias. Jurisdictions can attempt to monitor the racial/ethnic composition of offenders sentenced to alternatives to determine whether minority offenders are appropriately represented and if not, to conduct an analysis of the reasons for disparity.

3. Criminal Justice/Community Partnerships

Increase Community-based Diversion from the Criminal Justice System. Many young and first-time offenders are stigmatized by their contact with the criminal justice system, without necessarily receiving either appropriate supervision or support. Opportunities exist to divert many of these offenders to individuals and organizations which can better focus on problems that are most effectively handled in a community setting. These could include mentoring programs, counseling, tutorial support, and other options.

Strengthen the Link between Communities and the Justice System. The experience of community policing in recent years has demonstrated that a "problem-solving" approach to crime can be effective in increasing public safety while also building valuable links to the community. Variations on this model are now being explored by prosecutors, probation departments, and other components of the system. These approaches hold the potential of both increasing minority confidence in the justice system and building on community strengths to promote public safety.

Conclusion

The origins of the crisis of African American males as it regards the criminal justice system extend far back in the nation's history. Unfortunately, despite admirable progress in reducing racial bias in many areas of society during the past several decades, the overrepresentation of black males in the justice system has clearly worsened.

While the situation is urgent in many regards, there is some reason for cautious optimism. Support for change in criminal justice policies and programs has been growing in recent years. The introduction of drug courts, prison-based treatment programs, and community policing are all indications of public and policymaker support for problem-solving responses to individual and community crises. In addition, many communities are now engaged in locally based programs that provide support to young people. These include mentoring programs, recreational activities, and personal skills development. The challenge for the community at large is to engage in broad discussion of the mix of family, community, and government initiatives that can begin to reverse the cycle that has been set in motion in recent years.

Notes

1. A previous version of this article was presented as testimony to the U.S. Commission on Civil Rights on April 15, 1999.
2. Unless otherwise specified, all data on prison and jail populations throughout is taken from various reports of the Bureau of Justice Statistics.
3. Marc Mauer and Tracy Huling, "Young Black Americans and the Criminal Justice System: Five Years Later," The Sentencing Project, October 1995.
4. FBI, *Crime in the United States, 2000,* 2001. All subsequent data on crime rates taken from this and previous reports in this series.
5. Philip J. Cook and John H. Laub, "The Unprecedented Epidemic in Youth Violence," in Michael Tonry (Ed.), *Crime and Justice: A Review of Research* (Chicago: University of Chicago Press, 1999).
6. Alfred Blumstein, "Racial Disproportionality of U.S. Prison Populations Revisited," *University of Colorado Law Review,* Vol. 64, No. 3, 1993.
7. Robert D. Crutchfield, George S. Bridges, and Susan R. Pitchford, "Analytical and Aggregation Biases in Analyses of Imprisonment: Reconciling Discrepancies in Studies of Racial Disparity," *Journal of Research in Crime and Delinquency* 31 (May 1994).
8. David A. Harris, "'Driving While Black' and All Other Traffic Offenses: The Supreme Court and Pretextual Traffic Stops," *Journal of Criminal Law and Criminology* 87 (summer 1997): 562.
9. Delbert S. Elliott, "Serious Violent Offenders: Onset, Developmental Course, and Termination—The American Society of Criminology 1993 Presidential Address," *Criminology* 32, no. 1 (1994): 1-21.
10. David C. Baldus, Charles Pulaski, and George Woodworth, "Comparative Review of Death Sentences: An Empirical Study of the Georgia Experience," *Journal of Criminal Law and Criminology* 74 (fall 1983): 661-753.

11. Stephen Klein, Joan Petersilia, and Susan Turner, "Race and Imprisonment Decisions in California," *Science* (February 16, 1990).
12. John Hagan and Ruth D. Peterson, "Criminal Inequality in America: Patterns and Consequences," in John Hagan and Ruth D. Peterson, *Crime and Inequality* (Stanford, CA: Stanford University Press, 1995), 28.
13. James F. Nelson, *Disparities in Processing Felony Arrests in New York State, 1990-92* (Albany, NY: Division of Criminal Justice Services, 1995).
14. United States Sentencing Commission, *1996 Sourcebook of Federal Sentencing Statistics*, Table 29.
15. _____, *Cocaine and Federal Sentencing Policy*, February 1995, Table 18.
16. K. Jack Riley, "Crack, Powder Cocaine, and Heroin: Drug Purchase and Use Patterns in Six U.S. Cities," National Institute of Justice, December 1997, 1.
17. John M. Hagedorn, "The Business of Drug Dealing in Milwaukee," Wisconsin Policy Research Institute, June 1998.
18. Jonathan P. Caulkins et al., *Mandatory Minimum Drug Sentences: Throwing Away the Key or the Taxpayers' Money?* (Santa Monica, CA: Rand Corporation, 1997), xxiv.
19. National Research Council, *Understanding and Preventing Violence* (Washington, D.C.: National Academy Press 1993), 6.
20. David T. Courtwright, "The Drug War's Hidden Toll," *Issues in Science and Technology* (winter 1996-97): 73.
21. Jamie Fellner and Marc Mauer, "Losing the Vote: The Impact of Felony Disenfranchisement Laws in the United States," Human Rights Watch and The Sentencing Project, October 1998.
22. Paula M. Ditton and Doris James Wilson, "Truth in Sentencing in State Prisons," Bureau of Justice Statistics, January 1999.

References

Blumstein, Alfred. (1993). Racial disproportionality of U.S. prison populations revisited. *University of Colorado Law Review*, Vol. 64, No. 3.
Cole, David. (1999). *No equal justice: Race and class in the American criminal justice system*. New York: The New Press.
Kennedy, Randall. (1997). *Race, crime, and the law*. New York: Pantheon..
Mann, Coramae Richey. (1993). *Unequal justice*. Bloomington: Indiana University Press.
Mauer, Marc. (1999). *Race to incarcerate*. New York: The New Press.
Mauer, Marc, and Tracy Huling. (1995). Young black Americans and the criminal justice system: Five years later. Washington, D.C.: The Sentencing Project.
Miller, Jerome. (1996). *Search and destroy: African-American males in the criminal justice system*. Cambridge: Cambridge University Press.
Tonry, Michael. (1995). *Malign neglect—race, crime, and punishment in America*. New York: Oxford University Press.
Walker, Samuel, Cassia Spohn, and Miriam DeLone. (1996). *The color of justice*. Belmont, CA: Wadsworth.

16

African American Incarceration and Policy Initiatives: Concluding Remarks

R. Robin Miller

Introduction

Regardless of the thousand-plus papers on African American families published since the 1970s (see Taylor, Chatters, Tucker, and Lewis, 1990; Billingsley, 1992; and Staples and Johnson, 1993, for further reviews) there has been a paucity of research on the ways our "race to incarcerate" has affected African American families. Leading the macro policy initiatives to be made is the overwhelming need for an upward redistribution of wealth. Exacerbating (if not directly influencing) the problems discussed in this text is the rapidly widening gap between rich and poor in this country today. Wolff (1996) states, "The sharp increase in inequality since the late 1970s has made wealth distribution in the United States more unequal than in what used to be perceived as the class-ridden societies of northwestern Europe" (1996: 2).

African Americans are hit especially hard by this growing poverty. The loss of many of the post-World War II manufacturing jobs that once provided economic stability for black families presents one of the biggest threats to family stability. In fact, marital instability "...appears to represent the response of the poorest, most disadvantaged segment of the black population to the social and economic situation they have faced in our cities over the past few decades" (Baca Zinn and Eitzen, 1996: 357). And the relationships among economic hardship, unemployment, and contact with the criminal justice system have been well investigated. For policy to stem this rising tide, economic privations must first be addressed.

We, of course, need to publicly face the seeming apartheid-like system which has developed into a near war on the African American community in general and on the African American male more specifically. To this end, we must strive to end the war on drugs/crime that give every appearance of being a war on specific individuals in our society. Finally, as has been articulated better by others, we must desist in relying solely on singular, easy, and quick remedies to complex social problems that result in scapegoating and exploitation.

Implications for Research

The papers found here may lead one to conclude that, first, research into the impacts of incarceration on African American families must be developed to include more cross-sections of incarcerated populations. Very little research on the effects on families, spread out over the last few decades, has been conducted. And still fewer studies on the effects on the African American community have been done. Further, often because of lack of research funds, these samples have been limited. Are there differences in the effects between families separated for shorter versus longer periods of time? For different offenses? Do effects differ by state versus federal systems? By region? Research into the families of inmates has just begun to burgeon in recent years with our rapid increase in the number of Americans incarcerated. These studies obviously need to more fully include various subgroups in the population, and these studies must sample the population in a way that allows us to examine myriad factors.

In this vein, further work is needed to determine whether it is separation in general, or separation due to incarceration, that causes the most harm. In particular, clinical trials, or experimental/quasi-experimental models should be more widely employed to allow us to control for many variables and to make more causal connections than we are able to at present.

Lastly, research into the impacts of incarceration on the African American family must be developed that focuses on incarcerated African American women and their families. Record numbers of women are presently incarcerated, too many of them from the African American community. The majority of the papers included here examine impacts on the families of incarcerated males, and yet the most rapid increase in female incarceration has been for young women; many of these young women have children; and many of these women lose their children due to the incarceration (Belknap, 1996). At this point, how this affects the African American community is unfortunately largely a matter of speculation.

Institutional and Correctional Policy Initiatives Suggested by This Text

Leading this section, Anthony King points out that the majority of African American men incarcerated were financially supporting others and were further involved in family work. Losing these family members to incarceration is not only devastating to the one who is incarcerated; "real" families are harmed. King suggests the following programs to aid these men: (1) culturally appropriate family-support groups, (2) clinical services, (3) community-based family life education programs, (4) family life education programs in correctional institutions, and (5) family case-management services.

In a followup piece, Hairston and Lockett describe the landmark *Parents in Prison* program—which was first implemented in the early 1980s. In this program, these men take courses in family studies and parenting practices; engage in special discussion sessions and workshops; and participate in special projects designed to aid in healthy family functioning. By focusing on strengthening families, fathering skills, and relationship building, these men take on more active roles. This program has the added benefit of pulling together efforts from the inmates themselves, their families, corrections workers, and community members. While programs similar to this have been cut throughout the 1990s, this volume highlights the need for the widespread development and implementation of such programs.

Allen-Meares and Burman widen this discussion with a strong call to social workers. They contend that while the historic mission of the discipline of social work has been to intervene on behalf of the disenfranchised and oppressed, social workers have been largely silent on the matter of families of incarcerated individuals. "The profession needs to develop program strategies that strengthen social support networks and resources in the community....To provide impetus for change, factors that affect self-esteem, self-image, and self-worth must be addressed."

Finally, Marc Mauer discusses differential incarceration rates within the African American community, racial bias in the criminal justice system, the impact of the war on drugs and what all this may mean for future trends. As case in point, African American families are harmed in many ways, including the growing disparity in male/female ratios. He recommends a number of program/policy changes such as reconsidering mandatory sentencing, equalizing the penalties for crack and powder cocaine, and increasing the use of alternative sentencing and community-based diversion programs. He ends on a cautious note of optimism, citing increased support in drug courts, prison-based treatment programs, and community policing programs.

In summary, the policy papers included here have a few elements in common. They all express, at least implicitly, an urgency about the impacts of crime processing on the African American community. They all stress not only the financial hardships involved in this separation as a result of incarceration, but the social and psychological, as well. Because many of these men erect a psychological barrier between themselves and their family members, these emotional factors need to be addressed both within and without the criminal justice system. And these papers direct us to the conclusion that fathers do matter! As we have seen, father-absence leads to critical problems, for instance in the adjustment of children (particularly boys)—a finding established by myriad studies of many different types (i.e., from different disciplines, different types of separation, using different methodologies). While most of the earlier studies on father-absence looked at divorce adjustment and focused chiefly on the economic losses of these families, socio-emotional and psychological effects are found to exist as well. Robert Staples (1999) states, "The future of the Black family is inextricably tied up with the current and future status of the Black male" (1999: 287). And since African American males are by far the singular largest group incarcerated in the U.S. today, it is therefore incumbent upon us to see to the familial needs of these men and their families.

References

Baca Zinn, M., and S. Eitzen. (1996). *Diversity in families*. 4th ed. New York: Harper Collins Publishers.

Belknap, J. (1996). *The invisible woman: Gender, crime, and justice*. New York: Wadsworth Publishing.

Billingsley, A. (1992). *Climbing Jacob's ladder: The enduring legacy of African American families*. New York: Simon and Schuster.

Staples, R. (1999). *The black family*. 6th ed. New York: Wadsworth Publishing.

Staples, R., and L. B. Johnson. (1993). *Black families at the crossroads: Challenges and prospects*. San Francisco, CA: Jossey-Bass.

Taylor, R., L. M. Chatters, M. B. Tucker, and E. Lewis. (1990). Developments in research on black families: A decade review. *Journal of Marriage and the Family* 52: 993-1014.

Wolff, E. (1996). *Top heavy: The increasing inequality of wealth in America and what can be done about it*. New York: The New Press.

Name Index

Adams, P. L., 148
Allen, W. R., 147
Allen-Meares, Paula, 13, 40, 221
Azibo, D. A., 123

Baca Zinn, Maxine, 6
Bain, M. W., 114
Bakker, L. J., 107
Baldus, David, 204
Balthazar, Mary, 10
Bancroft, Carrie, 10
Beckerman, A., 94
Bell, C. C., 190
Benga, Ota, 75, 76
Bennett, L. A., 49, 50
Bernard, Jesse, 5
Bernard, Jessie, 158
Billson, J. M., 131
Bland, I. J., 190
Blos, P., 149, 151
Blumstein, Alfred, 202
Bosket, Pud, 125, 126, 127, 131
Bosket, Willie James, Jr., 124, 125, 127
Bridges, George, 202
Brown, S. V., 146
Browning, Sandra Lee, 10
Burman, Sondra, 13, 40, 221
Butterfield, E., 124, 126

Campbell, A., 145
Campbell, Angus, 159
Carlo, T. A., 94
Carlson, B., 36
Cazenave, N. A., 146
Cervera, N., 36
Chafe, W. H., 122, 123
Clark, Theresa, 10
Cokley, K., 76
Connell, R. W., 143
Connor, M. E., 141, 147
Converse, P., 145

Crutchfield, Robert D., 38, 202
Cushman, P., 149

De Saint-Exupery, Antoine, 82
Devore, W., 194
DuBois, W. E. B., 3

Earl, L., 148
Eitzen, Stanley, 6
Elliott, Delbert, 203
Emery, R. E., 113
Eshleman, J. R., 145
Esselstyn, T. C., 106

Faigeles, Bonnie, 10
Feagin, J., 189
Feldman, L. B., 151
Fine, Michele, 122, 123
Fishman, L, 36
Foucault, Michel, 73, 76, 142
Franklin, J. H., 190
Frazier, E. Franklin, 98, 144
Friedman, S., 106

Gabel, K., 4, 79
Gabel, Stewart, 11
Gary, L., 35
Germain, C. B., 34
Glenn, Norval, 159-161
Goldstein, H. S., 112, 113
Grinstead, Olga, 10
Grogan, D., 114
Grogger, J., 38
Gutman, H. G., 144

Hagan, J., 37
Hagan, John, 205
Hairston, Creasie, 12, 17, 18, 40, 49, 79, 221
Hannon, G., 106
Harm, N., 93

223